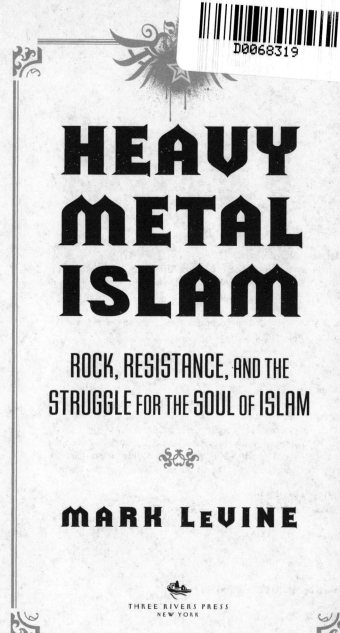

HEAVY METAL ISLAM

ROCK, RESISTANCE, AND THE STRUGGLE FOR THE SOUL OF ISLAM

MARK LeVINE

THREE RIVERS PRESS
NEW YORK

Three Rivers Press and the Tugboat design are registered trademarks of
Random House, Inc.

Library of Congress Cataloging-in-Publication Data

LeVine, Mark, 1966–
    Heavy metal Islam: rock, resistance, and the struggle for the soul of Islam /
    Mark LeVine.—1st ed.
    Includes bibliographical references and index.
    1. Popular music—Social aspects—Islamic countries.   2. Popular
    music—Social aspects—Middle East.   3. Popular music—Social
    aspects—Morocco.   4.   Popular music—Social aspects—Egypt.
    I. Title.
    ML3918.P67L48 2008
    306.4'8424091767—dc22   2008002801

ISBN 978-0-307-35339-9

Printed in the United States of America

Design by Mauna Eichner and Lee Fukui

10 9 8 7 6 5 4 3 2

First Edition

For Alessandro and Francesca, who are just
discovering music's ferocious joy, and Lola,
for helping to nurture it.

In memory of John Henry Bonham, without
whom I would have become a lawyer, and Albert
Collins and Johnny Copeland, who invited me
into their lives and taught me that it's not
how fast you can play that matters,
it's how deep you can bend the note.

HEAVY
METAL
ISLAM

CONTENTS

INTRODUCTION

Rock and Resistance in the Muslim World

We play heavy metal because
our lives *are* heavy metal.

— REDA ZINE, one of the founders of
the Moroccan heavy metal scene

"I stopped trying to define punk around the
same time I stopped trying to define Islam.
They're not as far removed as you might think."

MICHAEL MUHAMMAD KNIGHT,
Taqwacores

"Music is the weapon of the Future."

FELA KUTI

The first time I heard the words "heavy metal" and "Islam" in the same sentence, I was confused, to say the least. It was around 5:00 p.m. on a hot July day in the city of Fes, Morocco in 2002. I was at the bar of the five-star Palais Jamai Hotel with a group of friends having a drink—and only one drink, considering they were about twenty-five dollars apiece—to celebrate a birthday. Out of nowhere the person sitting across from me described a punk performance he had seen not long before we met, in the city of Rabat.

1

"There are Muslim punks? In Morocco?" I asked him. The idea of a young Moroccan with a mohawk and a Scottish kilt almost caused me to spill my drink.

"Of course," he replied. "And the metal scene here is good too." That the possibility of a Muslim heavy-metal scene came as a total surprise to me only underscored how much I still had to learn about Morocco, and the Muslim world more broadly, even after a dozen years studying, traveling, and living in it. If there could be such a thing as a Heavy Metal Islam, I thought, then perhaps the future was far brighter than most observers of the Muslim world imagined less than a year after September 11, 2001.

I shouldn't have been surprised at the notion of Muslim metalheads or punkers. Muslim history is full of characters and movements that seemed far out of the mainstream in their day, but that nevertheless helped bring about far-reaching changes in their societies. As I nursed my drink, I contemplated the various musical, cultural, and political permutations that could be produced by combining Islam and hard rock. I began to wonder: What could Muslim metal artists and their fans teach us about the state of Islam today?

And so began a five-year journey across the Muslim world, from Morocco to Pakistan, with a dozen countries in between, in search of the artists, fans, and activists who make up the alternative music scenes of the Muslim world. My journey was long, and sometimes dangerous. But the more I traveled and the more musicians I met, the more I understood how much insight into Islam today could be gained by getting to know the artists who were working on what might seem to be the edges of their societies. Their imagination and openness to the world, and the courage of their convictions, remind us that Muslim and Western cultures are more hetero-geneous, complex, and ultimately alike than the peddlers of the clash of civilizations, the war on terror, and unending jihad would have us believe.

It might seem counterintuitive to Americans, whose images of Islam and the contemporary Muslim world come largely from Fox or CNN, but an eighteen-year-old from Casablanca with spiked hair, or a twenty-year-old from Dubai wearing goth makeup, is as representative of the world of Islam today as the Muslims who look and act the way we expect them to. They can be just as radical, if not more so, in their religious beliefs and politics as their peers who spend their days in the mosque, madrasa, or even an al-Qa'eda training camp. In fact, if we think of what "radical" really means—to offer analyses or solutions that completely break with the existing frameworks for dealing with an issue or problem—then they are far more radical than are the supposed radicals of al-Qa'eda, Hamas, or Hezbollah, who are distinctly reactionary in their reliance on violence and conservatively grounded religious and political imaginations.

Follow the Musicians, Not Just the Mullahs

To understand the peoples, cultures, and politics of the Muslim world today, especially the young people who are the majority of the citizens of the region, we need to follow the musicians and their fans as much as the mullahs and their followers. The University of Chicago music professor Philip Bohlman argues that music's impact extends far beyond the cultural realm, for two reasons: first, because more than any other cultural product, music is "aesthetically embedded" within—reflecting and even amplifying—the larger social, political, and economic dynamics of a society; and, second, because political and economic power inevitably have "an aesthetic property" that the most socially relevant music in a society amplifies in order to move its listeners to action.

"Music affords power to those who search for meaning," Bohlman argues, but the same music can be amplified in very different ways: heavy metal and hardcore rap are blasted by soldiers going into battle, and used on prisoners as part of "enhanced interrogation." But when the metal or rap is played by young people trying to resist or even transcend oppressive governments or societies, its power and potential are much more positive, reverberating far outside the scenes in which the music is embedded.

Ever since 9/11, strategists and commentators on the Middle East have become obsessed with Islam's demographics: namely, that young people constitute a far higher percentage of the Muslim world's population—upward of 65 percent, depending on the age bracket and country—in the Middle East and North Africa (MENA), than they do in any other region of the world. These teenagers, twentysomethings, and thirtysomethings, are not just the future of Islam, but of the West and the world at large. That's why it's so important to listen to what young Muslims, and particularly those on the cultural cutting edge, are playing, and saying, even when they're playing and saying things the rest of us might not want to hear. Yet the range of voices that are heard today in the Muslim or global public spheres are both too narrow and far too black and white: the bad Muslim extremists versus the good

Muslim liberals and moderates. Reality, needless to say, is much more complicated—and hopeful.

The wide variety of music listened to by young people across the MENA reveals that the Muslim world is as diverse as are its music scenes: mainstream and underground, religious and secular, Sunni and Shi'i, Christian and even Jewish as well as Muslim. Governments in the MENA are naturally wary of the political potential of such hybrid "cultural" spaces and projects. They understand as well as the region's metalheads and hip-hoppers how the presence of heavy metal, other supposedly Western forms of hard pop music, and alternative cultures more broadly threaten the established order, and through it their political power. That's why most governments attempt to censor, and when that fails, either to co-opt or more violently repress these scenes. It's also why charting the conflicts between artists, censors, religious authorities, and the secret police (Mukhabarat) provides unique insights into the lives, struggles, and hopes of young Muslims around the world today.

❧

Getting people to pay more than passing attention to music in the Muslim world is not easy in the middle of a war on terror. So it's telling that when the U.S. State Department decided it needed to demonstrate that Muslims weren't so different from us, it commissioned a story about Dick Dale, born Richard Monsour to a family of Lebanese musicians, who, according to *Guitar Player Magazine,* is the "father of heavy metal." A generation before inspiring metalheads the world over, Dale created the all-American "Surf Guitar" sound made famous by the Beach Boys and Jan and Dean. The rapid-fire and twangy single-note picking style that is his signature is the basic technique for playing the oud, the centuries-old Arab lute, or fretless guitar.

In general, however, the attention given to the MENA has not led to greater understanding or cultural sensitivity in our policies or public discourse. Quite the opposite, in fact. The lack of knowledge about the Muslim world's complex histories and contemporary realities, coupled with an almost exclusive focus on conflict and violence, has made it harder for people around the world—including most Muslims, who don't have the chance to travel widely to other Muslim countries, never mind outside them—to understand what's really going on across the Muslim world. By expanding our perspective to explore Islam through music and other forms of popular culture, a much deeper and more positive portrait of the societies, histories, and futures of the Muslim world emerges.

As important, talking to Muslim heavy-metal, rock, hip-hop, and even punk artists and fans, listening to their music, and exploring their interactions with their families, neighbors, and larger societies, reveals the Janus-faced nature of globalization. Globalization has long gotten a bad rap in the Muslim world, and among many citizens of the West as well. The reality is much more complex: though it's true that globalization has reinforced the economic and political marginalization of most of the MENA, generating various forms of negative, resistance identities in response, it also has enabled, and in fact encouraged, greater cultural openness, communication, and solidarity across the region, and between Muslims and the West.

Nowhere is globalization's positive potential more evident than in the media and popular culture of the region today. Globalization may have brought *Baywatch*, late-night German soft-core porn, and Britney Spears to the Middle East, but it has also brought al-Jazeera, Iron Maiden, and Tupac Shakur. If the MENA functions as the primary global source of petroleum, arms purchases, and jihadis, it is also home to some of the most innovative cultural products and political discourses of the global era. And most of the people I've met in Morocco, Egypt, Iran, or Dubai are as discriminating in what they pick and choose from the innumerable cultural and political choices offered by globalization as is the average American. In fact, they are often more open to new ideas or products that challenge their identities and sensibilities. They have to be; the cultural and political chauvinism that has been the source of so many of America's troubles since 9/11 (and equally characterizes the mindsets of many conservative Muslims) is not a luxury most can afford.

Why Heavy Metal? Extreme Music as the Antidote to Extreme Religious and Political Systems

Metalheads and rappers were among the first Middle Eastern communities to plug into the globalized cultural networks that emerged in the 1980s. From the start, some have been fanatical about replicating the sound and styles of the American and European progenitors of metal or rap. Others gleefully violate the boundaries separating the global from the local, the religious from the secularly profane, the exotic from the mundane, and the hip from what those in the know deride as hopelessly passé. Whatever their approach, these artists have opened new avenues for their fans to reach outside their cultures, countries, and identities, and embrace the possibilities of globalization, a project that is still viewed with much suspicion across the Muslim world.

Cultural sophistication and musical innovation are not traits normally associated with heavy metal. Indeed, say "heavy metal" to the average American or European, and you are likely to conjure an image of a group of slightly deranged-looking white guys with long, crimped blond hair and leather outfits, whose primary talents are sleeping with underage groupies and destroying hotel rooms. Certainly there were plenty of bands like that, especially in the inglorious days of 1980s and early 1990s glam metal. But to define a genre as rich and varied as heavy metal by its MTV-lite version is equivalent to defining 1.5 billion Muslims by a few thousand turban-and-djellaba-wearing jihadis running around Pakistan's North-West Frontier Province (NWFP) hunting infidels and apostates. Both have given their respective cultures a very bad name, and deservedly so. But each constitutes only a small minority of believers, however seemingly powerful their influence over more-mainstream trends.

The term "heavy metal" as a musical term was coined in an early 1970s *Rolling Stone* interview by Alice Cooper, the patron saint of extreme rock (the term itself originated with the "Heavy metal kid" in William Burroughs's 1964 graphic novel, *Nova Express*). Heavy metal was influenced by a range of musical styles, from the counterpoint of Johann Sebastian Bach and the modern classical repertoire he helped to create, to the riff-driven, often equally virtuostic blues rock of Led

Zeppelin, Cream, Jimi Hendrix, and Deep Purple. But if there's one band that is most responsible for the sound of heavy metal, it's Black Sabbath. In the early 1970s, Sabbath produced a series of albums that literally defined a new genre of rock 'n' roll. The band's combination of relatively slow tempos, heavily distorted guitar riffs in various minor modes, half-tone and even tri-tone modulations (known since the Renaissance as the *diabolus in musica* because of the immoral, even lustful feelings it was felt to arouse), and morbid, death-inspired lyrics spoke to disaffected American and European youth. As guitarist Tony Iommi said about the blighted working-class landscape of his teens, "It made [the music] more mean."

By 1975 a new style of metal emerged, dubbed "the new wave of British heavy metal." Led by bands like Judas Priest, Motörhead, Venom, and Iron Maiden, the genre was distinguished both by the increased speed and musical complexity of the songs, and also by an explicitly working-class image that fitted the painful process of deindustrialization and economic adjustment experienced by working-class communities in Britain and the United States in the mid- to late 1970s. Some of the bands, particularly Def Leppard, played up their sexuality in their image and music videos, starting a trend that would become central to the popularity of 1980s glam or hair metal.

When you hang out with most metalheads in Casablanca or Lahore, however, you'll rarely hear names like Motley Crüe, Warrant, Poison, or other MTV hair-metal icons. Instead, bands like Metallica, Slayer, Deicide, Cannibal Corpse, Possessed, Angel, and other American and Scandinavian inheritors of British metal's new wave captured the ears and imaginations of musicians and fans alike. These bands created a style of music that was faster and far more intense, powerful, distorted, and technically difficult than any form of rock 'n' roll before it. Their music arrived in the region via flight attendants who spent their layovers trolling alternative record shops, expats from the United States or Europe, local record stores that sold illegal music under the counter, and the occasional courageous radio DJ.

Together, death metal and its sister subgenres of black metal (which, in contrast to death metal, features screamed rather than growled vocals and often deals with explicitly satanic themes), goth, doom, grind, grind-core, progressive, and ultimately nu-metal, reshaped the musical landscape of the MENA. Uniting all these genres was the military-style discipline it took to play them correctly at superfast tempos, and the violent, war-laden themes that dominated their lyrics. As one Israeli black-metal artist put it, "You play black metal like a warrior." Many bands, most notably Iron Maiden, designed their album covers and stage shows around the warrior image, although their warriors looked more like Orcs from *The Lord of the Rings* than the clean-shaven and telegenic young soldiers appearing in commercials for the U.S. armed forces.

Indeed, the warrior allusion is a bit ironic, since with the exception of satanic metal, most of the violence in heavy metal is depicted as part of a critique of the violence of society at large, especially its warlike propensities. While it might be hard to imagine when watching Ozzy Osbourne stumble around semi-incoherently in his pajamas on his MTV reality show, in its early days Black Sabbath could be a very political band, as exemplified by the seminal Sabbath song "War Pigs," in which Osbourne railed against "generals gathered in their masses / just like witches at black masses."

Osbourne was singing about the Vietnam War at a time when America was lurching toward a new, globalized "free market" that hit the industrial cities of the United States and Britain, and the working class that populated them, particularly hard. The foreboding and sometimes depressing music of Black Sabbath and the first generation of metal bands resonated with their fans, for whom deindustrialization and other economic problems were accompanied by a rise in alcohol and drug use, and a loss of community and hope for a better future. The same process would inspire punk in London and hip-hop in the South Bronx, a few years later, and gangsta rap and grunge on the West Coast of the United States a decade after that.

The community of fans these genres brought together reflected the widespread desire to drop out of, and in a few cases offer some kind of resistance to, a society from which they felt increasingly estranged. Today the aggressive nature of extreme rock and rap have won them fans across the MENA, where young people are facing dire economic conditions with the added burden of political oppression and, in some cases, occupation. The MENA's metal and rap fans are converting their musical communities into spaces where they can carve out a bit of autonomy, if not freedom, within which they can imagine alternatives to the status quo.

Ultimately, metal, punk, rap, and hard rock are giving their fans a feeling of self-respect and the courage to say to oppressive societies and repressive regimes, "Fuck you, I won't do what you tell me," as a famous Rage Against the Machine song of that title put it. Such a grassroots or do-it-yourself attitude is even more important in the MENA and the larger Muslim world, where governments and societies are strongly opposed—sometimes violently—to metal and everything it represents.

Music and the Struggle for the Soul of Islam

Metal and hip-hop musicians are at the center of the anxieties and even hopes of many Muslims in their teenage years through their late thirties. As a percentage of the population of most Muslim countries, this demographic, particularly its younger members, is close to twice as large as its counterparts in the United States or Europe. Musicians from these cultures tend to be much better educated and informed, and more socially active, than their Western counterparts. The music, politics, and lifestyles they embody are crucial to obtaining a full picture of the dynamics of Gen-X, Gen-Y, and "millennial" Muslims, a good many of whom, in the words of one Lebanese journalist, "love metal [and] freedom, and most of all, they love to live."

I have met musicians, activists, scholars, Islamists, and ordinary people in Morocco, Egypt, Israel/Palestine, Lebanon, Turkey, Iraq, Iran, the Persian Gulf, and Pakistan. This is a wide swath of the Muslim world, home to upward of 500 million people; but that's still only one-third of the Muslim world. The Middle East, and our journey, ends at the Pakistan-India border, but the Muslim world, and Muslim metal, hip-hop, and other forms of pop music, continue all the way to Indonesia.

Even within the region of the Muslim world I know best, I've still found it hard to overcome the clear imbalance in the preponderance of male voices versus those of young women. The most obvious reason for this is that, as with heavy metal, hip-hop, and other macho forms of music in the West, in the Arab/Muslim world these genres tend to be dominated by men, whether musicians or fans. The problem is so acute that the brochure for a 2006 rock and hip-hop festival in Morocco actually included an open letter from one of the female organizers titled "Girls Wanted," imploring young women to become more involved in this kind of music. But as one female artist lamented to me, as long as it's considered immoral, or at least unsafe, for young women to go out on their own to concerts, let alone to be on the stage playing "satanic music," it will be men who make up the majority of metal musicians and fans in the Muslim world.

Another preconception about Islam that is disturbed by delving into the extreme music scenes of the MENA involves the reality of a thriving secular Islam across the region. Contrary to what most westerners and conservative Muslims think, there are plenty of secular Muslims, even in Saudi Arabia and Iran. Some are in fact atheists, or at least agnostics. Most, however, prefer to separate their religious beliefs from their music or their politics, including those who use their music to deepen their personal faith (as opposed to a Christian metal artist who uses the music to evangelize publicly).

Those who identify themselves as religious are often followers of various Sufi, or mystical, forms of Islam. Their style of faith and practice goes against the grain of the Saudi-inspired orthodox vision of Islam that, thanks to decades of missionizing (*da'wa* in Arabic) by ultraconservative Saudis made possible by the kingdom's vast post-1973 oil wealth, is assumed by most non-Muslims to have always defined the religion. In fact, until the last forty years or so, Sufism was the Islam of the vast majority of the world's Muslims, including those in Taliban-controlled Afghanistan and Northwest Pakistan.

Why Metal?

Our discussion still elicits the question of why heavy metal has become increasingly popular in the Muslim world—popular enough that the Moroccan government, which has cracked down on home-grown metalheads, sponsored a metal festival organized by American evangelical Christians with ties to the Bush administration as a way of scoring points with both young Moroccans and its primary political and military sponsor. (Though lots of kids came, hardly anyone understood or paid much attention to the evangelizing lyrics.) The answer is quite simple. As Reda Zine, one of the founders of the Moroccan metal scene, explained to me, "We play heavy metal because our lives *are* heavy metal." That is, the various aesthetic qualities of heavy metal—its harshness, angry tone, and lyrical content—are enmeshed with the quality of life in contemporary Muslim societies. Even for well-educated and relatively prosperous Moroccans, the level of corruption, governmental repression, economic stagnation, and intolerance make it extremely hard to imagine a positive future in their country.

The metal life is not limited solely to metalheads. Young people who don't like metal can still *do* metal, as I learned when I brought Reda together at a conference with a young Shi'i sheikh from Baghdad named Sheikh Anwar al-Ethari (known to his people as "the Elastic Sheikh" because of his willingness to blend Western and Muslim ideas and practices). After listening to Reda describe why he plays metal, Anwar responded, "I don't like heavy metal, not because it's irreligious or against Islam, but because I prefer other styles of music. But you know what? When we get together and pray loudly, with the drums beating fiercely, chanting and pumping our arms in the air, we're doing heavy metal too." In other words, whether chanting for Ozzy, Osama, Najaf, or Moqtada al-Sadr, youth culture is crucial to the larger identity formation and debates within the Muslim world.

The difference between the two forms of metal—playing and praying—is that metalheads are generally quite accepting of outsiders and innovation; conservative Muslims, like their counterparts in most other religions, are not. But Sheikh Anwar, and many metal musicians who are deeply religious, are far from conservative, although figuring out how to categorize many of their relationships to orthodox Islam can be hard work. Beirut-based Iraqi researcher and activist Layla al-Zubaidi put it best when we left a clandestine meeting with a group of Moroccan Islamists on our way to the Boulevard festival to see De La Soul. As we zigzagged through Casablanca's nighttime landscape, she shook her head and complained, "Islamists don't even know who they are—so how can the people who study them, never mind the West more broadly, figure them out?" This is especially true when governments ban or otherwise restrict their activities so that their fellow

Moroccans or Egyptians rarely get the chance to explore their ideas firsthand. And the same problem is faced by metalheads, who, in addition to being arrested, jailed, and even tortured for being "Satan worshippers," have become the butt of national jokes and a foil for comedians, preachers, and talkshow hosts looking to assure mainstream Muslims of their own moral and cultural superiority.

Welcome (Marhaba) to the Global Agora

The variety of voices in Middle Eastern metal, rock, and rap, as well as the difficulties and rewards of bringing them together, became apparent when I wrote and recorded a song, titled "Marhaba," with Reda Zine, at the Beirut studio of Moe Hamzeh, lead singer of the Lebanese hard-rock band the Kordz. The song, whose title means "welcome" in Arabic, blends together hard-rock and funk-guitar riffs, with a Gnawa (Moroccan blues-style Sufi music) bass line and vocals, Lebanese-inflected melodies, and a hip-hop beat.

"Marhaba" was written only a few hours after Reda and I had met Moe, on the first night of the Muslim holy month of Ramadan. After a day of fasting, Reda was clearly inspired as he began playing his gimbri (a traditional Moroccan fretless instrument similar to but tonally lower than a guitar), over which his bandmate Amine Hamma and I started jamming on guitars. Amine played the supposedly Western-style funk line and I added an Arabized melody. Sitting at his dual-harddrive Power Mac G5, Moe came up with a drum track that mixed hip-hop and a bit of Arab percussion soon after the guitars and bass locked into a groove.

What makes the experience of "Marhaba" relevant here is not merely the first night of recording, but all the complexities and interactions that followed during the two years it took to finish the song. How to blend together the subtle but important differences in intonation, melody, and rhythm between North African and Middle Eastern music, not to mention the significant difference between the Arabic of the two regions, was the first issue that had to be confronted. But more challenging were the technological and logistical issues that arose from moving back and forth among various recording systems in Beirut, Paris, Casablanca, and Los Angeles, and finding engineers and producers who would understand how to capture a sound that would honor the different styles in the song.

The lyrics to "Marhaba" are equally as important. In essence, it is a deeply religious song, calling out to welcome a Sufi saint into the presence of the gathered devotees. Yet Reda's lyrics are also quite political, mixing Moroccan Arabic, French, and a smattering of English, recorded in a half-sung, half-rapped style that has come to define Southern rap in the United States (epitomized by the platinum-selling artist Outkast). They describe the numerous problems faced by his society, particularly the "many problems" that prevent the realization of any true democracy, before calling out, in true Gnawa style, to welcome the Sufi saint in the refrain.

What "Marhaba" was ultimately about, Reda reflected during a long night in the studio, was how collaborations such as the one we were engaged in could help forge what he described as a twenty-first-century "virtual agora": a public space in which communication among musicians across different cultures, whether in the studio, on stage, or through the Internet, becomes a model for communication and cooperation in situations where creating a physical agora, of the kind that was the cornerstone of ancient Greek democracy, isn't possible.

Such an agora is crucial in an environment of political oppression, and it's not just a concern for musicians. Egyptian bloggers and Moroccan religious activists alike have become expert at using the Web to disseminate information precisely because governments block other channels of communication. As the webmaster of Morocco's semi-outlawed Justice and Spirituality Association explained with a grin, "We're still better than the government at the Web, so they haven't been able to shut us down even after years of trying." Equally important, the kind of globalized agora that needs no permanent physical location to prosper is an antidote to the "seduction by Internet" that has become the preferred modus operandi for jihadi groups seeking to exploit impressionable young Muslims, for whom hanging around the Internet has become the equivalent of hanging out on the streetcorner a generation ago.

The collaborative building of an agora addresses one of the most important issues facing the Muslim world today—an acute sense of humiliation that is strong enough to turn young Muslims, in the West as well as in the Muslim majority world, into extremists and even terrorists. The Moroccan scholar and activist Mahdi Elmandjra coined the term "humiliocratie" to describe the continued sense of powerlessness, and the institutionalized "daily humiliation" felt by so many Muslims at the hands of the West, and the United States in particular. For Muslim rock and rap artists and activists, the treatment they receive at the hands of their governments and from many members of their societies adds another layer of humiliation, whose sting is often worse than that of their former (and, in a few cases, present) occupiers. These artists, secular and religious alike, are devoting their lives to creating an alternative system that builds an open and democratic culture from the ground up, against the interests of both the political, economic, and religious elites of their countries and, many believe, of the United States and other global powers as well.

§♋§

Not everyone can be a fan of death metal or hardcore rap. But appreciating how the people who are dancing, rapping, playing, and praying, at the seeming edges of their cultures, are transforming Islam and the Muslim world points us toward a deeper understanding of the past, present, and future of Islam. It might be hard to imagine a Muslim Martin Luther King Jr. sharing the stage with a Middle Eastern Ozzy Osbourne—the way Bob Dylan and Joan Baez joined the original MLK on the steps of the Lincoln Memorial at the pivotal moment of the civil rights era, inspiring an audience of tens or hundreds of thousands of idealistic young Muslims to dream of and work toward a hopeful and better future. But it's not so far-fetched; I have seen the various forces in play, in safe houses in Casablanca, in Palestinian ghettos inside Israel, in basements in Tehran, in middle-class neighborhoods in Peshawar, and on stadium-sized festival stages in Dubai and Istanbul. They are growing stronger and more vocal with each passing year.

The real question is not whether such a group can come together, but whether it can reach a large enough audience, and find a big enough stage to play on, before the toxic combination of government oppression, media manipulation, economic restructuring, violence, intolerance, and war drown out the rowdy, liberating new soundtrack of the Muslim world in a sea of hatred and blood.

In the end, *insha'Allah* (God willing), let's hope that it will be the kids with the long hair and black T-shirts who'll have the last laugh.

MOROCCO

When the Music Is Banned, the Real Satanism Will Begin

It's not easy being a headbanger in Morocco. If it's not the police arresting you for Satan worship, it's your guitar being stolen at a performance for high-schoolers, a flash-in-the-pan all-girl thrash metal band stealing the attention of the foreign press, or the corporate sponsor of the festival you created replacing your silhouette with a cell phone as the official logo.

But some nights make it worth all the trouble. This was one of them. It was the opening night of the eighth annual Boulevard des jeunes musiciens, the Boulevard of Young Musicians Festival, in 2006. The Stade du COC—Club Olympique de Casablanca—normally a rugby stadium where the national team plays, was packed with upward of 20,000 metal fans. Backstage, located on the grounds of the adjoining tennis club, were musicians, journalists, the odd filmmaker, the entire

Ugandan national rugby team, and a diverse crew of young, good-looking, and well-off Moroccans partying with great enthusiasm. It was definitely *l'événement* of the summer season.

Located a couple of kilometers from the sea, the Stade du COC sits in a border zone between several working- and upper-middle-class neighborhoods. To one side are rows of gated villas, some appearing to date back to the colonial era, with palm trees swaying in the sea breeze. If you walk just a block or two in the other direction, however, you'll arrive at a busy commercial street and the edge of a less affluent, working-class neighborhood. Early each June, when the festival takes place, the kids from the working-class neighborhoods, joined by tens of thousands of fans from all over Casablanca, Morocco, and even Europe, invade the streets around the stadium, hanging out in front of people's houses, drinking and smoking dope, and occasionally causing a bit of trouble.

Moroccans have coined a term for the kids who invade the Stade du COC each June: *khush pish* (or *bish*). The term is a Moroccan bastardization of the French phrase *les indigenes,* used to describe the native peoples of the countries colonized by France; it became popular in the 1990s to describe lower-class young people who engage in random acts of violence during soccer, other sporting events, and public gatherings. Their begging, harassment, and random attacks on middle- and upper-class Moroccans reflect the anger and nihilism that have driven extreme metal and rap since their emergence, and which are a major reason for their global popularity. This is no doubt why the *khush pish* turn out in force for the metal and hip-hop nights of the Boulevard, and become so rowdy during the shows.

Between the *khush pish* and their middle-class peers, bohemian artists and wannabes, and a sprinkling of hipsters and
hippies from Europe, the atmosphere at the Boulevard is part
Phish show and part NWA. And whether they come from Sidi
Moumen or other slums of Casablanca, the wealthy Anfa
neighborhood, or from Paris's funky 11th arrondissement, the
fans at the Boulevard clearly enjoy the chance to let loose in an
otherwise relatively conservative city. Poorer kids in particular
enjoy the few days of freedom to move, sometimes a bit men-
acingly, through neighborhoods in which they're normally not
allowed to congregate in large numbers. As one friend described it, the festival feels like a Moroccan Carnivale—one
crazy enough that organizers have to hire French-trained security personnel to handle the crowds.

Mostly, however, the tens of thousands of people who
flock to the Boulevard each year come to hear the music,
which is so loud that it reverberates for many blocks outside
the stadium. In fact, this year's sound system was even louder
than the year before, when a band I had just hooked up with,
Reborn, worked the crowd into such a frenzy that the police
almost had to stop the show. Word of last year's musical the-
atrics had spread across the Mediterranean, and a decent con-
tingent of foreign fans and reporters attended. They would
not be disappointed: the bands at the festival, from headliners such as the groundbreaking Portuguese goth-metal band
Moonspell and the American hip-hop pioneers De La Soul to
local stars such as the rapper Bigg and the metal band Syncopea, were all in top form.

When I arrived at the stadium, Moonspell had finished
its first song, and the crowd was going crazy. Their brand of
goth metal is a fusion of the older styles of death and doom

metal, often featuring fast riffs over low and slow grooves with growling, brutal vocals beneath. Lead singer Fernando Ribeiro barked the lyrics to the band's first single, "Finisterra" (Latin for "end of the world") as the crowd got sucked into the angry yet somehow still joyful spirit of Moonspell's music. As the energy level of the crowd grew to match that of the band, I wondered how many people in the audience knew that Casablanca was destroyed by the Portuguese in 1468 (in response to attacks on Portuguese vessels by Moroccan pirates based in what was then the town of Anfa), only to be rebuilt, renamed Casa Branca, and ruled by Lisbon from 1515 until 1755.

The seventy-five-foot viewing screens on either side of the stage and the multiplex light system suited a headliner of Moonspell's stature, while giving the local bands a welcome aura of rock stardom they hadn't yet achieved. Syncopea's music was a particularly fresh combination of progressive metal, funk, pop, and jazz. Both metalheads and those looking for a danceable groove were banging their heads with equal glee during their set, to songs that were at once strangely dissonant and harmonically rich. It became a little more difficult to party with abandon, however, if you actually listened to the words that lead singer Badreddine Otky, his close-cropped hair and goatee dripping with sweat, was screaming: "A world so fucking insane, injustice, abortion, and pain . . . a life so fucking disturbed and I can't avoid all this pain. Genocide, intolerable agony, politics, and wars"—the images upon which most good death-metal songs are built.

As I walked backstage, I caught sight of Reda Zine and Amine Hamma, two of the leaders of the Moroccan metal scene. We embraced and high-fived in celebration of how well Amine and the other organizers had pulled off the Boulevard despite all the financial, artistic, and security obstacles that had stood in their way. Amine reminisced about how far the metal scene had come in the last decade. Once upon a time, bands had rehearsed and performed in high schools, broken-down marriage halls, and nightclubs, and had suffered arrests, beatings, and legal prosecution. Now they were on a giant stage with international media attention and tens of thousands of fans.

Reda and Amine are my oldest friends on the Muslim metal scene. I first met Reda, who's in his late twenties, well over six feet tall, and thin as a reed, while doing Internet research. With his dark olive skin, angular face, and short, loosely wound afro, Reda looks like someone whose ancestors came to Morocco as slaves from Mali or Senegal. At least, I thought, that was the reason he sang and played the music of the Gnawa, who arrived in Morocco as slaves centuries ago, as if it were in his blood for generations. But in fact his family has lived in Dar al-Bayda, as Casablanca is known in Arabic, for as long as they can remember.

Soon after meeting, on the Internet, Reda and I came to understand that we shared what he calls "la même biographie" as musicians, academics, and activists. It was just a matter of time before we went from chat rooms to rehearsal rooms, the recording booth, and ultimately to sharing the stage. I had met Amine the year before, on the first night of the 2005 Boulevard festival, at a midnight jam in the apartment of a mutual friend. We passed around a couple of old acoustic guitars, gimbris, and hand drums, and started talking about the role of music in Morocco. I had long been a fan of Gnawa music, and had performed and recorded with celebrated Moroccan Gnawa artist Hassan Hakmoun. Reda and I had even jammed in

Sicily the week before, when we first met at a workshop on heavy metal and Islam that I'd organized in Messina. So I figured I could hold my own in a late-night session.

But I wasn't prepared for the kind of raw, roots-blues that Amine, Reda, and their friends started to play. As the music droned on and the warm sea air wafted in through the window, the musicians' voices drifted in and out of harmonies and the unique singsong of Derija (the Moroccan dialect of Arabic that is largely incomprehensible to Arabs east of Tunisia) interlaced with French, Berber, and West African dialects. I tried to imagine how heavy metal fit into this musical equation. A couple of days later, when Reda and Amine hit the stage with their band Reborn and 20,000 kids went crazy, the power and possibility of what Amine calls "Gnawa metal" became perfectly clear.

Reda is a few years older than Amine, and more experienced as a professional musician, but it's Amine who looks the part of a founder of one of the Muslim world's best metal scenes. He has the long, wavy black hair that describes the metal look from Morocco to Iran. And he plays guitar the same way he sings Gnawa and plays the gimbri: with a level of skill and authenticity that you'd rarely hear, for example, when an American metal guitarist tries to play the blues.

Like most metalheads, Reda and Amine got hooked on heavy metal in high school. When we first met, they were finishing degrees in Paris: Reda a PhD in Arab Media Studies at the Sorbonne, Amine an MA in the politics of leisure and cultural facilities at the University of Paris. They speak French fluently, as well as respectable English. They move back and forth between metal, Gnawa, jazz, and a variety of other musical genres even more easily.

This fluidity and openness to the world, while remaining rooted in Moroccan culture and concerns, defines the Boulevard festival. Other music festivals, such as the Fes World Sacred Music Festival and the Essaouira Gnawa Music Festival, are better known because they cater to foreigners as well as a large Moroccan audience, and sell an officially sponsored vision of tolerance and dialogue between the Muslim world and the West. The Boulevard is a much less sanitized and more Moroccan affair—a mass of contradictions and incongruities, musical and political. Its goal has always been to use the draw of a few well-known artists to give young Moroccan musicians the chance to gain exposure and experience. That such a festival can attract upward of 150,000 Moroccans over four days is a testament to the power of pop music and youth culture: it's organized almost entirely by young Moroccans, while dozens of volunteers and an increasing number of music fans come each year from across Europe (particularly France) to listen and perform.

The crowd is as interesting as the artists. People come dressed in strange combinations of metal, hip-hop, and punk attire. One can see a teenager with green spiky hair and baggy, hip-hop style clothing standing next to one in goth makeup, and a few feet away yet another in a black metal T-shirt who's watching the show with his mother or aunt, who may be dressed in a black, full-length abaya. The most startling sight of the festival, however, occurs when breakdancing competitions between fans erupt on the field between sets, with toprocks, downrocks, handstands, windmills, and other "power moves" being deployed with as much enthusiasm and proficiency as you might have seen on the streetcorners and basketball courts of New York City a generation ago.

Satan and Schizophrenia in Morocco

As Amine tells it, heavy metal arrived in Morocco in the mid-1990s: "In high school I followed all the trends, watching MTV's *Headbanger's Ball,* which was the most important show in the third world for metalheads who had access to satellite channels. Nirvana, Guns N' Roses, Machine Head, Cannibal Corpse, Morbid Angel, Carcass, In Flames, thrash metal from the Bay Area and New York." Most of the bands were formed by high-school students like Amine, and by the late 1990s the independent, grassroots spirit that is at the heart of most metal scenes also motivated Amine and other young friends to organize "mini-festivals" featuring the best bands from Casablanca.

Soon bands were forming with names like In the Nightmare, Guardians of the Moonlight, Despotism War, Killer Zone, Paranoia, Necrospiritual, and Tormentor of Souls. Among the best of the first crop of Moroccan metal bands was Immortal Spirit, established in 1996 by Amine and several friends. Immortal Spirit was at the forefront of Moroccan metal's eclectic and hybrid tendencies. The band was founded to "create a harmony between our Moroccan origins and the underground or avant-garde tendencies of metal." Think thrash with Dadaist ornaments: fast and dirty guitars, blasting drums synched tightly with the bass, with soundscapes and screamed vocals on top. There was hardly anyplace to rehearse; bands often wound up "squatting" in garages of friends whose parents were out of town, or rehearsing in nightclubs before they opened for the night. The only places to play for audiences were in high schools, rented halls, and the odd private party.

Then in 1999 the first Boulevard was organized; with its success, most big metal shows began to be organized by the grassroots organization that put on the festival. Not everyone stuck with the scene, though. Some metalheads "grew up" and left; a few even became Islamists. As Amine put it, "Our first guitarist was wicked at soloing, he was poor but fanatic, like us. But then he became fanatic about religion. He has a *barb* [beard] and doesn't play or even listen to music any-more." Immortal Spirit kept going. In the words of one re-view, its "pulsating and joyful" music reflected not just a "cultural revolution" for Morocco, but the realization that "music is undoubtedly a subversive language, free and har-monious," as well.

By the early 2000s, heavy metal was one of the major youth forces in the country. Kids would come from all over Morocco and camp out overnight to get good seats at metal concerts, which saw, according to one reviewer, "the unshaven and cosmopolitan Casablanca youth . . . coming to hear a music sure to piss off their mothers, who are stuck between Celine Dion and marshmallow pseudo-Lebanese pop . . . and to develop their own political consciousness." It wasn't their mothers who were pissed off, however. Instead, it was the Mukhabarat (security services), as metalheads discovered quite painfully when fourteen heavy-metal musicians and fans were arrested in February 2003, tried, and convicted of the ab-surd crime of being "satanists who recruited for an interna-tional cult of devil-worship," and of "shaking the foundations of Islam," "infringing upon public morals," "undermining the faith of a Muslim," and "attempting to convert a Muslim to another faith"—as if rock 'n' roll were a religion on a par with Islam. Similar raids have occurred against heavy-metal-listening "devil worshippers" in Lebanon, Egypt, and Iran.

Unlike these countries, however, the strategy of scaring musicians into silence did not work in Morocco. Invigorated human rights and youth groups sent hundreds of activists to a metal concert outside the Parliament building in Rabat a week after the Moroccans were sentenced. Even the unthinkable— a metal-yuppie coalition under the banner "Rockers, Dockers, Meme Combat!"—emerged, while one cartoon depicted Satan in a judge's chair with a red pentagram (which is, after all, part of the Moroccan flag) handing down a *verdict satanique,* a satanic verdict. But the religious community remained either apathetic and silent about the arrests, or spoke out against the young people, something few musicians have been willing to forgive, or forget.

Marock Sans Frontiers (Moroccan rock 'n' roll without borders) actually printed an open letter on their website to King Mohammed VI, asking him if the thugs who had arrested and jailed them "acted on your orders." Considering the penalties for insulting the king, the letter's boldness is reckless: "We want to believe with all our force, no. But in this case, one can't escape this fact: some among your subordinates escaped your control. That you have reasons not to clamp down . . . is, to a point, understandable. But to let the psychosis take hold isn't."

Reda's strategy for defeating what he called "the vampires of intolerance and superstition" was simple: "Trust each other, brandish our tolerance against these hideous visages of regression of all kinds." But the "each other" he's talking about is much larger than just Morocco. The "we" that needs to trust itself can come about only through a globalization of solidarity and sympathy. Yet however positive the outcome of the satanic metal affair was from an activist perspective, the incident pitted two forces who could and should be working together precisely because they recognize the same disease in Moroccan society and have a similar interest in building greater democracy and tolerance: rock-'n'-rollers and the country's oppositional Islamist movements. But government repression, coupled with religious conservatism and cultural stereotyping in society at large, succeeded in keeping these groups apart.

Ultimately the affair was resolved when the musicians were cleared—ironically leaving the music scene stronger than before. This is a very different outcome from the Arab world's first "satanic metal affair," in Egypt in 1997, which left the local music scene reeling for most of the next decade. In Morocco, however, within a year new bands such as the thrash-metal outfit Imperium began performing at smaller festivals such as the Sidi Rock Fest and Metal Gig 3, and even organized tours of cities like Meknes and Rabat. Each year, more people came to the Boulevard.

❦

In one of the best rock albums in a long time, the Moroccan rock/reggae/African/post-punk band Hoba Hoba Spirit sings that Morocco is a *blad schizo,* a schizophrenic country. When I asked lead singer and respected journalist Reda Allali why he gave the album this title, he responded bluntly, "Because it *is* a schizophrenic country." Centuries of power wielded by the Makhzen (the name long used to describe the Moroccan political and economic circle around the king), intensified by European imperialism and now globalization, have made it so. "You have to understand," he continued, "even our language is schizo. [Derija, the Moroccan dialect of Arabic, is a mix of Arabic, Berber, French, and its own grammar.] No one else, from the Middle East, Africa, or Europe, understands us. And our politics are twisted as well. That's why, in one song from the album, I sing that I just want a TV that will speak to me without twisting words, which is so important because after so many years of twisted words we've lost a feeling of social solidarity."

As Hoba Hoba Spirit's music makes clear, Morocco's painful political and economic realities are never far from the minds of artists and organizers. Everyone realizes that long after the stage, lights, and PA system are packed away from the growing number of festivals around the country, the Mukhabarat and the corrupt and still-oppressive system it serves, remain.

A History of Globalization and Exploitation

Although it involved some degree of violence, Morocco's struggle for independence did not involve anything like the bloody war waged by Algerians to obtain their independence from France. But the first two kings who ruled after independence in 1957, particularly Hassan II (the father of the current monarch, Mohammed VI) were no less corrupt than their counterparts in the Algerian republic. They curtailed the power of the parliament and other potentially democratic forces in order to ensure the survival and power of the monarchy and the Makhzen, which for 800 years has brought together attendants to the royal family, wealthy businessmen and landowners, tribal leaders, senior military and security officials, and politicians in a stable, if sometimes uneasy, set of alliances.

The Makhzen might seem removed from the metal scene, but in fact the relationship between the two is symbolic of the larger problems facing the country today. As one metal musician explained, it's the Makhzen that decides whether you can realize your dreams. Its long history of behind-the-scenes power has been crucial to the stability of the monarchy. But the price has been an equally stable system of corruption and authoritarianism whose roots are centuries deep, and which continues to make it extremely difficult to achieve real democracy and economic development in Morocco.

Whatever the democratic pretenses, there are limits to what a 2005 U.S. State Department report terms "tolerable dissent" in Morocco—meaning that nothing that represents a popular challenge to the power of the king, the government, or the Makhzen is tolerated—whether it's the main opposition and Sufi movement, the Justice and Spirituality Association, or the metal scene pushing the boundaries. These limits are clear from the increasing repression against journalists in Morocco in the last few years, even as the ruling elite has allowed increasingly "free and fair" elections to be held.

As exemplified by the Boulevard (and more recently by festivals in Europe devoted to Moroccan metal and rap), musicians and other marginalized groups (for example, Berber-rights groups, anti-globalization activists, and environmental and religious movements) have responded to the complex and often disheartening realities of life in Morocco today by using globalization to create alternative, often grassroots networks that provide the kinds of social, economic, and political space denied by the establishment. These global networks are among the best, if not the only, lines of defense against the toxic strains of globalization to Islam that circle like vultures over the politically and economically weaker countries of the Middle East and North Africa. They help the often young Moroccans who move within them to express their anger at the status quo, exercise autonomy from a system they find exceedingly hard to change, and even formulate a vision and strategy for doing just that.

In Hoba Hoba Spirit's anthem "El Caid Motorhead" (also known as "Morockan Roll"), the band calls out to anyone who'll listen that Morocco has developed its own rock 'n' roll, and with it a powerful community that's not afraid to take on all who dare attack it. Yet one of Allali's chief worries remains the loss of social solidarity in Morocco in recent years, and in expressing this concern he's making a pointed critique of a state in which the king, who is designated as God's appointed deputy on earth, is considered the binding force that unites the country's diverse population. This ideology has served the Moroccan political and economic elite surrounding the king quite well, but not the rest of his subjects.

Given its reach into Moroccan society, the Makhzen is well aware of how Hoba Hoba Spirit and other artists are creating new modes of resistance against it. At one of Hoba Hoba Spirit's concerts, "someone from the Makhzen was standing next to me in front of 100,000 people," Allali recounted, "and he said, 'We can't do this; only you can. Be careful what you say.' But he didn't mean this as a warning; he said it with a tone of admiration."

The man from the Makhzen was also wrong, or, rather, only half right. Yes, rock groups like Hoba Hoba Spirit can bring 100,000 people to a concert, but the only force in the country that can bring out similar and even far greater numbers into the streets for an explicitly political purpose is the Justice and Spirituality Association (JSA), the country's largest religious-political movement, founded by the famed Sufi sheikh and scholar Abdessalam Yassine in 1981. This is why, as a headline from the newspaper *as-Sahifa* on the second day of the 2006 Boulevard festival described it, the group was in "a war of destiny" with the government, even as metalheads and other cultural subversives in Morocco were finding their social and even political horizons a bit more open than before.

The JSA shares Allali's view of Morocco as a schizophrenic country. Moreover, both see the kind of tolerated dissent represented by most "alternative"-seeming music and/or religious forces—just edgy enough to seem critical or innovative, but avoiding a direct challenge to the system—as the antithesis of a true political opening. Instead, they point to how difficult it is to work for serious yet positive change in a system that has had centuries to cement its hold on power.

Indeed, the Makhzen does not tolerate dissent that would challenge its power. What it does tolerate, and what the government is regularly celebrated for, is the kind of "bold" economic, political, and social reforms demanded by the United States and international lending and development agencies, regardless of the steep social and economic

costs that accompany them. Such reforms have been imposed on Morocco for almost three decades, making the
country one of the Arab world's "early reformers" when it
comes to embracing neoliberal globalization. But it leaves the
country still behind the curve as far as democracy and freedom of expression are concerned.

There is a strong connection between the slum neighborhoods of Casablanca—home to the *khush pish* who flock to the
Boulevard every year—which have grown in step with Moroccan poverty and inequality, the radicalism they breed, and the
music that reflects this situation. As Omar Essayed, a member
of Nass El Ghiwane, one of Morocco's seminal musical groups
of the 1960s and 1970s, explained in a 2006 interview, mixing
great rhythms and subtle political critique has long been a
recipe for climbing out of the slums of Casablanca and onto
the North African pop charts. But back in his day, music also
had to give some hope, to reaffirm the strong bonds that
united Moroccans even during troubled times.

Today, he lamented, "Where can young people go? If they
have plenty of money, they go to nightclubs. Otherwise it's the
mosque." There are raves and smaller festivals and concerts,
but most of the musicians and activists I know—religious as
well as secular—agree with Essayed when he argues that the
social solidarity and modest ambition of previous generations
of Moroccans have been replaced by extraordinary wealth for a
few, and despair and violence for far too many. What's behind
this transformation away from a shared sense of belonging and
toward either individualistic ambition or a narrower, religiously
grounded solidarity (or both)? In a word, globalization.

As in most Muslim countries outside of the wealthy Persian Gulf states, the majority of Moroccans have been struc-

turally marginalized from the economic processes of globalization, such as increased trade, foreign investment, and adop-
tion of the latest technological advances to modernize industry.
And as in Jordan, Egypt, or Syria, whatever economic growth
these policies have produced has been accompanied by levels
of poverty, inequality, illiteracy, unemployment, and disease
that have either worsened, or at best remained anemic.

Moroccan and other peoples of the Muslim world have
been exposed to the full force of cultural globalization in other
ways as well. All of the satellite dishes you see from the train
as you pass by the slums of Casablanca and Rabat bring into
the homes of poor, and often religious, Moroccans an endless
stream of images, advertisements, half-naked and in many
cases fully-naked bodies, and fantasy depictions of life *outre-
mer* (beyond the sea), that few of the people watching them,
especially young men, can either resist or ever hope to afford.
This is a sure recipe for social anomie and psychological and
political distress.

Yet at the same time globalization also makes it possible
to watch MTV's *Headbanger's Ball,* and dozens of styles of
music from across the globe, which have inspired a generation of Morocco's best musicians to create some of the most
innovative new styles of music in the world. And it helps activists forge connections across the Mediterranean and beyond, which have opened up small but potentially significant
new spaces for critiquing and offering an alternative to the existing system.

❧

But whether it's globalization's negative or positive implica-
tions, one thing that became clear to me as I learned more

about its many roots and pathways is that the United States isn't always at the center of these processes. This became clear to me while drinking, I admit, Lipton tea—few people these days bother going through the ritual of preparing the traditional but far more delicious sweet mint tea—with two of Morocco's leading sociologists, Muhammad Tozy and Abderrahmane Lakhsassi. It was the third morning of the 2006 Boulevard festival, but it wasn't music that was on their minds. Instead it was the upcoming World Cup, most of which they weren't going to be able to watch after a Saudi company bought the rights to broadcast the World Cup in Morocco and then demanded that the Moroccan government pay $8 million for the signal (a tidy sum for a relatively poor country), which it couldn't afford. Only last-minute negotiations with the king ensured that Moroccans could watch a few important matches.

This, Tozy explained, was what globalization meant in Morocco, and it wasn't America that was behind it. Rather, it was the Saudis and their Persian Gulf brothers who were determining not just what Moroccans could watch on TV, but, increasingly, the shape of their economy and culture as well. The privatization of Moroccan television by foreigners is just one example of how an emerging "Dubai Consensus" is using the unprecedented oil wealth of the Gulf states to integrate other countries of the Muslim world into an OPEC-led regional economy with more success and less opposition than the largely discredited Washington Consensus before it. What we see in Morocco is how, if the United States and the other Western powers set the macro-level conditions for the globalized economy, today their Arab allies are acting in concert to solidify and even strengthen the system's power in the MENA.

To see the Morocco imagined by the Dubai Consensus, Tozy reminded me, visit the website of the Dubai-based Emaar Properties, perhaps the largest real-estate developer in the Muslim world. There you can fantasize about—or, if you're one of the few people lucky enough to afford it, actually consider—buying a home in a development like the "Bahia Bay" gated community on the Atlantic Ocean, the luxury golfing complex "Amelkis II," and "Saphira," the marina beachfront development in Rabat. Then visit the slums of Rabat, Casablanca, and other towns. Inside the gaping hole between vision and reality lies the cauldron that produces both Morocco's metalheads and its extremists.

Critiques of Arab neoliberalism are not offered just by curmudgeonly professors. Musicians are just as sensitive to the impact of Gulf hypercapitalism, which has made it even harder for Morocco's heavily politicized metal scene to travel across North Africa and into the Middle East, where the music is more depoliticized. Reda Zine explains this situation using the same language—an "invasion of foreign cultures"—bandied about by Muslim critics of Western globalization: "We're estranged from the dull Lebanese music clips that invade our media . . . In the end, it becomes a question of identity—musical and personal." In response, the Moroccan metal scene, and Marockan roll more broadly, has acted as a counterpoint to the domination of the production and distribution of popular music by a few Arab media conglomerates. It's not an easy struggle or a fair fight.

But it's getting harder to counter the power of global capital in Morocco, as became increasingly evident at the 2006 Boulevard. The festival was in many ways a more professional affair than in previous years. But that's because it was more corporate as well. Formerly free to the public, the festival now charged for entry (although only a modest fee, equivalent to about two dollars, just enough to keep the really poor out), and had enough security to ensure that those who couldn't pay couldn't sneak in. But something was also missing from the 2006 festival, and troublingly so. The year before, when I first attended it, the festival grounds were ringed by tents put up by grassroots NGOs from around Morocco. Many of them were associated with bands at the festival; the volunteers were often young women with headscarves, and they worked on issues ranging from homelessness to AIDS, drug addiction, and human rights. One of the musical highlights was the performance of an all-girl thrash-metal band, Mystik Moods.

In short, the 2005 festival pushed political and gender boundaries as much as musical ones. Walking through the various NGO booths was as exhilarating as standing on the stage. In 2006 all the booths were gone, save for a giant tent selling Red Bull at the back of the field. Few fans needed the energy boost provided by the drink; the music more than sufficed. But with the booths went the grassroots spirit that had made the Boulevard a unique combination of art and activism, and, because of that combination, a unique and valuable cultural and political space.

Perhaps the most telling image suggesting that the balance of power had shifted from the festival's grassroots organizers to its corporate sponsors was the logo. In 2005 the logo was a silhouette of Amine, in a guitar-god pose—legs apart, head bowed, long hair flowing, ripping into a guitar solo— which was also featured on seventy-five-foot banners on each side of the stage. The T-shirt featured the same image, with the logo of Nokia, the main corporate sponsor, relegated to the side of a sleeve. In 2006, however, Amine was replaced by a rip-off of the old Aerosmith logo, in this incarnation a winged cell phone with the word "Nokia" inside it. Both the T-shirt and the giant banners on each side of the stage bore the same image.

Amine wouldn't let on how annoyed or insulted he was to have been replaced by a cell phone as the logo of the festival he'd helped create. But he did rightly point out how expensive it has become to put such a festival on, particularly the battle of the bands that helps bring local talent from around the country to national and even international attention. But the activists who created the Boulevard didn't need Nokia to push them away from their original vision. By 2006 they were ready to leave the old-school, grassroots imagery behind, if the symbolism of the poster and the accompanying television ad for the festival were any indication. The image was of a beat-up old Mercedes taxi (the kind driven by taxi drivers across the Arab world), filled with a ragtag band of Moroccan musicians of various stripes, their incongruously ultramodern equipment on its roof, literally flying toward a beautiful, gleaming city of the future that towered above a more traditional cityscape of a Moroccan medina. On the surface, such imagery clearly signified the artists and organizers of the festival bringing Moroccan music, from Gnawa to metal, to the rest of the world. But look deeper and a more contradictory image appears, one in which the organizers see the festival as helping to modernize—but through it, whether the organizers want to or not, corporatize and commodify—not just Moroccan music, but Moroccan culture along with it.

Amine admitted that while the "militant spirit remained" among organizers, it has been at least partly replaced by a "new identity, based on image and notoriety—of the sponsors." Because of this, a scene that only a few years before had scared the authorities so much that a "satanic music affair" was needed to tamp it down, is now being patronized by the Ministry of Culture and sponsored by the biggest cell-phone company in the world. It's still a great festival, but its political force is getting harder to feel unless you already know where to look.

Yo Nigga! Moroccan Rap Hits the Big Time

Metalheads like to brag—and there's at least a measure of truth to their claims—that metal helped bring down the Iron Curtain by serving as an important source for alternative, antigovernment identities for young people in the last decades of communist rule. If heavy metal showed its global reach in the fall of communism, hip-hop has become *the* music of the age of globalization. From the projects of the South Bronx and Los Angeles to the slums of Lagos and São Paolo, rap's combination of sparse, menacing beats, angry and sometimes violent verses, and uneasy worship of money and power captures the experience of being poor and marginalized better than any other art form. But if American rap has largely been co-opted by profit-hungry entertainment corporations and rappers willing to trade in political relevance for a piece of the corporate pie, in Morocco rap still retains much of its subversive spirit. And no one represents this trend better than the new king of Moroccan rap, Bigg.

Bigg is, in fact, quite large, at about six feet and 280 pounds—certainly as big as Heavy D, Notorious B.I.G., and other "big" American hip-hop stars. Bigg has been rapping since his early teenage years, and it comes to him naturally. He can spit out rhymes in a variety of styles and cadences that remind one of Outkast one minute and Tupac the next, in a melange of Moroccan Derija, French, and English, and set to the latest beats from L.A. or Atlanta. Yet he fancies himself something of a Moroccan Frank Sinatra, if one can picture a sumo version of Sinatra rapping in Arabic. Watching him sashay across the giant stage of the Boulevard working the crowd with an expertise that belies his twenty-two years, it's not hard to imagine a bit of Old Blue Eyes in him. Bigg's lyrics, however, are uniquely Moroccan. At times he raps of the fear (*al-khouf*) so many Moroccans experience, whether warranted or not, of the emerging global system. Other times he discusses the humiliation they experience on a daily basis.

There's another reason hip-hop has quickly become so popular in Morocco and across the Muslim world—more so, in many places, than heavy metal or other genres of rock. Just as in the inner-city ghettos of the United States a generation ago, it's a lot easier to become a rapper and rhyme over pre-recorded tracks than invest a lot of money in a guitar or drums or a keyboard, spend years learning how to play the instruments, and then cart all the equipment around in a van to various gigs (which could then get destroyed or confiscated in police raids). Rapping and wearing hip-hop clothing is also a much better way of gaining the "street cred" that's important in urban ghettos around the world than would be growing long hair, wearing death-metal concert T-shirts, and playing guitar.

That is why, according to the manager of the rap group H-Kayne, the hip-hop scene is "the Big Bang right now . . . or at least similar to Brooklyn in the early 1980s. The number of practitioners is constantly growing. The local cultural or municipal organizations, who were quite good at turning hip-hop projects down, are now very keen on anything urban (thanks to the work of Boulevard des jeunes musiciens mainly). Even advertisers are recognizing its importance, and clubs are promising to start having hip-hop shows."

Whereas in the Occupied Territories, Hamas supporters have physically attacked rappers and their fans, in Morocco rappers have escaped the persecution by religious forces that has bedeviled their rocker comrades. Perhaps that's because rappers have focused on hip-hop's roots as political and especially social commentary, which in the United States have been all but buried under two decades of bling. According to one rapper (who asked that I not use his name), "The hip-hop spirit is not seen as an agnostic or atheistic one, and the fact that Morocco is a Muslim country has meant that MCs will generally avoid cursing or describing girls with negative words. Nor will they make the apology of guns, cars, and bling-bling, simply because that stuff doesn't reflect Morocco's reality."

This is not to say that all rap in Morocco is politically and culturally correct. Many rap artists, like the Mekness-based group H-Kayne, can be explicitly political. But there are also groups like Camelkos, who are content to copy the form and language of gangsta rap, with lyrics such as "Yo nigga, this is my life" and other stereotypical gangsta language, while avoiding the substantive critique of their society that made the genre so powerful and threatening in the United States.

What the best rappers are trying to create, however, is a kind of "hip-hop madrasa," what pioneering American rapper KRS-One calls a "temple of hip-hop"—a kind of public sphere for educating their young audience about the realities of the world in which they live. H-Kayne is clearly well schooled in hip-hop; its 2005 Boulevard performance blew the other bands off the stage (including the American headliner of the hip-hop day, Jah Stimuli). Mixing hard-core rap with traditional Moroccan Gnawa and other genres, H-Kayne represents hip-hop at its best.

With both Bigg and H-Kayne you get the feeling that, in Bigg's words, "Hip-hop isn't mediated yet in Morocco. We don't rap for money or nice cars, but to improve ourselves and our society." What makes the best rappers so good is precisely their recognition of how important music is as a "strong voice" for young people's struggles in Morocco. Yet while it's clear most rappers share such sentiments, if rap were this overtly political, it is likely we'd be reading about a satanic rap affair. Why such a crackdown hasn't occurred was explained to me by a young rapper performing at his first Boulevard: "The government doesn't bother you as long as you don't cross the lines." That's why most political rappers remain largely off the Mukhabarat's radar screen.

Morocco's Riot Grrrls: Caught Between Algeria and Iran?

One of the most talked-about performances of the Boulevard's eight-year history was that of the Moroccan hard-core metal band Mystik Moods. What made the band and their performance so special was not the music, which was in the early stages of development. Rather it was who they were and what they stood for: a bourgeois Arab all-girl version of the Sex Pistols, whose members, all in their teens, sported a goth-trash schoolgirl fashion style and a reckless disregard for the craft of musicianship. All this somehow managed to enhance the appeal of their music.

Certainly the band's performance caused quite a stir; much of the crowd of mostly young men spent the first half of the show screaming and gesturing "fuck you" at the band in anger at the very idea that girls would be playing heavy metal. But the sheer determination and courage of the band members, and their willingness to give the finger back to the crowd, eventually won over much of the audience. As one of the band members (who didn't want to be quoted by name) explained to me, "It's not easy to be a girl in the metal scene, no matter what country you're living in. But especially in Morocco. It's even hard for boys to play metal without being treated like shit by Moroccan society. But did you see our show? By the end there was a mosh pit, so the crowd moved past our appearance and gender and just dug the music."

And it wasn't just the crowd of rowdy teenage boys that dug Mystik Moods. The band's anarchic, disheveled "riot grrrl" act earned them a segment on the French channel Arte and, more important, fans in the royal family. Soon after the festival they were invited by some of the princesses to perform at the palace. Later that year they performed at a festival sponsored by the king (in fact, running along the bottom of the stage under the rock-'n'-roll light show were the words "Under the patronage of His Royal Highness, King Mohammed VI").

While the highlight of their career might have been the endorsement by a direct descendant of the Prophet Muham-

mad, they would never have come this far without the support
of their families. "Even our grandmas supported us, and
they're very conservative," said one of the singers, sixteen-
year-old Ritz. "Some people want to show off their religion,
but you know what, not everyone. Look at my father," she
added in explanation. "He prays *and* loves music too. In fact,
he's doing the sound for the festival!" Indeed, all the band
members have family members and friends who were "traditionally" religious, and none of them were opposed to their
music.

Given the support they've received, the members of Mystik Moods are naturally more sanguine about the prospects for
their future and that of Morocco than are most of the male
metal musicians I've met. As Mystik Mood's other lead singer,
Rita, put it, "In Morocco, women have more opportunities because our regime is more liberal than in other Arab countries."
(Despite this sentiment, however, most of the band members
were living and studying in France when I met them.) Bass
player Kenza elaborated, "This country is always moving, on
the way to developing. You know, they say that tradition and
modernity are supposed to be contradictory, that if they become more globalized or westernized, young people automatically become more European and renounce their tradition.
But this is a false idea of what religion and tradition are."

Perhaps, although nothing in the dress, language, or attitudes of Mystik Moods says that they incorporate "traditional"
Islam into their lives very much. As the band's guitarist,
Anaïs, saw it, "Young people are torn between two trends, two
kinds of extremes. On the one side are young people who
listen to everything Western, and on the other, they are only
religious, they can't be open. But it's wrong to call them

'traditional,' because tradition is more temperate than this."
Ritz added, "You know, young people who like metal also are
Muslims and pray." At the same time, however, the whole
band agreed that it was impossible to get along, or even have a
conversation, with extreme religious forces. In a clear dig at
the JSA's Nadia Yassine, Ritz explained, "The Islamists say,
'Yeah, we want democracy and a republic,' but what kind?
Like Algeria and Iran?"

Ultimately, Mystik Moods represents a very political moment in Morocco, but for the group's members the political is
most definitely personal: the freedom to dress, act, and play
however they want. Some scholars, such as the Columbia
University historian Thaddeus Russel, argue that such personal, sexualized politics is ultimately as powerful a force for
social change as the more overt politics of their male counterparts. As he put it after studying the regional popularity of pop
stars like Beyoncé, "in the Middle East, Beyoncé is a freedom
fighter." This may yet prove true. But in an environment
where DVDs of the latest porn movies easily outsell the jihadi
videos on the next shelf—even in Pakistan's North-West Frontier province—and *Sex and the City* has aired on Arabic Show-
time, there's as good a chance that sex will be as liberating in
the Muslim world as it is everywhere else—that is to say, liberating for women of a certain class and temperament, but irrelevant or even insulting and oppressive for their less
fortunate compatriots.

The King and the Witch

The members of Mystik Moods aren't the only mystical
women in Morocco. Nadia Yassine, "spokesperson" of the

JSA, is the heir to the most important mystical movement in the country. Although not technically outlawed by the government, its members are constantly harassed and its publications largely banned. Indeed, Sheikh Yassine spent almost two decades under house arrest for writing an open letter to King Hassan II in 1974, calling on him to repent of his autocratic ways. A little over two decades later, his daughter Nadia was indicted by the government for treason for daring to suggest, in an interview at a conference at UC Berkeley that we both attended, that a republic was perhaps a better form of government for Morocco than the monarchy.

Yassine is simultaneously one of the most nurturing and one of the most mischievously sarcastic people I've ever met. Such traits seem natural to someone who's had to simultaneously fight the Makhzen and be spiritual guide to several million Moroccans. She is a French teacher by training, and discussions with her send one running to the *Encyclopedia of Philosophy* and the works of Noam Chomsky and Howard Zinn.

The JSA has been thumbing its nose at the king and the Moroccan elite for more than two decades. While some metal artists get invited to the Royal Palace, the closest most JSA members get to the king is his photograph in a courtroom or jail, and that's fine with them. Between father and daughter, the JSA evolved into one of the most formidable religious and political movements in the Muslim world. Its commitment to nonviolence, its refusal to play the political game, and its focus largely on Moroccan rather than pan-Islamic issues (such as Israel or Iraq) make it unique and distinctly powerful. Yet while the JSA is interesting as a movement, it is Yassine who gives the group its high profile and edge. She is, one could say, more "heavy metal" than the young women of Mystik Moods.

Indeed, being called a witch puts her in the company of the country's metalhead–Satan worshippers, as they've been dubbed by the government and the courts. One thing is for sure, neither want to "suffer in silence" anymore, and both tend to be loud—the rockers and rappers with blasting music and searing lyrics, Nadia Yassine with her no-holds-barred attacks on Morocco's political system and her willingness to show up at court with her lips taped shut with an X to demonstrate the government's desire to silence her. As she defiantly explains, "Witches are witches because they think and act in different ways from other people. When people see a witch behaving differently, they get scared." Think Alice Cooper, Ozzy, or Marilyn Manson wearing a head scarf.

࿐

The difference between how Nadia Yassine and the girls from Mystik Moods view the world became clearer when I met with a group of hard-core activists of the JSA on the second day of the 2006 Boulevard. The first thing that strikes someone used to meeting with "Islamists" around the Muslim world is how much in dress (conservative), demeanor (usually very nice, polite yet formal), and worldview (conservative) they resemble conservative Christians in the United States. And their ideologies and rhetoric are similarly confident, and often hostile to divergent views. Discussions with JSA members are quite different, however; their focus on nonviolence and on critiques of neoliberal globalization make them appear to resemble more closely the long-haired activists of the Boulevard than the more dangerous but in many ways *less* radical groups such as Hamas or Hezbollah.

Because of constant surveillance of JSA members by the Mukhabarat, and standing orders to arrest members who congregate in groups larger than three people, meetings with the movement are usually clandestine, and can involve changing cars or taking circuitous routes to the meeting. Our meeting was in the home of an engineer and his wife, a teacher, who live in a working-class neighborhood of Casablanca. While the building was rather drab, the apartment was large and well furnished, reflecting the family's middle-class lifestyle. The fifteen or so members who came, most in their mid- to late twenties, were dressed in typical Islamist clothing—the men in off-the-rack suits, sporting closely cropped beards, the women in pantsuits or long skirts with loose-fitting jackets and full hejabs, which cover all their hair and neck, leaving just an oval around their face.

I was there to figure out whether the JSA's truly radical politics was matched by a more tolerant social ethos than is exhibited by most Islamist movements, regardless of their economic agendas: that is, could the JSA members get along and even work with their more musical peers in the metal scene to build the Morocco they both say they want? "Can you be a good Muslim and a good metalhead?" I asked. "Yes, definitely," one of the women, a schoolteacher, answered. "It's quite possible. But it's not just music, you know. Women should be able to do what they want, go to college, whatever. But . . ." And here I expected the sort of answer that Islamists often give to questions when they know what you expect to hear, want to say the opposite, but don't want to anger their guest. Instead, she continued, "The main question is, does music lead you to the Prophet and to God?"

Most of the musicians I know in the Muslim world, including metal and rap artists, feel deeply spiritual about their music even when they're not particularly orthodox in their belief or practice. It leads them closer to what they believe God to be. And since the JSA at heart is a Sufi—and because of this, a spiritually grounded—organization, the fact that most of the musicians I know approach Islam from a Sufi-like perspective creates more resonance between them. In fact, Layla al-Zubaidi, an Iraqi researcher, cultural critic, and metal fan who directs the Heinrich Böll foundation in Beirut, was astonished at the language of the JSA members when she accompanied me to the meeting. "You'll never hear the word *ruhani*, or 'spiritual,' used by Hamas or Hezbollah!" she exclaimed in the cab on the way to the show. "They're always too busy attacking Israel and other enemies."

I was also surprised at what they had to say, which didn't seem to square with what so many musicians have described as the JSA's support for repressive measures taken against them. "Why, if you believe musicians aren't necessarily bad Muslims," I pressed my hosts, "did you come out in support of the arrest of the Moroccan metal artists and their fans in 2003 by supporting the guilty verdicts against them in your papers?"

At this, the assembled group smiled. My host, the engineer, explained, "That's very interesting, since we don't have a newspaper! Our newspaper has been banned for years. Our only presence is on the Web. Look, this is a working-class neighborhood, right? You see all the Internet cafés around here? That's how we reach our people. And that's the only way.

If you read something in an Islamist newspaper, it's not ours."
In other words, the metalheads were confusing the JSA with
the government-approved Islamist groups such as the Justice
and Development Party, who substituted frequent rantings
against the supposed moral failings of Moroccan youth for a
sustained critique of the failings of the government.

While the vast majority of JSA members, young and
older, are clearly not metal or hip-hop fans, most members
don't seem to be working actively against popular music, either. Like the Muslim Brotherhood, its Egyptian counterpart,
the JSA has a lot more to worry about today than policing the
musical tastes of young Moroccans. And it seems as if many
musicians are actually even less discriminating in their understanding of Moroccan Islamism than the average JSA
member is about the distinctions among the various subgenres of extreme metal. "That's the problem," one young
woman at the meeting explained. "People have no idea what
we're about, so [they] accuse us of all types of things or con-
fuse us with other Islamist movements, like the Justice and
Development Party, which plays the political game and has
members in parliament, but who in fact was the group your
friend [that is, the metalheads] was so angry at." Indeed, the
few times I've offered to set up meetings between metalheads
and JSA members, it's always been the former, never the latter, who have told me to forget about it.

Such cultural and musical openness don't extend to the
JSA's most senior leaders, it seems. Unlike younger JSA
members, Nadia Yassine has fairly strong opinions against
both metal and hip-hop. While she admits in the introduction
to her book, *Full Sails Ahead,* that rock and hip-hop can "give
vent to the distress in the face of a shattered world," in the end

she argues that such music remains "crude" and "devoid of meaning," and is composed most notably of "groupies and spaced-out fans" who together represent the grand dismantling of the modern world. "Rap is a succession of desperate yelps; rock, hysteria; hard rock, insanity." Quoting Proust—rather than the *sharia* or another Islamic source, it's worth noting—she laments that "music can no longer be a means of communication among souls."

It seems that middle-aged bourgeois Moroccans can be as unwilling to accept Marockan roll as their counterparts on the other side of the Atlantic have often been when it comes to rock 'n' roll. Yassine's hostility to her country's most political forms of cultural expression is—aside from religion—all the more ironic (not to mention counterproductive) when it becomes clear how similar are both movements' critiques of the Moroccan government and its economic policies. Whether it's the activist-metal musicians of the Boulevard or the activist-intellectuals of the JSA, both focus on neoliberal globalization as a central threat to Morocco's future—"The point is not whether globalization is American or Saudi," a friend in the JSA put it, "it's whether it's neoliberal." Indeed, in the writings of the JSA's online publications (which are administered outside of Morocco and are hard for the government to block or filter out), and before that in its print journals, a critique of globalization is offered that is as detailed as those offered by Western scholars.

With their focus on democracy, poverty, corruption, and spirituality, metal artists and rappers could be the allies of the activists of the JSA, not their antagonists. If the JSA has little tolerance for mainstream Islam in Morocco, most of the country's best rock musicians have little tolerance for what passes for pop music, in Morocco and the Arab world more broadly. As Hoba Hoba Spirit's Reda Allali put it with a strong measure of exasperation: "We are all fed up with mainstream [music] . . . How can they still sing about romance, seeing what's going on in our region?" Nadia Yassine couldn't agree more, but an unwillingness to reach out to the other, coupled with the Makhzen's centuries-old policy of divide and rule, makes it unlikely that metalheads and Islamists will set aside their differences to work together toward common goals in the near future.

Satanic Angels
Save Civil Society

While hanging around the stage at the 2006 Boulevard, I heard talk of someone shooting a movie about the satanic-metal affair, but I wasn't able to find out who was behind the movie. Later in the year I was scrolling through the website for the band Tormentor of Souls, when I noticed a link to *Les Anges de Satan,* French for "The Satanic Angels" (in Arabic, *Mala'ika ash-Shaytan*). I pressed Play, and watched a trailer for a new movie directed by the iconoclastic Moroccan director Ahmed Boulane. It seems I wasn't the only person who thought heavy metal was a potential savior of Morocco.

The Satanic Angels is a fictionalized account of the arrest, trial, and civil society campaign to release the fourteen metalheads who were at the core of the 2003 satanic-metal affair. Watching the film, I was shocked that it was even made at all, never mind in Morocco—and in front of the very courthouse and prison where the kids were held and jailed (although Boulane had to shoot the courtroom scenes in a Protestant church, and his permit to film in the prison was canceled after the first day of a two-day shoot). The fact that a Moroccan film-maker was allowed to make and release a film depicting the torturing of teenagers by cops, protesters staring down the police, and cops and prosecutors making fools out of themselves, is quite remarkable. During one interrogation, a cop tries to get one of the metalheads to admit that he cooks and eats cats (for some reason, secret police across the Muslim world think metalheads eat cats), but he replies, "I don't eat meat, sir. I'm a vegetarian." During another interrogation, one of the fourteen is told that "In the seventies we used to stick bottles up the asses of people like you." I can't think of another country in the region except perhaps Israel where this would be allowed. Boulane agreed, explaining to me that the government's failure to stop the film reflects a political reality in Morocco today in which "there are two sides to the government. The justice minister naturally tried to censor the film, but the minister of communications is very progressive and supported us, revealing the delicate democratic balance in Morocco today."

Certainly Boulane was vindicated once the movie was released. With over 100,000 tickets sold in an unprecedented amount of time, it outperformed every American blockbuster in the theaters. "Kids who'd never think of going to a Moroccan movie because they tend to be boring flocked to mine, even sitting in the aisles," he said.

The Satanic Angels was an eye-opening film for Moroccans, owing to its sympathetic and even enthusiastic treatment of the metal scene, which at least until now most Moroccans have assumed was made up of little more than a bunch of drugged-out, dirty sinners. The film not only humanizes an oft-ridiculed group, but also captures the energy of the metal scene and shows how powerful, and much of the time how good, the music really is. More important, the movie offers a lesson to Moroccans, whatever their musical tastes, in how to take on the Makhzen, the police—indeed, the whole political and security and religious establishment— and win.

Boulane argues that when hundreds of metalheads and civil society activists chanted loudly in front of the courthouse, demanding the release of fourteen kids (in fact, when I discussed the film with Amine, whom one of the main characers was based upon, he pointed out that the real protests drew thousands of people), it's a message to the film's viewers that "the mobilization of civil society [can] free them. It's an example for our country to think about for future." But the most important point of *The Satanic Angels*—indeed, of the whole sordid satanic-metal affair—is expressed in the final words of the lead defense attorney's closing argument: "Your Honor, Islam can defend itself."

It's ironic, and a bit sad, that while Nadia Yassine shares Boulane's view of Islam, Boulane has little but contempt for Yassine and the other activists of the JSA, while she can't look past the distorted guitars and long hair to see the revolutionary potential of a bunch of kids who were willing to take on the Makhzen, and, unlike the JSA, won. And most "Marockans" feel, as Hoba Hoba Spirit's Reda Allali explains it, that religious forces "are antidemocratic and don't recognize our right to exist." For Allali, there are no forces in Morocco beyond rockers and their fellow secular activists who really want to "change the system." For Nadia Yassine, the JSA is "the only real opposition in Morocco today."

This debate over who is the only group working to de-
mocratize Morocco can seem parochial to an outsider, or even
egotistical—each side wanting to define itself as the main
hope for achieving justice and democracy in its country—
particularly when such alliances are already being forged
through the country's young NGO culture. The inability of
two movements of highly intelligent and politically committed people to find common ground speaks volumes about
how hard it will be for democratic forces in Morocco, and
across the MENA, to pry open corrupt and authoritarian systems that have spent decades perfecting the arts of repression, manipulation, and co-optation—the most important
skill set possessed by the region's leaders.

⁂

In *The Satanic Angels,* Boulane has one of the main characters
explain that "when music is banned, then the real satanism
will begin." This is surely true, but the problem with the
movie version of the satanic-metal affair is that the metalheads are no less cartoonish than the Islamists. If Nadia Yassine saw it, she'd recognize the metalheads portrayed in it as
her own worst nightmare: little more than spaced-out stoners
lost in the "spiritual vacuum" of contemporary Moroccan society. Their function, as one of the wealthy, French-speaking
"establishment types" who comes to their defense explains, is
little more than that of canaries in the political coal mine,
serving as "a wake-up call for all those living in the euphoria
of the Internet . . . Thanks to these young people, we have
learned that no one is really safe."

The fourteen metalheads of the satanic-metal affair were
certainly not angels, satanic or otherwise. At least back in

2003, there's no doubt that many of them liked to drink beer, get stoned, and generally slack about as much as their teenage or twentysomething counterparts in the United States or Europe. But many of them were—and today are even more so—incredibly talented, intelligent, well educated, and politically active citizens at the forefront of their country's struggles for social change. As much as their peers in the JSA, or the older generation of journalists and activists who have patronized them, they were, and are, agents of their own destiny—and of Morocco's as well.

EGYPT

Bloggers, Brothers, and the General's Son

"Listen, I don't wanna worry, but I'm really afraid that some of the stuff that I—we—have told you could get us into a lot of trouble. Do you think that you could use different names when you mention us in your book?"

Marz (not his real name) made this admission to me at around two in the morning as our tour bus sped along the mist-covered road connecting Alexandria to Cairo. Tall, with narrow features, a short ponytail, and the stubble of a beard, he normally speaks with an arresting voice that alternates between plaintive whispers and barked orders.

Marz is the lead guitarist of Hate Suffocation, for my money the best death-metal band in Egypt, if not the Middle East and North Africa, and he had a lot to lose if my account of the burgeoning Egyptian metal scene brought Hate Suffocation unwanted—as well as much-wanted—publicity. A well-known California-based metal producer was considering producing the band's new demo, and with each gig its fan base was noticeably increasing. And gigging, Marz explained, is crucial for Egyptian bands since hardly any of them have record deals. Their popularity rests on their live performances and the buzz created from songs downloaded from their MySpace sites. What would happen if he couldn't gig, or if the government blocked his website?

Taking a drag on his cigarette, Marz peered nervously out the window; to ease the tension, I mentioned his far blunter warning then posted on the "about me" section of his MySpace page—"Know This! Fuck you, you don't need to know anything about me! So fuck you!" He grinned while our fellow passengers discussed the differences between the Cairo and Alexandria metal scenes, which had come together that evening for an impromptu "metal summit" in my honor.

In Egypt today, Marz's obnoxious attitude is not only understandable but reasonable (in fact, he's quite sweet). Living on the political and cultural margins of Egyptian society, refusing to conform to its norms, metalheads—or "metaliens," as they often refer to themselves—have long been the object of ridicule and attacks in newspapers, on television, in live comedy, and in conservative religious discourse. This situation is aggravated by the policies of a regime that is expert at tolerating and even encouraging a manageable level of dissent by those who don't question its legitimacy, while regularly deploying pinpoint violence to slap down anyone, including the metal community, who directly defies or challenges its authority. (According to Human Rights Watch, this policy has resulted in between 6,000 and 10,000 political prisoners in detention at any given time, "pervasive" police

torture, including rape, and the routine beating of and sexual assault on peaceful protesters.)

Metaliens naturally worry about once again becoming
easy targets for attack from the government or conservative
forces, as they were in 1997, when more than a hundred metal
musicians and fans were arrested in the Arab world's first
satanic-metal scare. As they move through the hardscrabble
streets of Cairo and other major cities with their strange, menacing T-shirts, long hair, and guitars slung over their shoulders, they present a direct and public challenge to the regime
and the values it pretends to uphold. But they are not the only
group to do so. Egypt's burgeoning blogger scene, one of the
most prolific in the Muslim world, is the newest group attempting to create an independent social and political space,
albeit largely on virtual terrain. This hasn't stopped the government from jailing prominent young bloggers even as it
boasts of sponsoring a high-speed Internet infrastructure for
the country's growing middle class.

The biggest threat, however, remains the Muslim Brotherhood. Until recently, the government could count on playing these two poles of Egyptian society, secular and seemingly
westernized versus religious and traditionally conservative,
against each other in order to deflect any challenges to its
power. Today, however, a new generation of Brotherhood
members—the peers, and occasionally family members of
the metalheads (and in some cases it turns out, former metalheads themselves)—have become far more interested in
pushing the boundaries of political expression for their members than in limiting the expression of metalheads or other
non-mainstream groups within Egyptian society. Yet, as in
Morocco, the opposite sides of youth culture have yet to con-

sider working together toward the goal of greater freedom and democracy. Part of the reason is the wide cultural gap between them, and the mistrust of religious forces by musicians who have suffered through "satanic metal" affairs. But Egypt's metalheads are also far less sanguine about the possibility of political change than are their counterparts in Morocco. Less willing than Brotherhood members to risk their freedom to push for greater democracy (which, despite accusation by the government, today's Brotherhood is clearly doing), they would rather hold on to the slowly increasing freedom they have to play their music.

❦

I had arrived in Egypt at the time of Hate Suffocation's biggest gig yet, at the fourth installment of what has become known as the "Metal Accord." The space was the legendary Villa Hassan Fahmy, known as "the Mecca of Egyptian metalheads" because of the many great concerts that have been held there. New venues have opened up in central Cairo, such as the Sawi Culture Wheel, celebrated for its professional sound system (still a rarity in most smaller music halls in Cairo) and for sponsoring metal nights even though the owner is devoutly religious. But it is at the neglected old villas of the country's elite, lying upward of an hour outside Cairo's urban core, where Egyptian metalheads feel most free to be themselves.

Located not far from the pyramids, off one of the ring roads that surrounds Cairo, Villa Hassan Fahmy was packed with upward of 1,000 fans for the Metal Accord. Shouts of "Metal till we die!" and "That's so fuckin' brutal!" were punctuated by enthusiastic fist-pumping and metal horns. The bands plowed through sets of originals mixed with classic metal hits as the black-T-shirt-clad fans headbanged and slam-danced their way into metal Firdaws, or Heaven.

From the stage, Marz screamed into the microphone, "Welcome to the new era of death metal in Egypt." The crowd went crazy. While the majority were young men—as is the case at metal shows the world over—a far larger share of the crowd was female than would be the case at a typical Moroccan metal concert. Some of the girls headbanging and scream-ing were wearing headscarves. The energy, never mind the air, was hot and sticky; the fans lapped up the fleeting mo-ments of freedom. The concert, like the other mini-festivals organized by the metal community, was naturally a place for the best-known artists to meet, party, and strategize. Mem-bers of almost a dozen bands came to check out the show and show their support, and for several hours the Villa Has-san Fahmy rocked.

But even a decade after the 1997 crackdown, the Mukha-barat still routinely comes to metal shows to spy on the scene. Who exactly was that taking pictures of the bands and audi-ence? Would plainclothes security people suddenly pounce on a fan perceived to be sporting an inverted cross or pentagram on his neck or T-shirt? Some younger fans, with no memory of the crackdown, joked about how cool it would be if they were arrested. My friend Slacker, official archivist of the metal scene, shook his head in disbelief. "Man," he said to them, "you're such poseurs. Do you have any idea what it means to be arrested by the Egyptian police?"

❧☙

Egypt has long been home to one of the most vibrant centers of cultural production—in film, music, and television—in the Arab world. In fact, one of the first international conferences of musicians and composers, the Oriental Music Conference, took place in Egypt in 1932. Because of this, it's not hard to imagine there being space for metalheads to play and listen to their music without interference from the government or self-appointed gatekeepers of public morality. But as in other Arab countries today, the music scene in Egypt is dominated by "porno devil" divas singing the kind of cheesy and sex-saturated pop music produced by Arab entertainment conglomerates such as the Rotana. As one Egyptian observer of the scene described it to me, "If we judge by numbers, then Arabic pop music sells the most, dudes with cars and sound systems mainly listen to rap (gangster wannabes), and people who are on drugs mainly listen to electronic music—trance/house/techno and rave."

The rap scene best illustrates the shallowness of most Egyptian music today. While powerful local styles of hip-hop have developed in Morocco or Palestine, in Egypt the biggest star among the "popular" class and young people more broadly is Sha'aban Abdel-Rehim, a working-class hero from Cairo (he started life as an "ironer," or *maqwagi*, in a laundromat) who used to be a nightclub singer before becoming an Egyptian phenomenon with his song "Ana bakrah Isra'il" ("I Hate Israel"). In the song he famously boasts, "I hate Israel and I'll say so if I'm asked even if it costs me my life or I get arrested."

Unlike his compatriots on the metal scene, however, Sha'aban has no need to worry about being arrested despite his occasional criticism of government ineptitude. That's because he also sings of his love of Hosni Mubarak's "broad mind" (in fact, the president has long been the butt of jokes depicting him as stupid). Sha'aban's Mubarak-good/Israel-bad rap is held up as the epitome of "authentic" Egyptian popular culture today because it allows people to vent anger at Israel that otherwise would be directed at the Egyptian regime.

Metalheads have had to struggle to be accepted as authentically Egyptian against the same political-cultural forces that crowned Sha'aban the prince of Egyptian pop. Even more difficult has been their struggle against so-called traditional popular religious identities that are viewed as authentic by the lion's share of Egyptian society. Such identities have been the basis for the social and political power of the Muslim Brotherhood, the social movement created in 1928 by Hasssan al-Banna, which, more than any other movement, is responsible for the rise of political Islam.

The good news (for metalheads, if not the government) is that as the Brotherhood moves cautiously into mainstream politics, its leaders, but particularly its younger members, are coming to realize that the best chance for them to answer skeptics is to recognize the plurality of Egyptian society, to stop defining other points of view (particularly those not grounded in their reading of Islam) as being alien and dangerous to Egypt, and in so doing, finally to let the metalheads be.

This marks a fundamental change compared with the mid-to-late 1990s, when Egyptian Islamists played a prominent role in the Arab world's first genuine satanic-metal affair. The crackdown was initiated by the government on January 22, 1997, after newspapers published a photo from a metal concert allegedly showing someone carrying an upside-down cross. Both Muslim and Christian clerics smelled blood; the press, always looking for a way to boost sales, had a field day with the "satanic" musicians and fans and their fantastical sex-and-death-filled orgies.

Upward of a hundred metal fans and musicians were arrested (some of them as young as thirteen), including dozens who were caught hanging out illegally at the decrepit, cobweb-filled Baron's Palace, a dilapidated nineteenth-century villa located on one of the main streets of Cairo's Heliopolis district. The villa was built by a wealthy Belgian industrialist and amateur Egyptologist named Baron-General Edouard Louis Joseph Empain. The Palace had become a favorite haunt of metalheads looking for a creepy place to hang out, spray-paint graffiti, and party. The Egyptian media decided the goings-on were far more macabre (one article imagined how the Palace was "filled with tattooed, devil-worshipping youths holding orgies, skinning cats, and writing their names in rats' blood on the palace's walls").

"All of a sudden I was seeing pictures in the newspapers of my friends, with captions under them describing them as the 'high council of Satan worship,' " Hossam El-Hamalawy, one of Egypt's most prominent bloggers and a metalien from the old days, recounted to me. "It was all quite frightening." It was even more so after Egypt's state-appointed mufti, Sheikh Nasr Farid Wassil, demanded that those arrested either repent or face the death penalty for apostasy.

To make matters worse, the satanic-metal affair occurred when the government was struggling to deal with a surge in extremist activity that culminated terrorist attacks by radical Islamists on tourist locations in Luxor and Cairo later that year. In its battle for the hearts and minds of the average Egyptian, the Mubarak regime couldn't be seen as standing by while a growing swarm of westernized and, it goes without saying, Zionist-sponsored vampires shook the foundations of Egyptian morality. With Egypt's highest religious authorities literally calling for their scalps, the metal scene came screeching to a halt.

The crackdown, and the fear of jail or even execution, was so frightening that some musicians destroyed their guitars and cut their hair to avoid arrest (which is, to look on the bright side, still better than Iran, where the police drag you to jail and cut your hair for you). A decade later, such are the scars of the satanic-metal affair that the majority of musicians I know are scared to speak on record about their music, never mind politics. Marz and several other artists wouldn't even give me copies of the lyrics to their songs when I first met them. They're not about to cut their hair or sell their guitars, but they're also not going to risk setting the scene back another decade just to score a few meaningless political points.

One History, Two Cities—at Least

Most tourists or casual visitors to Cairo get only a circumscribed view of the city. But the experience of living there is central to understanding how and why Egypt's metal scene developed. It's not just that the Egyptian government is more repressive than Morocco's; size matters too. Compared with Casablanca's population of about 4 million, Cairo's nearly 24 million people make it the most populous urban center in Africa, with twice as many people as Istanbul and Tehran, and more than all but four of the Arab world's twenty-two countries.

Tourist attention is focused on such Pharaonic and Islamic monuments as the famed pyramids or Muhammad Ali's mosque. Tourism brings in about $7 billion annually in revenues, but the city's economy lives through the networks connecting upscale island neighborhoods like Zemalek, Gezira, and Geziret El Rhoda to the bustle of Cairo's downtown, and to slightly more dépassé neighborhoods such as Heliopolis, Garden City, and Giza. Surrounding the inner city are middle- and working-class neighborhoods such as Medinat Nasr, the largest residential district of Cairo.

The majority of metalheads I know live in middle- and upper-middle-class neighborhoods like Zemalek or Muhandasin, filled with high-end coffee shops that provide free wi-fi access, as well as numerous bars and pubs bustling with expats and well-off middle-aged Egyptians out for a drink with their friends or mistresses. At heavily secured five-star hotels such as the Nile Hilton, wealthy American tourists mingle with the country's burgeoning Islamist bourgeoisie over pastries and coffee.

Yet few of the metalheads I know feel at home in these neighborhoods, at least during daylight hours. They live in a kind of twilight world; like denizens of an Anne Rice novel, they come alive after the sun goes down, when the city exhales 4 or 5 million workers to the suburbs, the pollution has settled down for the evening, and the city becomes livable—or almost. More important, darkness is when a metalhead can walk around with a ponytail, earring, and concert T-shirt, and even carry a can of beer, without fear.

Just how different night and day can be for Cairo's metaliens became clear as I strolled through Cairo with Stigma, acclaimed as one of the best singers in the Egyptian metal scene. Despite his prodigious talent, however, Stigma can't walk the streets of Cairo, particularly in his own middle-class neighborhood of El Haram, without suffering some form of abuse. El Haram is a mixture of conservative working-class and petit-bourgeois residents on the one hand, and musicians and nightclubs—of the "traditional" belly-dancing kind—on the other. "There is *no way* I can walk around Haram Street without tying my hair," he explained to me, "or else people are going to stare at me, make fun of me, and maybe insult and swear at me.

"If you look like an Egyptian and you have long hair . . . that's a disgrace," he says. But it's not just in El Haram. Walking around greater Cairo or Alexandria with Stigma at most any time of day puts one on the receiving end of unwelcome, sometimes utterly disdainful glances that remind you that you're not legitimate members of Cairo's cityscape. In London of the 1970s or the Southern United States of the 1980s, kids had long hair or mohawks, and dressed in punk or metal outfits with the specific goal of ruffling their societies' feathers. But in Egypt today it can be quite frightening; only in Iran and Gaza have I felt more eyes focused angrily upon unconventionally dressed young people.

The same angry eyes that can make Stigma's life so uncomfortable also inspire his voice with its anger and power, qualities that don't quite fit his rather diminutive frame and delicate Egyptian and Indian facial features. His style of singing is literally "brutal," the technical term for the low and guttural screaming—which one friend described as sounding like the Cookie Monster singing high on angel dust—made famous by seminal American death-metal bands such as Death and Morbid Angel.

When you watch Stigma scream his lyrics in concert, rid-ing the harsh, syncopated guitar riffs and rapid-fire bass-drumming of Hate Suffocation to even higher levels of intensity, the last thing you think about is the first lady of Arabic music, Oum Kalthoum—who worked hard to identify herself with the traditional values and cultural tastes of the Egyptian peasant or villager, or her onetime partner Muhammad Abdel Wahab, with whom she defined the contours of classically inspired Arabic-language popular music. But if Egypt's metal bands show little interest in blending heavy metal with their local musical traditions (it's mostly at the edges of the MENA—Morocco, Iran, and Pakistan—that you find this phenomenon), they are inspired both by the same iconoclastic spirit, and by Oum Kalthoum's improvisatory artistry: her ability to lead her audiences into *tarab,* what in Arabic music is known as a state of musical surrender and ecstasy that has all but disappeared in contemporary Arab pop music—although not at metal concerts.

But the still-shadowy existence of Stigma and so many other Egyptian metaliens also reflects the less celebrated part of this heritage: the realities of Mubarak's rule, a half-century of military domination of Egypt's political life, and the legacy of British colonial rule. Western involvement in Egyptian politics began with the brief but violent Napoleonic invasion of Egypt in 1798, the failed attempts at industrialization by the Ottoman viceroy Muhammad Ali and his successors in the first half of the nineteenth century, and increasing European control over the economy that culminated with the British invasion and occupation of 1882. Although Egypt was formally granted independence in 1922, the British effectively controlled the country for the next thirty years, until the Revolution of July 1952.

The Nasserist era of the 1950s and 1960s saw the implementation of a quasi-socialist "authoritarian bargain," in which the Egyptian people traded democracy for significant gains in social development and welfare. However, Nasser's successor, Anwar Sadat, "reopened" Egypt to Western capital and influence with his *infitah* (open-door) program that began after the October War with Israel in 1973, when Egypt turned away from the Soviet Union and toward the United States.

Hosni Mubarak's almost-thirty-year rule has only intensified the drive toward economic liberalization and privatization, which is more accurately described as the handing over of control of key industries to members of the country's elite. As has occurred elsewhere in the developing world, the structural transformation of the Egyptian economy has transformed the country from a breadbasket of the Mediterranean and the Near East—a position it has held for some 5,000 years—to a net importer of food (this in turn caused the Arab world's first anti-globalization riots, against an IMF-imposed reduction in food subsidies in 1977). All told, as one of Egypt's most respected journalists put it to me, almost a century of authoritarian politics and three decades of neoliberal economic policies have today made Egypt a "sick and decaying place."

The extent of the country's problems is evident on the drive from downtown Cairo to the villas outside the city where metal concerts and raves usually take place. If you happen to go the wrong way, you wind up driving through the sometimes desperate city that surrounds Cairo's fashionable neighborhoods, with dilapidated buildings, smog-filled air, decrepit cars running without headlights, a sea of uncollected garbage, and the smell of more than 4 million residents without a functioning sewer system.

How a Music About Death
Overcomes Suffocating Hatred

There was a palpable sense of relief as our bus arrived in my neighborhood in Zemalek at the end of the four-hour drive back from Alexandria. Most of the trip was spent driving through the rain on a poorly lit highway, with a driver who had a predilection for hashish-laced cigarettes and an inability to notice the giant twin-cab trucks making illegal U-turns across the divider until it was just about too late to slam on the brakes without going into a spin. It had been a long ride.

As we pulled up to the Hotel Horus, on Ismail Muhammad Street, I was forced to admit something I'd been hoping not to have to disclose. I still couldn't tell the difference between death, doom, black, melodic, symphonic, grind-core, hard-core, thrash, and half a dozen other styles of metal that make Egypt among the Muslim world's most eclectic metal scenes. Most bands here reject the blending of metal and local styles that has helped define the scenes in Morocco, Lebanon, Pakistan, and Israel. Even after observing rehearsals and gigs and listening to their demo, I didn't have a clue to how to describe Hate Suffocation.

Marz answered emphatically that the band is a combination of death metal, a style known for chromatic progressions with detuned guitars (Marz is one of the few guitarists I know who plays a seven-string guitar; the added B below the low E string gives even more power to his power chords), rapid-fire drumming, dynamic intensity, and growled lyrics about death, and black metal, which tends to use screamed vocals and more-melodic and fluid grooves. "But it's not blackened death metal!" he clarified for me.

However you want to describe the band, it's clear that Hate Suffocation is one of the best of the new generation of metal bands in Egypt. Considering the complexity and intricacy of the music, one of the most important reasons for its success is the military-like discipline with which Marz manages the band and its rehearsals, a trait that he no doubt inherited from his father, a retired general in Egypt's Air Defense Command.

Being a general's son has shaped Marz as a person and as a musician. He lived in Miami for six years, until high school, and later in Poland. In fact, while pirated copies of metal albums were available in kiosks across Egypt as far back as the 1970s, Marz fully embraced metal in Krakow rather than Cairo. "But I always hung out with the wrong people, like my friend Amira, who introduced me to heavy metal in the ninth grade. She was considered a loner and was discriminated against by her schoolmates because of how she looked and the music she listened to. One day I came up to her and she was wearing a band T-shirt for Korn. I asked her what she was listening to . . . and it was all so raw and powerful. Bands like Morbid Angel, Iron Maiden, W.A.S.P., Opeth, Pantera, Sepultura, Bathory, Benediction, Vader, Megadeth, Metallica, Annihilator, Cannibal Corpse, Death, Deicide, Monstrosity, Slayer. Basically from thrash to death metal. I just went crazy."

What was it about heavy metal that drove him crazy? "I was a confused teenager and had many problems trying to blend into Egyptian culture because I had lived in the U.S.

and my cultural norms were different. In fact, I was discriminated against by teachers and other students for being open-minded, especially about music, and I was constantly being force-fed religion in school and by society in a way that really turned me off."

Many Egyptian metal musicians have a similar life story. They are the well-educated prodigal sons (and in a few cases, daughters) of diplomats, military officers, or other members of the country's elite—a bit strange if you think about it, since metal is supposed to be the ultimate outsiders' music. Most of them, including Marz, also have university and even graduate degrees.

So why are these sons and daughters of the Egyptian elite checking out of a system designed to enable them to join the global elite of tomorrow? As Marz tells me, it can be summed up in the band's name. "I chose Hate Suffocation to reflect the suffocating level of hatred across Egyptian society. The rich and poor hate each other, conservatives and liberals hate each other, cops and metalheads hate each other, religious and secular hate each other." At least that's how Marz and many of his fellow musicians experience Egypt today. "People pretend to love when in fact they really hate. That's why we title our songs 'Confused,' 'Corrupted Virtue,' 'Human Betrayal,' and 'I Hate.' "

Their music can't avoid dealing with the problems of Egyptian society, but the goal of Marz and his fellow metalheads is not to transform the country. It's much more modest: to be left alone by both the government and society—to be able to play their music and walk down the street without being harassed by the Mukhabarat or the Muslim Brotherhood. They also want to become famous, or at least successful enough to tour outside of Egypt and not have a day job. Achieving such a level of success would place these bands directly in the public eye, which would make them even more of a target for a government that regularly exiles anyone who becomes too popular and won't publicly support the regime.

Just being a metal musician is enough to get you in trouble. As Marz recounted: "A few months ago my band got dressed up in our best metal gear and went to the pyramids to do a promotional photo shoot. It happened to be October 6, the anniversary of Egypt's launching of the Ramadan, or Yom Kippur, War. While we were setting up to shoot, a couple of cops came over and started harassing us, and when they found that one of us didn't have proper ID, we were all arrested. Just for trying to take a picture in front of the pyramids. All we wanted to do was show fans that we were from Egypt and support our country, but to the cops we were like enemies of the state."

❧❦❧

"Enemy of the state" is an apt description of how anyone is regarded who challenges the Mubarak regime. One of the best-known Egyptian political figures to be slapped down—but not silenced—by the regime, is the former presidential candidate Ayman Nour, whose Tomorrow Party was the standard-bearer of the Egyptian reform movement. His teenage sons Shady and Noor dealt with the pain of watching their father rot in jail by founding Bliss, which for a brief time was one of the best up-and-coming metal bands in Egypt. Nour is a gentle, affable man with an impeccable reputation for honesty, a steel resolve, and little fear of the consequences of taking on the Arab world's longest-serving dictator. He was convicted of forgery in the 2005 presidential election, a cruel joke, since it was clear that Mubarak had rigged the vote against him.

Largely abandoned by the United States and Europe, both of which initially supported his push for real democratic reform, Nour was still being held in solitary confinement, without proper treatment for his diabetes, when I went to see Shady and Noor at their apartment. Their building has the kind of post–World War I eclectic architectural style that gives the Zemalek district its charm. Their apartment, one of the building's penthouses, has a commanding view of the surrounding neighborhood, yet its elegant but slightly tattered furniture, and empty swimming pool on the terrace, hints at the sacrifices their father has made trying to bring democracy to Egypt.

Both of Nour's sons are blessed with the kind of rock-star looks and attitude that would stand out in any scene. Their sense of style and their energy as performers—which they documented by pulling out their video iPods and cell phones to show me clips of recent shows—are remarkable, given how young they are. But Shady and Noor have been forced to become wise far beyond their years because of their father's imprisonment. Watching their father paraded in and out of sham trials (whose proceedings they secretly record on their video phones and show to friends and journalists), and grow sicker each month he remains in jail, has taught them that music and politics can and should come together. This is still very much a minority position within Egypt's metal scene, but as the brothers expand their musical horizons, performing with more established bands, they hope to encourage their largely teenage fan base to translate their cultural individualism into political activism.

Can Metal Help Heal a Sick Country?

If Morocco is a *blad schizo,* or schizophrenic country, this is largely a result of French colonialism and France's effort to assimilate conquered peoples into French culture. As a result, many Moroccans have some measure of affection for France. England had a very different attitude toward Egypt—rule without assimilation—and as such, the English language, and British culture more broadly, never became part of the Egyptian soul.

Yet metal in Egypt is almost entirely an English-language affair. Few can articulate exactly why, but most musicians I've met feel that while rap can work in Arabic, metal works only in English. In other countries, particularly Turkey, Iran, Israel, and Pakistan, there's a growing hard-rock scene that not only sings in Turkish, Persian, Hebrew, and Urdu, but even includes overtly religious lyrics. Even the *shahadah,* or Islamic testament of faith (*La illaha illa-llah,* "there is no god but God"), has been recorded over a driving hard-rock groove by one Turkish rock group.

Egyptian metal's "English only" policy points to how important the influx of foreign, and particularly Anglo-American, music has been there. Despite the unwillingness of most metalheads to mix metal with Egyptian or other Arabic styles, there are strong local roots for what sonically might seem like a foreign style of music. This became clear to me about fifteen minutes into watching a popular movie from the 1980s, Samir Seif's *Al-Halfout* (*The Nobody*), on Egyptian television. The movie's star, the well-known comedian Adel Imam, enters the home of a provocatively dressed woman, followed by a group of middle-aged women and men. Suddenly the women pick up traditional drums and tambourines and begin chanting, and banging out a driving beat while they dance around in a circle, heads swaying up and down and back and forth. As the circle breaks up, the men pair off with the women and go into different rooms, apparently to have sex.

What millions of Egyptians and I had witnessed was a bastardized version of a *zar* ceremony, an ancient magical ritual meant to cure mental or physical illnesses by contacting and hopefully placating what is believed to be a spirit (or spirits) possessing a woman, and which are believed to cause various types of illnesses, including infertility. Though prohibited by orthodox Islamic law because of its roots in pagan African religions, the *zar* has long been an essential part of Egyptian culture. The ritual is traditionally performed in private settings that are free from the prying eyes and ears of outsiders, especially those in political and religious power. The heavy, sexualized, beat-driven music and swaying head movements that make up the *zar* ritual are used by one of the country's most marginalized groups—women—to cope with the stresses of living in an oppressive society.

The parallels with the metal scene are striking, and run a lot deeper than just headbanging, heavy drumming, and alcohol-driven sex. Chief among them are the "psychological issues" that a lot of the metalheads I know say motivated them to become metal fans and musicians. "Most everyone who plays metal in Egypt has some kind of psychological problem," Marz explained one night as we left a marathon six-hour rehearsal for two of the bands he plays in. Although that is surely an exaggeration, it is accepted as true in Egyptian pop culture. In fact, in his long-running one-man play, *A Witness*

Who Witnesses Nothing (Shahid ma Shafish Haga), Adel Imam does a skit depicting metalheads as mentally disturbed. The slightly crazy—and therefore either amusing or dangerous—metalhead has become part of Egypt's cultural vocabulary, to be feared, censured, or ridiculed depending on the political or cultural needs of the moment.

The reality, however, is that like the female practitioners of the *zar* ceremony, the metalheads are using the "ritual" of playing or listening to music as a way to cope with the stress they face as a marginalized group in an oppressive society. When Egypt's metaliens describe problems such as loneliness, alienation, or having little hope in the future, I don't see a psychological issue as much as a social and political one that can't be expressed politically because of the country's patriarchal, highly authoritarian political system.

A good example of the connection between psychological and political problems can be seen in a young, Cairo-based band called Enraged, one of the few Egyptian metal bands with a female lead singer. When I arrived in Egypt, the band had just released a powerful song dealing with this issue, titled "The Truth Is Concealed." It blends together the haunting vocals of the band's lead singer, Rasha, with the brutal growling of Stigma, who guests on the song. Giving the song its tension and sense of movement are alternating soft and hard sections. Rasha's vocal over an arpeggiated piano melody surrenders to Stigma's brutally vocalized chorus, which is sung over a super-distorted guitar riff. The lyrics take on Egyptians who hate metalheads, especially those in power. Rasha accuses them: "Nothing you justify is real. The only reason you hate is that I am a part of you," while Stigma counters, "This hate is all that I know, and it runs in my every vein.

Under the shadows of a deserted throne." Finally, Rasha replies, "If this is just a dream, I hope it never becomes a reality. There is a fine line between knowledge and insanity."

According to the lead guitarist, Wael Ossama, the song is meant to be a critique of a political and social system based on "hate propaganda . . . living in fear and ignorance, under an iron fist." The song's protagonists believe that without hate, their world will fall apart. Hatred has become their identity, and their madness.

To an outsider, these songs might well seem political. They represent the kind of messages that some artists confided to me they like to slip into their songs without being explicit enough to get censored or arrested. But the majority of the bands won't go as far as these moderately critical songs. When I asked Marz why this was the case, he looked at me with near disdain for even asking the question. Didn't I know that doing so would lead to another crackdown by the government on the metal scene, just when it was picking up again? And anyway, where was the evidence that real political and social change were possible in Egypt, so that he should risk his freedom—and his music—to pursue it? Where exactly was Shady and Noor's father as we spoke?

Slacker, the metal scene's chief archivist, was even more honest, although wistfully so. At around six feet tall and well over two hundred pounds, with a round, shaved head that crowns the contours of his body, Slacker is one of the most imposing presences in the metal scene, but his physical appearance is completely at odds with his jovial and gentle personality, and he is anything but a slacker. He seems to be in perpetual motion, running from gigs to rehearsals to photo shoots to document the evolution of Egypt's metal scene.

Unfortunately, his day job was not nearly as interesting when we first met. As part of the fulfillment of his army service, Slacker was working for a defense contractor (he's since finished his service, but is unable to find a job despite his prodigious talents as a web designer). The contradictions between the two worlds through which he's been forced to move back and forth—between the metal scene and the military establishment that has long helped suppress it—tear at Slacker's soul. "Look, my father is very, very religious, and I used to work with human-rights groups. But the government came after me and eventually I moved on. Just this past summer, one of Egypt's biggest newspapers ran a story after a big metal concert describing us—and using my name!—as 'servants of Satan.' Can you imagine what this did to my family?"

Whatever the costs of being a metalhead, Slacker isn't about to walk away from the metal scene. Its members have become a surrogate family, not just because his parents and siblings are scattered across the Persian Gulf emirates, but because, as a Coptic Christian, it's difficult for Slacker to feel at home in a country that increasingly defines Egyptianness through Islam. The metal scene is one of the few places where it doesn't matter what religion you are, since it's your fidelity to metal that determines your place in the hierarchy. That's why, for Slacker, "Metal is what keeps me sane, what keeps me feeling like Egypt is still home." It's what keeps most of its adherents feeling like Egypt can still be their home, despite the disdain that so many of their fellow Egyptians have for them.

In fact, Slacker pointed out, there were hints of political activism within the scene, albeit of the virtual kind. To prove it, he opened his laptop and pulled up one of the two main websites for the Egyptian metal scene, "metalgigsforum.com." Slacker created and manages this site, which has become his life's work. Navigating to the site's members-only forum, we began reading through one of the most active threads, which involved a debate over just the issue of "why we don't bring more politics to music."

The main question faced by metaliens is whether or not they are "smart enough" to outsmart the government and politicize the scene without destroying it. The majority of participants believe, in the words of one posting, that if a band becomes political, "the cops will F**k u." The article from the summer of 2006 that "outed" Slacker as a satanist only reinforced such fears in the metal community, and led one participant in the forum to argue that it would be better to keep the scene more underground. But Wael pointed out that the bad press "actually refutes your argument to stay low, since, as you see, if the press or Amn el Dawla [state security services] or anyone wants to get to us they can do so very easily. Mesh hanetnase7 3aleehom lama ne3mel concert fel badeya aw Hassan Fahmy aw 7atta ta7t el ard" ["We can't pretend to be smarter then them [government] by doing concerts in Badya, Hassan Fahmy, or even under the ground." The numbers represent Arabic letters that don't have corresponding English sounds].

The fluidity with which Wael moves back and forth between Egyptian Arabic and English is striking, and is a part of the trend in which Arabs, Iranians, Pakistanis, and other peoples normally using non-Latin alphabets have combined their spoken language with English—the lingua franca of the Internet—into hybrid languages that reflect their cultural heterogeneity. In fact, it is the normal way the Egyptian metalheads communicate with each other in person as well, even when they don't have to speak English. In rehearsals, on the phone, in chat rooms, at the local yuppie coffee bar or pub, the borders between what could be considered "Egyptian" and "foreign" or "Western" culture are impossible to define, which is precisely why other, more powerful groups want to define the borders for them.

For Wael, the main problem is that the security services are too pervasive to avoid by keeping the scene underground. In his opinion, the best strategy is to make the scene more legitimate by doing shows at "respectable" locations like the Sawi Culture Wheel in Zemalek, where they can be regulated according to cultural and political norms, rather than at more-clandestine spots like the Villa Hassan Fahmy, where "tons of law violations" (mostly involving drinking and drugs) occur.

Another, and perhaps better, option than playing by the government's rules is to play by global capital's. This was the option chosen by the organizers of the SOS Festival held in Cairo in late 2006, which followed the lead of the Boulevard des jeunes musiciens festival in Casablanca and sought out major corporate sponsors. With support from over a dozen large Egyptian and foreign corporations, the festival attracted more than 15,000 people and saw the launch of a relatively new metal band, Wyvern, to national prominence with a well-received set centered around its song "Sex for Sale." The BBC and organizers heralded the festival not just as a renaissance of heavy metal in Egypt, but as "a new musical revolution . . . that will return [Egypt] to the days of musical legends like

Oum Kalthoum." This comment made my friends laugh, for it's precisely against the culture of Oum Kalthoum that most metaliens are rebelling.

It's revealing of the weakness of opposition movements across the Arab world that giant multinationals are the only force capable of ushering in much-needed revolutions, albeit of the musical, not the political, kind. But for many of the metalheads in attendance, the sheer size of the audience and positive response to their music trumped any concerns about the inexorable advance of neoliberal globalization. Egyptian metal, people began to think, was back. Perhaps still on a high from the show, Wyvern's drummer, Seif El-Din, explained that the festival even proved that metal could once again connect with the people in a way that hadn't been possible since the satanic-music affair.

The SOS Festival proved the positive potential for corporate-metal synergy, but such a combination was never part of the core vision of the Egyptian metal scene. Instead, authenticity and power are what matters most to bands in the scene, and both were on display the week before at a concert by Wyvern at the Sawi Culture Wheel. It was evident in the smiles on the faces of the young male and female audience members, in the way they put their arms around one another's shoulders, danced sensually, and created a visceral sense of community that for Egypt was quite unique. And nearby was al-Azhar University, the most important Islamic university in the world, where calls for the death penalty were heard during the 1997 satanic-metal scare. The music was powerful enough to exorcise the demons of a rotting political culture—at least for the duration of the concert.

Can't Two MBAs Just Get Along?

Egyptian metalheads are one of the most closely knit groups of people I've ever met. But in terms of sheer size, the metal scene is dwarfed by the largest social network in Egypt, the Ikhwan, or Muslim Brotherhood. Founded in 1928 by Hassan al-Banna, the Brotherhood has been a thorn in the side of Egyptian governments ever since. Its political and social power has increased considerably since it won a surprising eighty-eight out of 454 seats in the 2005 parliamentary elections, the first time it competed more or less openly in an Egyptian campaign.

Since then, Brotherhood parliamentarians have been impressive for their discipline, professionalism, and, for the most part, moderation. The movement's newfound political clout makes it the biggest threat to Egypt's ruling elite. Its leadership has broadened the core base of support from the working and middle classes to the emerging class of "air-conditioned Muslims"—the new Muslim business class and a younger yuppie Muslim bourgeoisie that is Western-educated and politically liberal, yet socially conservative.

This new Brotherhood was on display, sans air conditioning, on an unseasonably warm December day when I met Omar (not his real name), the Cairo Bureau Chief of the Brotherhood, at the Gropi Café in downtown Cairo. Located in a grand but slightly dilapidated storefront, the Gropi is one of the most famous patisseries in Cairo. When I arrived, at least three tables were filled with men in their thirties and forties sporting close-cropped beards and dark business suits—the standard Ikhwan look these days—who were speaking in

English with well-dressed foreigners about Egypt's political situation. At least two other tables were occupied by men pretending not to be listening in on their conversations. Whether they were spying on them or providing security for them, I couldn't be sure.

As I waited for Omar, I listened to a new song, "Human," by the all-female Egyptian symphonic metal band Massive Scar Era (aka "Mascara"). What better way to prepare for the Brotherhood than an all-girl metal band that sings about the destruction plaguing Egyptian society and the tragedy of living lives that are little more than "imitations of the West"?

But Omar, whose neat-trimmed mustache and mischievous smile don't quite mesh with his bland Eastern European–style suit, didn't take the bait. He had no interest in denouncing female metal bands, or any music for that matter, a change in attitude that the metal community would do well to recognize. Omar wasn't even interested in talking about Islam per se, or, as sometimes happens when I meet with Islamists, in converting me. Instead, he wanted to discuss the political situation in Egypt and why the Brotherhood was the only group able to take on the system. By the end of our talk I almost believed him.

"There's no political life here," Omar began after we exchanged the complex set of salutations and kisses that Arabs often use when meeting for the first time. The afternoon sun poured into the restaurant through the floor-to-ceiling windows. The smell of burnt coffee mingling with the smell of sickly sweet honey-coated pastries of every imaginable description hung thick in the air. Eyeing the other tables from our position at the back of the room, Omar stirred yet more sugar into a cup of mint tea that he'd ordered with extra sugar to begin with, and continued, "The regime goes after everyone who tries to be political. The kids are scared; there's so much fear, censorship, and then self-censorship."

An increasingly popular alternative to direct political or social engagement is, of course, the Internet. The problem for Omar was what young people found on the Internet or in other informal social networks. "They go on the Internet, angry and frustrated, looking for an escape, and what do they find? Porn or bin Laden, or both. And those who don't go to extremes often become little more than 'negatively religious.' And Islam can't be just negative." Omar took another sip of tea, sighed, and explained, "You know, in the old days, before Qutb took over, Ikhwan members used to play the oud! We were cultured." He cringed slightly as he said Sayyid Qutb's name, as if the mere mention of the man who, more than any other Muslim thinker of the last century, was responsible for creating and popularizing the ideology of violent, jihadi Islam would bring a curse on him.

As Omar continued talking, I wanted to point out that many young Egyptians found more useful things on the Web, from political blogs to heavy-metal forums, that help them resist, or at least survive, government oppression. But before I could say anything, he stunned me by declaring that as far as he was concerned, the Brotherhood had gone to hell in the 1960s, when the movement became increasingly militant. "It's really the Salafis' fault," he explained, referring to ultra-conservative orthodox Muslims who base their actions on what they believe to be the model of the earliest generation of Muslims (and which therefore can often include a big dose of jihad). This was the first time I'd heard an Islamist essentially blame everything on Islamism, but Omar wasn't done. "And in some ways it was also al-Azhar's fault for not correcting this tendency before it was too late."

I was starting to become a bit incredulous at the conversation. Not once did Omar cite the Qur'an, the Hadith (the sayings of the Prophet Muhammad that are the second source of Islamic law after the Qur'an), or famous figures from Islamic history to back up his arguments. I couldn't help thinking that he was spinning me, telling me what he thought I, as an American, wanted to hear.

He must have sensed my lack of trust in his words, because he gripped my arm, looked at me, and said, "What we need to combat people like them are more freedom of speech, more trained judges, more human rights." This agenda is in fact quite similar to that of the Egyptian left, but Omar dismissed the left with a wave (except, he clarified, for the surprisingly popular Trotskyists, who apparently include more than a few Brotherhood members). "First of all, the left can't motivate most young people, even if its ideas are good. More important, we are making up for the clear lack of bravery by much of the left . . . as there are some people, particularly secularists, who argue that if the choice is between Islamists and dictatorship, they'll choose dictatorship. Can you believe that? But it's a false choice." That may be true, but it's a choice I've heard non-conservative Muslims, memories of the violence of 1980s and 1990s still fresh in their minds, make across the region.

❧❧❧

Despite its change of tune, the Muslim Brotherhood still scares most metalheads. Just how much became clear one afternoon when I invited Slacker, Stigma, and Seif, the drummer for the band Wyvern, to meet me at the Horus Hotel for a drink. The hotel had come highly recommended by several friends, but not because of the décor or cuisine. It is a nondescript, slightly shabby floor-through accommodation with an unplugged metal detector in front of the door that suggested a slightly more illustrious past. The owner, a sixtyish amateur painter who spends his days sitting on the hotel's small terrace practicing English, French, and German with guests, gives the place an old-world, cosmopolitan air. One guest explained that, like the advertisements for Las Vegas, what goes on inside the Horus stays there—meaning that you don't have to worry about having your activities reported to the Mukhabarat, or your phone tapped, as long as you're not inviting any particularly nasty or politically dangerous guests for tea.

No sooner had Slacker, Seif, Stigma, and I sat down to talk, however, than I got a phone call from someone named Ibrahim, saying he was on his way to meet me. I thought it was one of the metalheads I was trying to meet, but when a clean-cut twentysomething in a suit showed up and introduced himself as an editor of the official website of the Muslim Brotherhood, it was clear that I had been mistaken—but also, I reckoned, quite lucky, as I had long been trying without much success to bring together metalheads and Islamists in the same room.

The metaliens did not share my enthusiasm. In fact, the moment Ibrahim introduced himself, they started fidgeting in their seats and glanced around the room nervously. And yet, Ibrahim's round, boyish face and British-accented English couldn't have been more different from the media image of bearded, scowling Islamists.

Slacker seemed surprisingly uncomfortable, considering that earlier in the day he'd explained to me that the Brotherhood wasn't focused on metal anymore, "because they now have bigger fish to fry." But he and Ibrahim are more alike than he imagined, and not just because both come from very religious families. They also have many of the same cultural tastes, heavy metal aside, and live their lives through their computers and the virtual worlds they create with them. Seif has even more in common with Ibrahim; they both are graduates of English-language universities with MBAs and hi-tech-related jobs. Equally important, Seif and Ibrahim are both searching for an alternative yet authentic identity to the one offered by the Mubarak regime.

Given these similarities, I wasn't surprised that Ibrahim was happy and perhaps even anxious to hang out with the artists sitting around the lobby's shabby coffee table. Seif, Slacker, and Stigma were not, and their wariness is understandable, at least regarding the Brotherhood as an institution. For all its talk of moderation, the "new" Brotherhood can still seem a lot like the old one, as it did in the fall of 2006 when Brotherhood members of Parliament tried to have the minister of culture fired for suggesting to a veiled reporter that the headscarf was a step backward for Egypt. Even if such relapses are infrequent, in Egypt's still-undemocratic political environment, there's no way to test whether the movement really is sincere, which is why, much to the disgust of Omar and Ibrahim, so many Egyptians—and Arabs more broadly—prefer to continue dealing with the devil they know (corrupt and autocratic regimes) than to risk the even less appealing alternative of a religious state.

Ibrahim, who was forced to flee to the Gulf in 2007 to avoid arrest, wasn't unsympathetic to my friends' fears when I asked him—after Slacker, Stigma, and Seif had left—why he thought they were so nervous around him. "But still, they're being naïve. They should know that the movement is more diverse and less strictly hierarchical today. Women are more involved, and young members have even started blogs, like 'Ana Ikhwan' [I'm a Muslim Brother], where they criticize the leadership."

As an editor of the Ikhwan website, Ibrahim has himself engaged in some not-so-subtle criticism of the actions of other Ikhwan members—indeed, he would agree with a colleague of mine, Samuli Schielke, who's spent several years studying youth culture in the Egyptian equivalents of "Smalltown, U.S.A.," that while a growing number of twenty- to fortysomething Ikhwan members like Omar and particularly Ibrahim exhibit a "very surprising openness" toward more-liberal moral and political ideas, the more conservative Islam of their elders is still "prevalent and powerful, at least in Egypt," including among a significant share of the Brotherhood's younger generation.

But for me, it's the conflict between the two Brotherhoods that's important, as became apparent when a conservative-reading draft of a potential party platform for the Ikhwan containing troubling language about *sharia* and Egyptian law was leaked to the press, and was immediately criticized by many members, especially younger ones. As important is the personal dimension of the transformation of the Brotherhood's younger generation. This became clear in my conversations with Ibrahim, when I realized how similar his experiences of alienation and suspicion as a Brother are to those of Marz or

Stigma as musicians. For Marz, being a metalhead is "demeaning after a while. We work so hard but get no money, no respect, only harassment by police." Ibrahim's experiences are no different: "People don't see me, as an Islamist, as a man. I am discriminated against because I'm a politically active religious Muslim."

The difference between them is in how they respond to this situation. While Marz wants a space to be left alone, Ibrahim argues, "Here's the thing I know: If I fight just for myself and my rights, then I'll never get them. Only if and when I'm ready to fight for everyone's rights can I hope to have my full rights as a religious Muslim in Egypt." This is a radically different approach to politics from the one that has traditionally existed among Islamists in the Muslim world, who haven't been very interested in the rights of other oppressed groups in their societies, particularly those that don't follow their conservative views on religion and morality. It's also quite different from the depoliticized metalheads, who have given up on the idea that their struggles could be society's. Yet giving up on society is precisely what has made the metaliens' music so dark and their sense of possibility so narrow. "We want to confront the regime," Ibrahim continued, "not to impose *sharia* or wage jihad against the West or Israel—but to bring real democracy and social justice to Egypt and the region as a whole."

Such an attitude puts him in direct confrontation with extremist versions of Islam, but also with an "air-conditioned Islam" that is both depoliticized and very accommodating toward consumerist lifestyles. As Ibrahim explains, "Air-conditioned Islam is creating a culture of shadows. Take this new advertisement from the Gulf that's regularly on TV. It shows two kids playing on their PlayStations when the call to prayer comes. They jump up, and while they run to pray, their joysticks stay floating in the air until they come back and pick up right where they left off. What message is this supposed to send? Is this Islam? The Kuwaiti Ministry of Religion [which sponsored the TV spot] has become more secular than the communists!"

Enough Is Enough!
Egypt's Bloggers Enter the Fray

Egypt's metalheads are not on the Brotherhood's radar screen at the moment—and that's fine with them. But in the last two years the Brotherhood has been reaching out to other secular groups within civil society, most notably the movement of civil society and political activists and bloggers that have coalesced around Kefaya, which has justly received a lot of attention and praise in the Western media for its advocacy of real democratic reforms. But most commentators don't realize that as reasonable as its goals seem, the movement's roots are much more radical.

What makes Kefaya dangerous to the Egyptian government and the political elite more broadly is its combined critique of Western foreign policy. It calls for an end to the U.S. occupation of Iraq and the "Zionist devastation wreaked" upon the Palestinian people, and, even more threatening, for an end to the monopoly on political power by Mubarak and his cronies and the establishment of the rule of law. The government has gone to great lengths to weaken Kefaya, from jailing Ayman Nour to arresting, imprisoning, and sometimes torturing hundreds of activists involved in the high-profile protests in support of incarcerated judges.

Perhaps the core of the Kefaya movement is the burgeoning blogger community, which has become the most compelling and threatening social force in the country by bringing together Egyptians of vastly different political, social, and economic backgrounds. But bloggers aren't just operating in a virtual terrain. They train fellow activists in computer technologies, attend demonstrations and pass out new website information, and—especially important—have energized what was a moribund mainstream opposition with their defiant attitudes and willingness to go to working-class neighborhoods and involve people normally ignored by the country's opposition elite.

Some of the most important bloggers in Egypt emerged out of the country's metal scene. Prime among them is Alaa Abdel Fatah, who, along with his wife, Manal Hassan, runs what is likely the best-known blog in Egypt, "Manal and Alaa's Bit Bucket." Alaa's arrest in 2006 and jailing (forty-five days for protesting without a permit) earned him international recognition, awards from groups such as Reporters Without Borders, and regular appearances on Egyptian and Arab TV. He has one uniform whether he's meeting you at a café or appearing on al-Jazeera: a T-shirt (usually with some form of political symbolism or slogan on it) and a pair of old jeans. His uncombed hair and days-old beard remind me of the twenty-something computer geeks who were at the core of the anti–corporate globalization movements in the 1990s, which is not surprising, since that's exactly what Alaa is.

But long before he started blogging, Alaa was headbanging. He's a longtime metal and hard-rock fan, and traces his love of music and computers back to the bands he was turned on to as a precocious thirteen-year old: Pink Floyd, Nirvana,

Portishead, Radiohead, Prodigy and, of course, Metallica. "I was mildly harassed when they cracked down on the black-clads and long-hairs in the infamous satanic incident," he explained as we sipped cappuccino in yet another overpriced coffee bar populated by students and *Lonely Planet*–lugging tourists. "While [the abuse was] comparatively minor, I felt firsthand what my parents tried hard to explain to me: you can't avoid politics, you can't just pretend this country is not fucked up. I developed a strong hate of those who wronged the metalheads, and I still fantasize about fragging them all with bazookas."

Alaa and Manal were among the major advocates for free/open source computing in Egypt. For Manal and Alaa, the Web serves the same function as does the Brotherhood for Ibrahim: it's a vehicle and a movement through which they can reach a lot of people and help bring about much-needed social change.

Hossam El-Hamalawy, another of the top bloggers on the Egyptian scene and a core member of Kefaya, has been investigating what happens to people who wind up on the receiving end of the government's "pinpoint violence" for several years. As a journalist and researcher with the *Los Angeles Times,* AP, Human Rights Watch, and now his blog, "El-3Arabawy" (the 3 represents the Arabic letter *ayn*), Hossam has helped break several stories about the routine abuse experienced by democracy activists at the hands of the Mukhabarat.

Although his shaved head and sloppy-chic clothes place him more readily in SoHo than at a metal concert, Hossam's formative experiences were, like Alaa's, immersed in heavy metal. "I went to Islamic school, even though my parents were secular, because it was the best in the area. Yet despite being religious it was known as the most metalien school in Cairo, with its own gang, the Immortals of Doom, who had access to the best metal, because we knew stewardesses who'd buy it for us." But however exciting the scene was for a teenager in 1990s Egypt, it was ultimately too upper-class and apolitical for Hossam. "It was pathetic. And politics and street protests were dead because the government broke the back of the insurgency by cracking down on everyone." Having no desire to become a musician, he turned his energies to journalism and activism.

Metal may have been too apolitical for Hossam, but his metal background and attitude have helped shape the philosophy behind Kefaya, which he describes as being "very in your face." This position has no doubt helped make Kefaya fairly popular with more-militant young activists, secular and religious alike. If you surf around Hossam's site, you'll see why: exposés on the corruption of the Mubarak regime, photos of the "other Cairo"—the city's vast shantytowns that the president doesn't want you to see—and most recently, disturbing video of people being tortured and sodomized by the police.

One of the comments on Hossam's blog read: "All I can say is Fuck to the silent people." Yet among the many groups who are remaining publicly silent are, of course, most of the metalheads. Not because they don't care, but because they're too scared that the next torture video could feature one of them. As Stigma explained, "Making music is the best we can do."

The Future Wears Black...

One night after a marathon six-hour rehearsal with Marz
(which was so loud my ears hurt after jamming with them for
only twenty minutes), I walked the few blocks from my hotel
to the home of Shady and Noor Nour. Shady met me halfway
to his family's penthouse apartment. On the way we passed
the local Hardee's, which—as in New Jersey when I was growing up—has become the place for Cairo's metal population to
meet after dark. At 1:00 a.m. on any given night, at least a
dozen kids with long hair and black T-shirts hang out in front
of the restaurant, while half a dozen military policemen look
on with bemused detachment. A few kids semi-clandestinely
drink beer bought from a nearby store or smoke hashish-
spiked cigarettes.

A metalhead came up to us and announced that he had
just finished his thirteenth beer. I had to laugh. How many
times in high school had friends and bandmates announced a
similarly ludicrous accomplishment? It seems that metalheads are truly the same the world over.

Well, perhaps not exactly. Growing up, I don't remember
any metalheads playing music to deal with their father dying
in jail after being imprisoned by their country's dictatorial
leader. But somehow Shady and Noor seemed to get stronger
each time we met, even as the prospect for their father's release dwindled, despite his increasingly dire medical condition. "We listened to metal before our father's arrest, but it
helps us deal with the anger since then, and to convert it to
useful forms." It also seems to have had a therapeutic effect

for their mother, Gamila, a well-known journalist, who went to all their shows and stood in the middle of the mosh pit, videotaping her sons.

Shady and Noor are certainly unique in the metal scene, and not just because of their age and precocious talent. Although their band, Bliss, broke up soon after we met, the name remains the best way to describe the expressions on their faces when they're playing guitar or singing. What is truly different about Shady and Noor, however, is that they are openly, though not conservatively, religious. Shady's Friday-afternoon ritual is to go to Juma' (Friday afternoon) prayer at the local mosque with his band and then rehearse for four hours. "We go pray, and then play black metal," he said with a laugh, knowing how that probably sounded to a foreigner.

The brothers are among the first in what will surely become a trend—as it has in other Muslim countries—of religiously grounded hard rock, or at least a metal sound that doesn't violate more-traditional religious and moral sensibilities. "Look, you can be a metalien and a good Muslim at the same time," they explained, without a hint of the internal conflicts over their identities that plague so many of their musical comrades.

Besides, Bliss had a strangely upbeat sound, among the first metal bands in Egypt that consciously sought to play something resembling the "oriental doom metal" made famous by the Israeli band Orphaned Land. It's only fitting that Shady and Noor would be big fans of Orphaned Land, whose members come from mixed Middle Eastern and European Jewish backgrounds, and feel like orphans in a country that is claimed by all but belongs to none. Shady and Noor clearly

feel similarly; their eyes lit up when I mentioned I'd be seeing Orphaned Land in a few days. "Can you send them a
'horns' from us? We love them."

I asked Slacker about the importance of Orphaned Land
when I noticed that the band was listed as a friend on the
MySpace sites of a lot of Egyptian bands. "I know it seems
weird, but they're awesome." Shady Nour was even more em-
phatic that Orphaned Land was a band to be emulated. "The
main reason for their success is that despite everything, Israel
is comparatively free and democratic, even though Egyptians
hate to admit it."

To emphasize the difference between Egypt and Israel,
Shady explained that the police had recently threatened his
father that if he wasn't more cooperative, his sons would be
arrested as satanists. "And as you've seen, we're watched
twenty-four hours a day, even coming to our house with you,
we were followed," Shady cautioned. "We can't even go into
the studio to record, because the police might plant drugs and
then have us arrested."

I couldn't help thinking, as I walked home from their
apartment, that maybe the metal scene's search for autonomy and authenticity—that is, to be left alone—was in fact
a political act in an environment where direct political action
is a risky endeavor. Hardly anyone agreed with me, however,
inside or outside the metal scene. Blogger Nora Younis
summed up the problem best when she explained that for
musicians to stay apolitical is exactly what the government
wants, because music then becomes a safety valve for young
people who might otherwise join more politically subversive
groups like Kefaya or the Muslim Brotherhood.

Mohammad Said, editorial writer for *al-Ahram* and a

generation older than Younis, went further, explaining that "the political sphere is and will remain relatively empty until culture can become more politicized." But politics could be taken to a whole new level if culture became more positively political. "What Egyptian politics needs is more 'civil guerrilla action'—learning to adapt to whatever fits the situation."

Heba Raouf, perhaps the most famous "Islamist-feminist" professor in Egypt, summed up the problem best when we discussed why Slacker, Stigma, and Seif were unhappy sitting down—never mind working—with Ibrahim. "There are no overlapping spheres here. These two groups, young metalheads and young Brothers, are completely isolated from each other and uninterested in communication. Even enemies can become friends because through conflict you communicate. But they're not at that point yet. Until they are, they'll be fighting their battles alone, and they'll lose." It's not just that bringing these two groups from the opposite ends of Egyptian society together would win the day, it's that such a process would act like a net, helping to bring other marginalized yet opposing groups together in the common struggle for democracy and economic equality.

... Under the Dark Blue Alexandrian Sky

It took about three and a half hours to drive from Cairo to Alexandria. Marz, Slacker, Stigma, a few of their friends, and I had come to meet up with their counterparts in Alexandria's metal scene. On the way I practiced the vocabulary and grammar invented by the metaliens to describe their scene in Egyptian Arabic. To headbang: *bangara.* I'm a headbanger: *Ana babangar.* This song really headbangs: *Lughnaiti babangar.* I'm a metalhead: *Ana metil.*

As we arrived in the city center, the sun had just begun to set over the Mediterranean. It shimmered off the windows of the spectacular Great Library of Alexandria, historical symbol of a city that's been famed for its learning and cosmopolitan personality since the time of Aristotle, and whose recent "reopening" was intended to symbolize Egypt's intellectual and scientific renaissance. This sent a small tingle up my historian spine, even though there's little in the present-day collection I couldn't find online or through my university library. Alexandria is also famed for its food, and after so many meetings in Cairo's coffee bars and European-style restaurants and pubs, I was equally excited about the possibility of eating something more authentic than pasta or hummus. "Maybe some *foul* or *mujedara*?" I asked Marz. "Mark," he said, laughing, "that's so five years ago."

The sea and some good Egyptian cooking beckoned a few blocks away, but I wound up going to yet another soulless yuppie café-restaurant, which blasted the air conditioning and the Eurotrash dance music with equal disregard for the comfort of its customers. It didn't matter once the musicians started arriving, maybe a dozen of them from Alexandria's best bands, including Erebus, Chronic Pain, Ammattammmen Bas, Hellchasm, Massive Scar Era, and Worm, which was one of the first Egyptian bands to be noticed in Europe.

As we moved to a bigger table to accommodate everyone, Ahmed, a member of the band Erebus—in Greek mythology, Erebus is the embodiment of primordial darkness and the son of Chaos—sat next to me. His opening words made clear that the scars of being a metalien run as deep in Alexandria as in

Cairo: "If the government just sees you playing guitar, they think you're a satanist," Ahmed explained. "But we're Muslims, we do our prayers. We don't violate Islam." Sitting a couple of feet away, Marz rolled his eyes at Ahmed's testament of faith.

"No one dares to fuck with the government because no one fucks with the government and gets away with it. Even at metal shows, everyone is tense, waiting for something to happen. So you see the musicians with less long hair, while the poseurs come and go because they don't appreciate the music for what it is." At the same time, however, succeeding in Egypt as a metal artist brings a great feeling of accomplishment. "Despite the fact that the government is trying to fuck you, repress you, and control you—did you know that Egypt is like the twelfth most corrupt country in the world?—you have your fan base and you, not the government, are in control."

Women, of course, face a bigger challenge. The members of bands like Massive Scar Era have to deal with conservative fathers who strictly enforce 8:45 p.m. curfews (Massive Scar Era's guitarist had to rush home soon after explaining this to me, to make hers), and fans who don't want to accept girls playing metal. Male or female, being a metalhead is a daily struggle to affirm one's identity against a host of forces—the government, religious leaders, the music business, and economic pressures.

It was sad to sit across from Alexandria's Library, so recently reopened after more than 1,600 years, hearing story after story of ignorance and oppression at the hands of Egypt's present-day rulers and society. Perhaps that's why everyone seemed a bit subdued on the ride home later that evening, if not downright emotional as we sat down in the lobby for a farewell drink.

After the usual promises to stay in touch and perhaps work together on some new music, Marz, Slacker, and Stigma stood up to say good-bye to me. As they headed out the door, past the beat-up metal detector, Marz turned around, his voice choking just a bit, and said, "Despite everything, Egypt is my country and I love it." At least for Marz, Egypt is still the promised land.

※☆※

A few months after our "summit" in Alexandria, Massive Scar Era and other local bands organized a metal festival on the steps of the Alexandria Library. The event was by most evaluations an important steppingstone in the public legitimization of Egyptian heavy metal. Artists were interviewed by international Arabic news channels, who compared the evening favorably with the Dubai Desert Rock festival that Marz and I had attended a month earlier. More high-profile gigs came every few months, and Stigma, Slacker, and even Marz started to sound optimistic about the future of metal, if not of Egypt. But Ayman Nour remained in solitary confinement without proper medical care, while bloggers, Brotherhood members, and other civil society activists were being arrested with increasing frequency.

Hate Suffocation also changed its name—to Scarab. Soon after the Alexandria festival, either emboldened by musical success or having had enough of Egypt's poisonous politics (or both), Marz sent me the following e-mail:

MArk YOU KNOW WHAT!

I WANT TO DO SOMETHING i was thinking over a million times!

WRITE MY NAME!

WRITE WHAT WE ARE GOING THROUGH HERE!

SAY WHAT EVER YOU THINK IS RIGHT

i want people to know that we are struggling! . . .

am not afraid anymore FUCK IT!

USE MY FULL NAME AS YOU WANT!

We are who we are we are not hurting our culture in fact we are an evolution

let the fucking world know what we are doing!

please feel free

We decided the band to suffer what ever consequences i believe that we should be activists and musicians at the same time!

please make it happen even though am afraid BUT AM NOT SO FUCK IT!

Mark! use my full name if you want

AL SHarif Hassan MArzeban

ISRAEL/ PALESTINE

Hard Music in an Orphaned Land

"If you're lucky, you can say you were here for the start of the Palestinian civil war," joked my friend the Palestinian sociologist May Jayussi. She jumped into a taxi and sped out of downtown Ramallah, where our expensive lunch had just been interrupted by a firefight between Hamas and Fatah fighters that left thirty-three people shot and me sliding ever lower in my chair as we hurried to finish eating before the cab arrived. (The restaurant staff had already abandoned us to get a better view of the fighting.) A demure, chain-smoking dynamo with an angular Chanel-girl haircut, May is the director of the most important Palestinian think tank, Muwatin, the Palestinian Institute for the Study of Democracy.

May's concern that day, however, was to make it to her house on the outskirts of town without running into any of the pickup trucks overloaded with young men brandishing Kalashnikovs and cruising the city for someone to fight. I ran around the block and jumped into my friend Sami's car. Fortunately, despite its slipping transmission, we caught up with May's taxi, whose driver knew a safe route out of downtown. As we careened through the backstreets of Ramallah, Sami and I had to laugh. This wasn't what we'd expected to be doing when we met, both of us students, more than a decade ago.

Even then, Sami's unfailingly calm demeanor and pleasant smile belied an activist streak that had earned him a "Shabak education," a euphemism Palestinian citizens of Israel use to describe the sometimes violent harassment that so many of them experience at the hands of Israel's security services. (I use "Palestinian Israelis" to refer to Palestinian citizens of Israel, and "Palestinians" to refer to Palestinians living in the West Bank, Gaza, and the Diaspora.) In those days, before the collapse of the Oslo peace process and the more or less permanent closure of the Occupied Territories, I'd think nothing of popping over to Ramallah on a Saturday afternoon or evening with Sami and other Palestinian Israeli friends from Jaffa (the onetime economic and cultural capital of Palestine) and even an Israeli Jew or two, to have lunch at my favorite hummus restaurant, shop for the latest Arab pop CDs, or even go to a nightclub that featured the latest underground house or trance music spun by European DJs.

Today the drive to Ramallah can take hours. The hundreds of checkpoints set up by the Israeli Defense Forces (IDF) in the Occupied Territories, some permanent and heavily fortified, others temporary, have nearly destroyed the Palestinian economy by making it impossible for Palestinians to move freely throughout the West Bank and (before the Israeli pullout in 2006) Gaza, or between them and Israel. Meanwhile, 400,000 settlers speed between Tel Aviv and Jerusalem and the settlements on Israeli-only bypass roads.

Once you get across the Green Line—the internationally recognized border of 1949 that separated Israel from the West Bank and Gaza until 1967—the roads are a disaster, having been crushed under the weight of innumerable sixty-five-ton Merkava tanks since the outbreak of the al-Aqsa intifada in September 2000. The situation and the roads have become even more surreal in Gaza, as I had discovered the previous day on my way to the town of Khan Younis, capital of "Hama-stan" and perhaps the most dangerous town in the Middle East after Baghdad or Fallujah.

I was trying to see the Gaza Strip's most famous rapper, Mohammed Farra of the group Palestinian Rapperz. Mohammed is a lanky twenty-two-year-old with close-cropped hair, who favors well-creased hip-hop clothing (baggy pants, sports jerseys) over the Eastern European–looking slacks, jeans, and dress shirts most of his peers wear. Mohammed has never been able to find a real job, thanks to the disastrous economic situation in Gaza, and now he's finding it impossible to finish his degree in English at Gaza's al-Quds Open University, thanks to his burgeoning music career.

Considering the amount of violence Mohammed has experienced in his brief life, I am still surprised at how warm and open he is to anyone who shows interest in his music, in Gaza's plight, or in both. Unfortunately, on the day I was first to meet him, Mohammed's cousin, an Islamic Court judge and Hamas leader named Bassam al-Farra, was gunned down. With the family gathering at his house to pay their respects, and with Gaza even more tense and violent than Ramallah, it was clearly not a good time to visit.

Gaza is home to at least 1.5 million people, the large majority of whom are descendants of Palestinian refugees who live in overcrowded and woefully underdeveloped camps that were established in 1948 as temporary shelters. Today it has the dubious distinction of being one of the most densely crowded, fetid, violent, and poverty-stricken places on earth, and one of the youngest demographically (more than 55 percent of Gaza's residents are under nineteen, and 76 percent are under thirty).

Seeing friends and relatives killed almost weekly was taking a toll on Mohammed. Physically he was still recovering from being shot by Israeli snipers, and emotionally he was reeling from the refusal of the Israelis to allow his band to travel to France for a tour. It was, Mohammed explained, "hard to see into the future." The growing Palestinian-on-Palestinian violence only added to the general level of despair for Gaza residents. "But what can I do?" Mohammed asked me rhetorically. "This is, in fact, why I became a rapper. Rap came from struggle, and at least being a rapper allows me to take the realities of the occupation and transform them into songs." And when local producers and technology can't quite capture the intensity of his experiences, Mohammed heads to Egypt—which, tellingly, is easier to get to from Gaza than is the West Bank—to collaborate with underground MCs and producers in Cairo.

But wherever they're writing, recording, or performing, Mohammed and his fellow rappers cannot escape the social and political context of their music. And taking any political stand automatically puts them into conflict not just with Israelis, but also with their more conservative elders and peers in Palestinian society who hold different and often more violent views than theirs. Slowly, religious leaders are beginning to recognize that the music of Palestinian Rapperz inspires young people to continue a seemingly hopeless struggle, rather than simply providing an escape from the realities of life in what remains of Palestine.

Cosmopolitan Ramallah's rap scene is naturally more open and innovative. There, rappers work with visual artists and poets in collectives that stretch the boundaries of art as a means of resistance. Boikutt, a rapper who's part of the "Ramallah Underground" collective of MCs, visual artists, and "soundcatchers" (sound engineers who roam the streets recording random sounds to incorporate into songs) that Sami and I were going to see when the Hamas-Fatah firefight erupted, explains the situation this way: "Ninety percent of what I rap is political because eighty percent of life in Palestine is political." (The heading of his MySpace site begins by declaring that "Palestine is not listed [in the official MySpace countries list], so FUCK United States.")

In such a hyperpolitical environment as Palestine today, it's not surprising that crews like Ramallah Underground and Gaza's Palestinian Rapperz have hit a cultural nerve by weaving together the postindustrial protest sounds of hip-hop, with its commitment to using words as weapons, and the Palestinian tradition of passing down history through music and storytelling. And they're reaching young people around the world at a time when the mainstream media rarely presents an unfiltered Palestinian point of view.

Ramallah Underground's MCs rap over some of the most

haunting tracks I've heard since the early days of gangsta rap. The grooves evoke early 1970s funk, but its discordant tonality is generated by descending chromatic bass lines, crackling soundscapes, Arab instruments like the oud or nay (flute), and the sounds of gunfire recorded by local soundcatchers. A mélange of Arabic and English rhymes can be incredibly un-settling—especially if you're listening to them in the Occu-pied Territories, during a gunfight, which is when many of them were inspired and even recorded. Capturing both the complexity and violence of the occupation, they rap in their song "Almadeel Mustamerr" (Past Continuous): *"They at-tacked, they endured, they bombed . . . They built, they destroyed, they parked and honked. No one moved out of the way so they kept going . . . And while you're sitting here contemplating . . . They widened their borders."*

But Boikutt, Stormtrap, and their comrades don't just rap as an alternative to throwing stones or building bombs. Being musicians offers these artists opportunities that most Palestinians are denied. They are able to travel outside the country (something Mohammed and the other members of Palestinian Rapperz have a harder time doing because they're from Gaza), tell their stories to a wide audience, and meet with people from around the world.

With Jerusalem increasingly out of reach for most Pales-tinians, Ramallah has become the de facto capital of Palestine. It is the epicenter of what the Palestinian sociologist Salim Tamari terms the age-old conflict between "the mountains and the sea" that has defined Palestinian culture and identity for centuries. If you stand on one of its hills and look east-ward, the biblical landscape of the West Bank opens before you. If you look to the west, the Mediterranean Sea and the lights of Tel Aviv and Jaffa glimmer in the distance. In the mid-1990s, the early years of the Oslo process, Ramallah became home to the majority of the Palestinian elite and thousands of foreign NGO workers. Other than Bethlehem, Ramallah is one of the few Palestinian cities where one can openly drink alcohol, or go to a nightclub dressed in the latest b-boy attire and bump and grind the night away. As Stormtrap said, "Without music we wouldn't have much hope for the future. We don't want to end up leading boring office lives. We're looking for something beyond that—and music is the key."

Hardly any Israelis travel to Ramallah or anywhere else in the Occupied Territories these days, unless they're soldiers, settlers, or peace activists. The peace activists have the hardest time, because their presence makes it more difficult for soldiers and settlers to carry on with the business of occupation. But the drive is worth it, if only because it brings into clear relief the differences between Israel, with its First World living standards (the country ranks twenty-third in the Human Development Index, far above almost every country in the Arab/Muslim world) and cookie-cutter Jewish settlements on either side of the Green Line, and the much poorer and densely populated Palestinian towns of the West Bank (whose HDI ranking sinks further below 100 with each passing year).

Equally disheartening are the permanent checkpoints like Qalandiya. Little more than an ad-hoc series of barriers a decade ago, today it is a permanent border crossing with hours-long lines and soldiers who scream and point their weapons at any car carrying a Palestinian, even when it's approaching from the Israeli side and the Palestinian is an eighty-year-old woman, as Sami and I learned when we picked up an old woman carrying a huge package on her head a few hundred meters from the checkpoint on our way to lunch with May.

Long, Hard History

Fifty years of Zionist colonization of Palestine, and with it intensifying intercommunal conflict, culminated in the first full-scale war between Israelis, Palestinians, and the surrounding Arab countries in 1948. The result: the establishment of the Jewish state on 78 percent of Palestine, and the exile of three-quarters of a million Palestinians. This was followed by four wars in four decades, resulting in the conquest of the remainder of Palestine in 1967, the rise of the PLO, the signing of the Israeli peace accords with Egypt, the transformation of Israel from a heavily state-managed economy to a neoliberal one, and the outbreak of the first intifada in December 1987. Finally, in the wake of the 1991 Gulf War, the Oslo peace process began in 1993 and continued until the outbreak of the al-Aqsa intifada in 2000.

It's impossible to understand Israeli and Palestinian music today apart from the abysmal failure of Oslo to deliver on its promises of peace, independence, and development for either Palestinians or Israelis. As important, and linking Israel/Palestine to similar trends across the MENA, was that Oslo coincided with increasing globalization along neoliberal lines of the Israeli and Palestinian economies. This had the predictable consequences of creating increased wealth for some Israelis and for their clients among the Palestinian elite (especially senior officials of the Palestinian Authority). But the majority of citizens in both societies faced a sharp rise in inequality and poverty and a decrease in average salaries for blue collar/unskilled workers. (Israel's poverty rate jumped from 10 to over 25 percent between 1990 and 2005; today, half of all Palestinian citizens live below the poverty line. Palestine fared worse, especially with the constant closures of the territories that decimated the economy.) The squeezing of both the Israeli and Palestinian working and middle classes created fertile ground for conservative or radical movements on both sides to preach violent confrontation as the best way to solve their problems. More positively, it helped produce some of the best hip-hop and heavy metal in the world.

Finding Your Way in an Orphaned Land

Palestine might be burning, and Jewish and Palestinian workers might be suffering, but you'd never know it sitting in a café at the beach or your apartment in southern Tel Aviv, where Kobi Farhi is working on a new song. Kobi is the lead singer of the Israeli Oriental death-doom metal band Orphaned Land, whose vibrant Arab and Muslim fan base surprised me during my trip to Egypt. The day before I was supposed to meet Mohammad Farra in Gaza, I had dinner with Kobi at a fashionable restaurant in Tel Aviv's Florentin neighborhood. Tel Aviv is known the world over as the White City because it has more ultramodern International Style buildings than any other city in the world. But in its southern part, near its mother town of Jaffa, Tel Aviv gets funkier and more bohemian. Florentin has the feel of New York City's Tribeca, but with even more picturesque buildings and the added bonus of a warm Mediterranean breeze.

The restaurant was filled with good-looking Israelis in their twenties, but even in that company, Kobi stood out when he walked through the door. With his long, dirty blond hair and a two-day beard, he looks as though he could have played Jesus in the movie version of *Hair*. "I actually used to try to look like Jesus," he admitted to me. "And why not? He was a great person, a great Jew." Not to mention that Orphaned Land is steeped in religious symbolism, so having the lead singer look like Jesus (or more accurately what most people imagine that Jesus looked like) doesn't hurt the band's image.

Kobi exudes the kind of aura that comes with being, if not a rock star, then a successful musician in the prime of his creative life. He's in one of the most influential bands in the world metal scene; he believes that his music can help bring peace between Jews and Muslims; and, most important, he doesn't need a day job. He is, refreshingly in this country, at peace with himself and the world, and has none of the arrogance, ego, or anger that seem to be staple personality traits among successful rock-'n'-roll musicians.

But then, Israel's metal scene has been a study in contradictions for more than twenty years. The music began with the extreme metal band Salem in 1985, who made it onto regular rotation on MTV's *Headbanger's Ball* as one of the ten best up-and-coming metal bands in the world. Salem brought the headbanging and mosh-pit experiences to Israel, and were soon followed by bands like Substance for God, Executer, Explicit, Betrayer, Providence, Amxxez, Phantom Pain, and Sword of Damocles, and the Palestinian Christian band Melechesh. The early 1990s were perhaps the biggest years for heavy metal in Jerusalem. At least half a dozen bands, with names such as Seppuku, Leviticus, and Incarnation could fill up theaters, while the local press reviewed new albums by local Death, Doom, Thrash, Grind Core, and even progressive thrash metal.

Orphaned Land was formed in 1991 in what Kobi and lead guitarist and primary songwriter Yossi Sassi-Sa'aron affectionately refer to as their marriage. Kobi's long hair and Ashkenazi looks are balanced by Yossi's darker hair and Mizrahi (that is, Middle Eastern Jewish) face and vibe. With a father from Libya and a mother from Iraq, Yossi grew up in an Arabic-speaking house where Oum Kalthoum mixed with just enough Jewish rituals to create the aesthetic sensibility behind Orphaned Land.

Together with Salem, the two bands form the two poles of Israeli metal, politically as well as sonically. While Salem was very nationalist and patriotic, for Orphaned Land, music has always been as sacred as land and territory. The band doesn't throw its Israeli—as opposed to Jewish/religious—identity into their music; in fact, none of the members of the band completed their army service, a rare and implicitly political act in a country where the army is the most important social bonding experience for young Israelis.

If, politically and spiritually, Orphaned Land is far more oriented toward peace than are most other bands, its music is anything but peaceful. In fact, it's quite violent: the biblical imagery, huge guitar sound, complex sonic textures and shifting grooves, and vocals that veer between prayers and grunts, have had a powerful impact on the metal scene. The fruitful mix of Ashkenazi and Mizrahi culture that makes Orphaned Land—and Israel—so musically unique, was abundantly clear at a sold-out show the band did in Tel Aviv in late 2006 as part of the *Global Metal* documentary film. Well over 1,000 fans jammed into Tel Aviv's Theatre Club for the show. Hardcore goth rockers headbanged next to kids swaying in trance-like traditional Jewish prayer. Kobi's vocals veered from harsh and brutal to soaring and fluid, while the band pounded away at grooves that merged Metallica and Megadeth with their own, unique blend of "Oriental" instruments: stringed instruments like the oud, lute, saz (a three-stringed Turkish guitar played expertly by Yossi), and Arabic drums.

For two hours the Theatre Club was truly a temple—more accurately, a synagogue—of heavy metal. The complexity and strange power of the music reminded me of the concerts put on by seminal art-rock bands like Yes and Rush. Yet here were young fans wrapped in prayer shawls and tfillin—the small boxes worn on the heads of religious Jews when they pray. And when you scan the titles and lyrics of Orphaned Land's songs, you understand why: the band's music is saturated with religious and biblical themes.

Watching kids pray at a metal concert is quite a sight. Then I remembered Sheikh Anwar al-Ethari's comment that when he and his fellow Shi'is pray, "we're doing heavy metal too," and the Noor brothers' admission that they love to pray before they play. But Orphaned Land is not seeking to bring kids back into the traditional religious fold. Instead, Kobi explains, "We're the next level of religion, because we're more open. We take things that are in conflict and bring them into harmony rather than driving people apart."

Kobi's argument is clear from the lyrics to the band's songs. In the band's 1994 first album, *Sahara,* Kobi sets up the main human and political dilemma the band has been exploring ever since. In "The Storm Still Rages Inside," he sings, "This land is barren, it does not feel / Our self-made slaughter / By our own hands / Here lies the orphaned land." In subsequent albums a more positive view of religion emerges, and "God's divine call" is exclaimed as a source of love and peace. But it's in the 2004 "Birth of the Three," from the album *Mabool,* where the band's desire to bring the three Abrahamic religions back into harmony comes together. Arguing that it was earlier attempts at unity that drew God's wrath, after "a thousand incarnations . . . the time was now at hand. A prophecy fulfilled so he may save this sinful land."

What's most compelling about Orphaned Land's lyrics is that unlike most metal bands from the region, they openly bring Muslim religious themes into their music. Kobi has a strong desire to explore Islam as both a religion and culture, a drive instilled in him growing up in the mixed Jewish–Palestinian Israeli neighborhood of Jaffa: "I was so influenced by hearing the call to prayer when I was growing up," he explained. "To this day when I hear Muslims say *Allahu Akbar,* I love it; in fact, my dream is to go to a mosque and sing the call to prayer. When I did it in the Taj Mahal [which is a mausoleum, not a mosque], it brought me closer to God."

Yossi also "feels Muslim," when he hears Muslim music or goes into a mosque. Kobi and Yossi may be more at home in Muslim culture than many of the Arab or Muslim metal artists I know. But is their Islamophilia ultimately a luxury easily afforded by two bohemian Jewish Israeli musicians who, when push comes to shove, are not directly involved in the conflict? I certainly couldn't imagine Mohammed Farra declaring that when he hears Jewish music or goes into a synagogue he "feels Jewish"—if he wasn't shot by Israeli soldiers upon entering the synagogue, he'd likely be shot by Palestinian militants upon leaving. Yet the unmistakable sincerity of Orphaned Land's music makes it hard to be cynical about Kobi and Yossi's embrace of the Muslim cultures surrounding Israel.

Tupac Lives On, from Ramla to Gaza

Ramla is one of the oldest towns in Israel, having been founded by one of the early caliphs of Islam, Suleiman Ibn Abd al-Malik, in 716. He liked the city so much he chose to remain there rather than move to Damascus, the imperial capital, when he was chosen as caliph. It remained one of the most important Arab cities in the country until 1948, when most Palestinians fled or were forced into exile.

Today only about 16,000 out of Ramla's 70,000 people are Palestinian. The rest, including the mayor, are Israeli Jews, most of them supporters of right-wing, anti-Palestinian Zionist parties. Not surprisingly, it was in neglected Palestinian neighborhoods of towns like Ramla and Lydda where Palestinian rap was born.

I was in Ramla to see one of the best young rappers in Israel, Sameh Zakout, aka Saz, a baby-faced MC with a linebacker's body, who is also a cousin of Tamer Nafar, a founder of the seminal Palestinian rap group Dam. As we walked through Ramla's decrepit souk, Saz gesticulated wildly as he spoke, filling me in on how the poverty and closed horizons that define life in Israel for the 1.4 million Palestinian citizens have impacted his life. "We wanna feel human," he explained in rapid-fire Arabic punctuated by Hebrew and English. "But instead the Jews are against us and call us a threat, a 'cancer' [as many senior Israeli officials have called Palestinians over the years]. They don't want to accept that we have the same dreams as them. And how can we achieve them when we're closed into these ghettos with little hope of improving our lives and the government treats us as a danger who isn't worth shit?"

Saz is clearly a political rapper, who barely gets by on income from his music. Yet his financial difficulties don't stop him from walking around with the swagger of a rap star—and from the way people greet him in the souk, or market, it seems as if he's one of Ramla's most famous sons. "Look at this shit," Saz explained, motioning to the crumbling market and dirty streets around us. "You want to know why I rap? Don't you listen to Tupac?"

Tupac Shakur is without a doubt the greatest single influence on Arab, and especially Palestinian, rappers. If you think about the violence that trailed Tupac literally from the cradle (his mother and uncle were involved in murders of police officers and armed robbery) to the grave (his own gangland-style murder), you can understand why he's idolized by aspiring rappers from Brazil's favelas and South Africa's shantytowns to the decaying Palestinian neighborhoods of Israel.

Tupac's powerful intersection of political and gangsta rap has served as the perfect model for young Palestinians whose neighborhoods are similarly drug- and crime-ridden, whose schools are underfunded and subpar, and who are surrounded by a hyperconsumerist culture that is out of reach for most. His tragic and meaningless death resonates strongly with young people who have little hope for the future, however talented they might be.

Saz dropped a verse for me: "My beats are my M16 / and my rhymes are my bullets / Each rhyme is a bullet and it's going somewhere." The music he records under these lines doesn't quite match Tupac's lushly produced sound, but it captures the same grittiness and intelligence that initially made Pac's thug-intellectual persona so appealing.

Just as Egyptian activists and metalheads describe their country as a "sick and rotten place," Saz smells the rot at the heart of his society. As he raps in his song "Yooma": "History has changed / It is the era of weapons / Do weapons bring victory? Our youth are lost in ridiculous customs and traditions. You smell it at first, this is not the smell of our country; its rotten root has entered inside us." But as bad as the situation can be for Palestinian Israelis, Saz is the first one to admit that it's not nearly as bad as in the Occupied Territories, where the construction of the so-called separation barrier or apartheid wall, and the more or less permanent closure of the Territories from Israel, have made the West Bank and Gaza a series of prisons for Palestinians.

When the Dam Bursts

The impossibility of regularly moving through the Occupied Territories has meant that the globalizing force of the Internet has become perhaps the most important way for rappers to communicate with one another, their fans, and the wider world. Dam's most famous song, "Min Erhabi" ("Who's the Terrorist?"), has been viewed on YouTube or otherwise downloaded over 2 million times. Without the Internet, Palestinian rap would still exist largely in obscurity; because of it, it has become the most important hip-hop in the Muslim world. Yet before Dam's Web success is celebrated as an example of the liberating power of the Internet, it's worth noting that from the perspective of the Israeli government, a cyber-intifada led by Dam and Palestinian Rapperz is far less threatening than the real one, which is precisely why more-militant Palestinians don't see much to be gained from political hip-hop unless it's directly motivating an even younger generation to take up the struggle, usually armed.

Unlike foreign rappers or those across the Green Line, Dam, Saz, and other Palestinian Israeli rappers and singers have no choice but to carve out a musical and, through it, political identity that can move back and forth between the Palestinian and the Israeli. Dam (in both Hebrew and Arabic, *dam* means "blood," and is also an acronym for "Da Arabic Microphone Controllers") titled one of its biggest Hebrew language hits, "We're Born Here," as a direct response to the song "Bladi ve-ardi" ("My country, my land"), by the ultra-Zionist Jewish rapper Subliminal. The song's video drips with the kind of anger and contempt for the symbols of the Israeli government—especially the police—that used to populate rap videos during the heyday of American rap in the late 1980s and early 1990s. The group is rapping in Hebrew, but the female rapper and R&B singer Abeer Zinati adds a chorus in Arabic.

That the video was shot in Lydda, which looks an awful lot like the West Bank, only adds to the song's power. "Maximum Jews, maximum land. Minimum Arabs, minimum land" the rap goes, in a summary of Israeli strategy vis-à-vis Palestinians for the last century. To counter it, Dam regularly crosses the Green Line for concerts in Ramallah and other Palestinian towns, uniting Palestinians on both sides of the Green

Line and fostering a sense of solidarity that is all but absent on the political level.

Men come to Dam's shows wearing their best hip-hop bling, kaffiyeh (the traditional Palestinian scarves), and American football or basketball jerseys. Headscarved women can be seen dancing next to their more-secular sisters and brothers as well. Some dance the *debka,* the Palestinian national dance, with the same fervor that the latest moves from J-Lo or Shakira are imitated at concerts in New York.

Yet if songs like "We're Born Here" and "Who's the Terrorist?" challenge the positive self-image most Israelis, Diaspora Jews, and supporters of Israel have of themselves, Dam's goal is not merely to be provocative. As Tamer Nafar explains, "I don't ask people to be pro-Palestinian or anti-Israeli. I just ask them to listen, read about the situation, and then decide." Picking up the famous line from Chuck D about rap being the "CNN of the street," Tamer argues that Arab hip-hop is the "al-Jazeera of the street."

Abeer Zinati's goal, by contrast, is precisely to provoke— not just the Israeli establishment, but Palestinian society, and even her own family. As we sat at a café on the campus of the Hebrew University of Jerusalem, Abeer explained that her stage name is "Sabreena Da Witch." She fingered the witch necklace—a figurine of a little witch on a broomstick—that she wears both as a symbol of her power over men and a not-so-subtle buzz-off to anyone (especially family members) who tries to label her or tell her what she can and cannot do. When not working on a new R&B or rap tune, Abeer is a photography major at Hebrew University. She's also one of the most beautiful singers in the Middle East, but with a roughness— or as she calls it "rudeness, hey, I'm from the 'hood"—that would never be tolerated in more-traditional Arab divas in Lebanon or Egypt.

As she describes her hometown, "You come to Lydda and you feel like the Separation Wall is here, even though we're well inside Israel. On the one side, beautiful houses and lawns, and on the other—our—side, shit. I don't know how a rat survives here, how kids aren't constantly sick. The police put drugs in our neighborhood and let the collaborators deal them, then they surround our 'hoods with checkpoints in order to police us, using the drugs as an excuse. I mean, you're telling me this is a country that can kill with precision Sheikh Yassine or Abd al-'Aziz Rantisi [two assassinated Hamas leaders] in the middle of a crowd, but the cops can't figure out where the drugs are in my neighborhood?"

Abeer is not the only Palestinian Israeli female rapper, but she's without a doubt the most talented. Her voice sounds as if it's been through a life of pain and joy far longer than her twenty-three years should have given her. Although we'd only just met, her cadences were familiar to me, even when speaking in Arabic. I understood why as soon as we began discussing her influences: "I sing most every type of black music: hip-hop, R&B, whatever. Because I'm Arab and I'm Palestinian, I'm black." Her home, located in the same poor neighborhood as Dam's in Lydda, is festooned with pictures of her idol, Tupac, and her musical heroes—Lauryn Hill, Bob Marley, and, most of all, Michael Jackson. "The sadness in MJ's breath moved me, literally, to sing and dance too. And when I saw vids of Tupac or other gangsta rappers running from the police, it seemed so much like my experiences that I was hooked on hip-hop."

Abeer is adamant about the negative role organized

religion—but not, she's quick to point out, Islam or the Qur'an—plays in Palestinian Israeli society. Her flouting of "traditional" Arab cultural norms—dressing provocatively, titling a song "I'm a Witch," and boasting in her lyrics that she casts spells and can enslave listeners—has meant that despite her presence on YouTube, MySpace, and several Dam videos, her work and identity must remain, for the most part, underground. "My family doesn't know what I do. I have to be sure who's at a gig and if it's being covered on TV. But at least I have a choice."

And it's the choice that matters to her. Abeer would rather be a closet witch who sneaks out every now and then to a gig or recording session than be like so many other Palestinian women who, despite having some of the highest educational levels in the Arab/Muslim world, remain trapped in what is still a patriarchal culture that values them primarily for their roles as mothers and housewives, rather than as individuals with the power and creativity to contribute to their society and change it in a positive way.

Channels of Rage, but Where Do They Lead?

If Tamer Nafar is one of the most famous rappers in the Arab world, the biggest rapper in Israel is his Jewish doppelgänger, Subliminal, born Kobi Shimroni. If you saw them on the street, it would be hard to tell which one was Jewish and which one "Arab." That's because Subliminal is Tunisian and Iranian by heritage. "We're not white like Europeans. We're the sand guys from the Middle East," he explains.

As recounted in the 2003 Israeli documentary *Channels of*

Rage (*Arotzim shel za'am*), when Subliminal and Tamer first met, around 2000, the more established Subliminal—perhaps the biggest pop artist in Israel—took Tamer under his wing. It was an incredible learning experience, Tamer admits, and the two became good friends for a time. But then the al-Aqsa Intifada erupted in October of that year, thirteen Palestinian citizens were killed by the police in protests that occurred in Palestinian towns and neighborhoods inside Israel, and a string of suicide bombings in Israel left scores of young Israelis dead. As with Jewish-Palestinian relations more broadly, Subliminal and Tamer's relationship quickly deteriorated into open hostility.

In an age of constant national soul-searching, Subliminal uses hip-hop to provide a renewed and largely uncritical nationalist narrative for Israelis, one that appeals especially to working-class Mizrahim (Jews whose families immigrated from Muslim countries), whose Middle Eastern heritage and culture the European-dominated Zionist movement and then state worked for generations to delegitimize. Not surprisingly, Subliminal's raps depict Israel as the main victim and the weaker side in the conflict with the Palestinians, "dangling like a cigarette from Arafat's mouth," according to a lyric from one of his biggest hits. This belief is very attractive to young Israelis conflicted about serving in an occupation army, for whom the idea of a powerful Palestinian leader manipulating Israel into signing on to its own destruction justifies the routine humiliation and violence that Palestinians suffer at the hands of the IDF.

But Subliminal's narrative has little basis in reality—Arafat was imprisoned for the final years of his life in his decrepit Ramallah compound, while Palestine disintegrates into chaos more each year. Since this fact doesn't fit into Subliminal's narrative, however, it is ignored. Moreover, any criticism of Israeli policy by Palestinians, including citizens of the state, is illegitimate in Subliminal's opinion, because in the end all Palestinians want not just to "divide and conquer us . . . they want us dead. That's it."

Yet while Subliminal's language and rhetoric can be harsh, he is not an especially right-wing Israeli. He even raps about "respecting Islam," and when fans at a concert started chanting "death to Arabs" he shouted, "Fuck you!" back at them, declaring, "Not death to Arabs, but life for Jews." But for Subliminal and his fans, Israel's life-or-death conflict with Palestinians justifies continued discrimination against Israel's Palestinian population, and worse for Palestinians across the Green Line.

With such an attitude, there is little wonder that when he took the stage after Tamer had performed at one of their last joint appearances, Subliminal asked the crowd, "What do you say if we make Palestinian ID cards for Tamer" and then shouted, "Fuck you if you badmouth Zion. You're in Zion, in Israel, in Tel Aviv, you asshole." The crowd went crazy. Tamer just sat at the back of the club staring at the stage. Four years later, however, it is Tamer who's the bigger international star, bringing his no-holds-barred critique of Israeli society and its Palestinian policies to Europe and the United States in almost monthly tours outside Israel.

Keep Doing What You're Doing

"I was at the Wailing Wall one day and I met a rabbi," Orphaned Land singer Kobi Farhi recounted between sips of organic tea. "I explained what we did as a band, and he listened very intently. 'You must keep doing what you're doing,' he said. 'Even with all my Kabala and power and religious training, I can't reach the kids like you.' And he's right. We take songs from the synagogue and get thousands of metalheads to bang to them. It's a religious experience."

In Morocco and Egypt, metalheads and religious authorities view each other with great suspicion, if not outright hostility. In Israel/Palestine, the relationship between rock and religion is more complicated. For one thing, Judaism doesn't have the obsession with Satan that Christianity and Islam do. But an even more important reason metal and hip-hop aren't looked down upon by many religious authorities is that the musicians are seen as serving their interests, whether it's Kobi leading otherwise secular metal fans toward religion, or Subliminal supporting the government's policies and propaganda.

There is, as far as I can tell, only one Palestinian metal band today in Israel/Palestine: Khalas. They have not had many problems with Muslim religious figures, perhaps because they don't have enough Palestinian fans to be on their radar. Hip-hop is a different matter. When Palestinian rappers first started out in the late 1990s, they encountered a lot of hostility from religious forces. In Gaza, Mohammed Farra received death threats, and his band's concerts were forcibly stopped by Hamas, even when the band performed at "liberation" rallies.

Israeli Palestinian rappers like Dam and Saz haven't received death threats, but early religious opposition has left them wary. Yet as rappers have become more popular, religious leaders have started to view them in ways reminiscent of the rabbi at the Wall. Explained band member Mahmoud

Jreri, "Now some sheikhs support us and tell us to keep doing what we're doing. 'You deliver a message we can't.' " Israeli Palestinian artists can bring hope and galvanize into action kids who might otherwise turn to drugs or crime.

The road to social acceptance has been harder in Gaza. As Mohammed recounted to me, "At first people in Gaza didn't know about rap, and when we started they thought we were just trying to be American. They didn't like us because of the way we looked and dressed. They didn't understand that we were doing this for Palestine. But once they hear our lyrics, most people start to like us, and now we have a lot of fans in Gaza."

When Mohammed raps "Allahu Akbar" ("God is Greater"), it is a chant of defiance against the occupation. When Kobi Farhi of Orphaned Land hears Muslims say the same phrase before every *sallah,* or prayer, he "feels Muslim." In fact, in his songs Kobi invokes "Allah"—the name he frequently uses for God—to save Israel from the "damnation" of endless violence. But moving beyond such generalizations to direct criticism of the occupation, he and guitarist Yossi agree, would be counterproductive. "If we become political and make statements, we will lose our audience," Kobi explains. Yossi adds, "Music can be a cure, but only for those who want to listen. We can't make the blind see."

What Orphaned Land's music can do, Kobi explained, is help humanize Muslims and Jews in the eyes of the other. "One Saudi fan came up to me at a show and said, 'Dude, I was brought up to hate you, but I love you, man.' Then he showed me a tattoo of our logo on his arm. What can you say to that? They listen to us, hiding in their basements." At the end of the day, Kobi and Yossi are operating under the same paradigm as Marz and the metaliens of Egypt: in a situation where it seems impossible—or at least not worth the considerable risk—to take on an oppressive or corrupt system, you can opt out of it so that at the very least you're not part of the problem. What remains to be seen is how bad it will have to get before, like their acolytes in Hate Suffocation, the members of Orphaned Land decide to say "fuck it" and, to quote Marz, become "activists as well as musicians, and suffer the consequences."

Enough with Silence!

Mohammed Farra raps in his song "History Book" that Palestinian history is like "an outdated book" that refuses to go out of print. Instead, it just "repeats itself day after day." The group that has best memorialized Palestinian history is not Dam, Palestinian Rapperz, or any other Palestinian band. Rather, it's the Israeli hard-core band Dir Yassin, the most famous product of the Israeli punk scene. Formed in 1997, Dir Yassin was a punk "supergroup," made up of members of some of the best (or at least most notorious) punk and hardcore bands in Israel.

The band took its name from the Palestinian village Dir Yassin. Located a few miles west of the old city of Jerusalem, it was the site of the worst massacre of the 1948 war, when members of several Jewish militias, including those led by future prime ministers Menachem Begin and Yitzhak Shamir, killed more than a hundred Palestinians, most of them women, children, and old men. In taking the name of the village as its name, Dir Yassin explicitly chose to force fellow Israeli Jews to remember an event that has been excluded from, or at best explained away in, the country's history, and in doing so "question the legitimacy of Zionism itself . . . It's a positive provocation."

With few exceptions, questioning the legitimacy of Zionism is rarely good for one's career in Israel. It's equivalent to questioning American values and motivations the day after September 11, 2001. Except that most days in Israel are treated as if they are September 12. But the band struck a nerve with young Israelis at the precise moment Oslo was falling apart. During its heyday from 1999 to 2002, Dir Yassin concerts were exercises in the cathartic futility that characterizes life in a permanent state of 9/12. Mosh pits steamed with anger against the very system most fans would soon be joining when their military service began. Lyrics screamed with a piercing honesty and clarity of style that few journalists or activists can rival. As the band sings in "All Our Planes Have Returned Safely,"

> *We are better than them, because we apologize when we kill innocent people.*

> *We are better than them, because we . . . work the land dropping bombs from airplanes.*

Dir Yassin's lyric sheets even come with a short explanation after each song that describes the historical or political event to which it refers. In a sense, Dir Yassin decided, like Abeer, Dam, and other Palestinian artists, that the best way to confront the Israeli occupation was not through physical terrorism, but through what could be called "cultural terrorism," a practice first adopted by Dadaists and Surrealists almost a century ago. Judging by the failure of Palestinian violence to achieve even the minimum Palestinian goals, the powerfully in-your-face message of Dir Yassin and Dam at least forced their fans—and occasionally politicians—to confront their role in creating the mess in which Israelis and Palestinians continue to find themselves.

The problem is that it's extremely hard to keep up that level of anger without either burning out, which is what happened to Dir Yassin, or getting "lazy" about forefronting the conflict in one's music, as other political punk bands admitted to me had happened with them. Meanwhile, Orphaned Land lets its music do the talking, its members satisfied if their songs keep one more Israeli soldier from shooting a Palestinian, and one more Muslim from hating Jews.

"It Keeps Getting Harder..."

It used to take about seven minutes for me to drive from Jerusalem's Old City to Abu Dis; now it's impossible to reach it directly because the Separation/Apartheid Wall cuts across the main road right at the entrance to the village. The town, which is slated to become the official Palestinian "Jerusalem" if a peace agreement is reached, has today become a Palestinian village-sized jail, completely cut off from Jerusalem.

Despite four roadblocks, Sami and I took the long way to Abu Dis to see one of the people who inspired this book, my old oud teacher Ghidian Qaymari. Ghidian can ring more sustain out of a cheap, Syrian-made oud than can Eddie van Halen out of his custom-made Kramer guitar and a stack of Marshalls turned to full volume. He's also one of the few traditional Arab musicians I know who can hold his own with (and is willing to play next to) an American rock guitar player,

and an Israeli accordion virtuoso and singer, such as the
esteemed world music artist Sara Alexander, with whom we
both played for several years.

Ghidian has thick black hair, a typical Palestinian mustache, and a face that reflects unfailing kindness mixed with
weariness and anger at a situation that has grown worse each
year since he was born, just weeks after the Six Day War in
1967. When the Israelis first put up the wall a block from his
house, it was only about eight feet high. Palestinians quickly
used rubble and garbage to build makeshift steps up to the
still-unfinished top and climb through an opening between
two of its support beams. Ghidian was too big to fit easily
through the hole. He couldn't do the weekly gigs at weddings
and hotels in Jerusalem that had made him one of the most
sought-after musicians in the Jerusalem region. Now the wall
is about twenty-five feet high and no one can climb over it.
The most direct available route from Abu Dis to Jerusalem
takes a half hour and usually involves at least two checkpoints.

As Ghidian and his wife, Manal, prepared lunch, I sat in
the spacious foyer of his home, staring out at the "Jerusalem
Hall" across the street, where eleven years earlier he and I had
watched Yasir Arafat and thousands of other Palestinians vote
during the first elections for the Palestinian Authority, on January 16, 1996. Ghidian took out his oud and played some of
the songs we used to perform together. In the heady days of
the Oslo nineties, Ghidian and I played several times a year
with Sara Alexander. Israeli Channel 2 television even did a
documentary about us. An American Jewish guitar player
working with an Israeli peace singer and accordionist (who as
a teenager played in the personal band of founding prime
minister David Ben-Gurion before "going Arab" and being

forced into exile for her views), and a Palestinian oud player with a silken voice, seemed to be a sign of a hopeful future. We even shot a video performing a song in Arabic and Hebrew at the Damascus Gate entrance to Jerusalem's Old City. Children danced around us and we smiled as we sang because we really thought the future was going to be bright. Sara toured Palestinian refugee camps, teaching children peace songs in Hebrew. Ghidian and I made trips to Paris, where Sara lived, to record and perform together.

In fact, it was the combination of Sara's acoustic guitar, accordion, and gypsy–Middle Eastern melodies with my distorted guitars and Ghidian's oud that inspired the journey that has produced this book. Although I didn't realize it at the time, it planted the musical seed that would allow me to imagine the possibility of heavy metal taking root in the Muslim world a few years later in that expensive hotel bar in Fes.

The three of us don't play together anymore. Sara hardly comes to Israel from France, and Ghidian risks arrest and a huge fine if he accepts the weekly offers he still receives to be sneaked into Palestinian East Jerusalem to play at a wedding or hotel. ("It's not a Palestinian wedding without you," he's often told.) So mostly he stays in his house and plays for the walls, Manal, and the regular stream of local and foreign friends passing through the Territories, who somewhat masochistically like to spend an hour or two reminiscing about a time when peace seemed to be on the horizon.

"Mark, it keeps getting harder," Ghidian confided to me as Manal served us a delicious meal of homemade hummus and rice with almonds. "My brother keeps offering to bring me to Australia and get me a job at the university where he's a physics professor, but this is my home. I was born in this house. My father sat under the same grapevines where they filmed us and Sara playing together so long ago." The problem for Ghidian is that the Israeli government has adopted a policy that strips Jerusalem, West Bank, and Gaza Palestinians who have taken up residence outside the country for more than a few years of their residency rights, essentially making them foreigners in their own countries—a fate far worse for Ghidian than being imprisoned in his hometown. It's this terrible choice that has drained the smile from Ghidian's once-cherubic face, and made his playing more plaintive than it used to be.

As the sun began to set, Ghidian suggested that Sami and I head back to Jerusalem in order to avoid the long lines at the checkpoints. We arrived just in time for a concert by the Israeli hard-core bands Useless ID and Betzefer. I was excited by Betzefer's new concert shirt, which had the phrase SILENCE IS DEADLY emblazoned on the back. But then the band's lead singer, Avital, explained that the silence referred to is a lack of music, not a lack of political engagement.

Not long before the show, Useless ID did a rare interview for the weekly magazine of *Yediot Ahronot,* the biggest newspaper in Israel, in which, as guitarist Ishay Berger proudly showed me, they spouted outrageously critical comments about "spitting on Zionism," and warning kids to "think hard before going into the army." Their remarks landed them on the cover, proving the old dicta that it pays to be outrageous, and that bad press is good press if it's *your* press.

But the sense of political urgency in the interview was missing from the show. Whatever their political inclinations, which, judging from their clothes and the ubiquitous smell of marijuana, were presumably on the "left," the fans at the sweat-inducing show were clearly not interested in lectures about the occupation. As the increasingly large crowd writhed and moshed across the floor and jumped up and down with happy abandon, my friend Sami turned to me and said, "There's no point preaching to these kids. They can get whatever news they want on the Web or in the newspaper, and anyway, most of them are too fucked up to care what happened in Ramallah or Nablus today." Before the show Ishay admitted that these days his activism is geared more toward saving the local vegetarian restaurant than ending the occupation. At least there was hope for the restaurant.

The music did give me an itch to play some guitar before I left for the States. Luckily, the Palestinian-Israeli metal band Khalas was rehearsing in Tel Aviv not far from Sami's house, so we hopped in his wife's car, put on the Oum Kalthoum, and drove effortlessly home on the spacious and checkpoint-free highway to Tel Aviv. I was keen to meet Khalas because they are one of the few heavy-metal bands—perhaps the only one—I know in the MENA that sings entirely in Arabic.

Khalas (the band's name is another way of saying "Enough!" in Arabic, like *kefaya*) was in the middle of working out some new songs when I arrived. Not wanting to break the rhythm by sitting them down for an interview, we decided just to jam for a while and then talk. The rehearsal room stank of sweat, cigarettes, pot, and beer. But the members were happy and satisfied with their progress on the new material. While Orphaned Land likes to incorporate Arabic music into its songs, Khalas does so in its membership: two Muslims, a Christian, and a Jew. Khalas's sound, however, is pure metal, with very little in the way of the Arabesque ornamentation that Orphaned Land and Salem helped make a signature sound of Israeli metal.

One thing was certain, the band wasn't going to endear it-self to Sami; Bassam is not a fan of Oum Kalthoum. "I re-garded her as a fat woman," he once said in an interview. The band decided to open its first album with an instrumental metal version of the classic Oum Kalthoum/Abdel Wahab song "Inta Omri" (which Sami, ever the purist, didn't find very convincing). Bassam and bass player Rooster are more into Led Zeppelin than the native music of the Middle East. Yet as we blasted through a few more songs, an image of an old building Sami and I had passed on the way to the studio came into my head: Jaffa's once-famed al-Hambra theater, where, over six decades ago, Oum Kalthoum used to perform. Back then she was the future of Arabic music; for Khalas she's a past better left behind.

For Bassam and Abed, Oum Kalthoum was a kind of opium for the masses that "lulled crowds into . . . complete inaction while they listened. We made people move when they heard [our version]. At the very least," Abed explained, "we can be loud and provocative—and in Arabic, which no one else is doing. But we're not so directly political because we feel it's important to focus on social problems, to fix family and social issues first."

I was in the middle of a discussion with Rooster about what it's like to be the only Jewish member of a Palestinian metal band that sings in Arabic when Sami tapped me on the shoulder and told me it was time to go. His uncle—it seems wherever I travel in the Arab world, my friends always have an uncle who drives a taxi—would soon be at his house to take me to the airport for a 6:00 a.m. flight home.

A couple of hours later, after my usual interrogation by airport security (being a Hebrew-speaking American with a journalist ID and a passport with stamps from most of Israel's enemies is a sure invitation to a preflight grilling at Ben-Gurion Airport), I settled into my window seat and scrolled through all the new music I'd just finished arranging on my computer. As the flight attendant did the usual safety demonstration, I thought of something Saz had said to me as we walked through the Ramla market a week earlier. "If one of my lyrics goes into your heart, it's worth more than a thousand stones thrown at your head. If my raps make the Jews open their eyes and the Arabs open their eyes, then I've done my share."

If only I could get Saz, Dam, Orphaned Land, Abeer, Palestinian Rapperz, Ramallah Underground, Useless ID, Betzefer, Ghidian, Sara, and Khalas to do a show together—set up a stage on both sides of the wall, crank up the amps and turntables, and do a hard-core, oriental-tinged, rap-metal version of Pink Floyd's "Another Brick in the Wall" so loud that it would literally blow the wall down, the way Joshua had done a few millennia before (although for very different reasons). Maybe ten bands and 100,000 watts could change the face of Israel/Palestine where ten years of failed negotiations and ten times as long of violence could not. As the plane settled in at cruising altitude, I opened my computer and put on a track from Ramallah Underground's latest project, *No Borders*, which features Arab MCs rhyming over tracks by European producers, and European rappers dropping rhymes over tracks by Palestinian producers, while I read about the latest "Hip-hop Sulha," this one in New York City, bringing together Israeli and Palestinian rappers in a musical version of the traditional Arab ritual (the *sulha*) for mediating and reconciling a conflict. For a moment my idea didn't seem so crazy.

LEBANON

Music and the Power of Blood

Of all the countries I've visited in the Muslim world, I've always felt most at home in Lebanon. Perhaps it's because of the cosmopolitan atmosphere of Beirut, a city that seems at once fully Arab, European, and quintessentially Mediterranean. Or that, like its neighbor and enemy to the south, Israel, Lebanon's geography is among the most beautifully diverse in the world, especially for a country no bigger than New Jersey. Or it could be that Lebanese Arabic is one of the dialects of Arabic I know best.

Maybe it's the abiding warmth of the people despite the war, violence, and political disappointments they've had to endure in the last two generations. Ultimately, however, I think I love Beirut because, like the New York I came of age during the 1980s and early 1990s, its vibe is just a bit more intense, hedonistic, and dangerous than most cities. Within, at most, an hour's drive from downtown Beirut you'll find a hyper-consumer culture obsessed with copying the latest Euro-American trends in fashion, music, and plastic surgery, a resurgent Shi'ism nurtured on poverty, political discrimination, and military discipline, a foreign-sponsored Sunni radicalism spreading virally through the Palestinian camps and Sunni areas, and the shifting alliances of Lebanese politics— Shi'a Muslims with Maronite Christians, Sunni Muslims with the breakaway Druze sect, conservative Hezbollah with secular Syria. Lebanon is the Middle East in miniature.

Beirut is also one of the most open cities in the MENA. Friends from Egypt or Morocco are shocked at how young women walk around the streets, even in Hezbollah-controlled neighborhoods, in tight jeans, often without headscarves. "They could *never* walk around like this in Cairo," Egyptian blogger Alaa Abdel Fatah exclaimed as we toured the rubble-strewn streets of the Hezbollah stronghold of Haret al-Hreik, in the south of the city, less than a year after the Israel-Hezbollah war.

But Beirut is also a supremely divided city, just as Lebanon is a divided country. If people are relatively tolerant of each other on the street, Lebanon has one of the most toxic political environments in the world, having been poisoned by two centuries of foreign meddling, war, and corruption. In a way, the country was created by the French to establish a Maronite (the 1,500-year-old Eastern Catholic Church) enclave in Syria that would be loyal to France. It suffered over a dozen years of civil war (1975–1989), almost thirty years of de facto Syrian political and economic control of the country (1975–2006), eighteen years of Israeli occupation (briefly in 1978, and then 1982–2000), and most recently the short but incredibly destructive Israeli-Hezbollah war (summer 2006).

The bombing that killed billionaire developer and former prime minister Rafiq Hariri on February 14, 2005, split a country that had never fully healed from the wounds of civil war and Israeli occupation. On the one side stood most Sunnis, the majority of Maronite Christians, the Druze, and much of the educated upper middle class more broadly. At the initiative of thousands of young activists, artists, scholars, and NGO workers, upward of one million citizens thronged the streets in several mass protests after Hariri's assassination. They blamed his murder on Syria, and used it as the spark for what became known as the Cedar Revolution or "Cedar Spring" (the Lebanese flag has a cedar tree in its center).

The huge rallies, and the sprawling tent city that emerged overnight at the site of Hariri's murder, achieved the previously unimaginable dream of ridding Lebanon of its thirty-year direct occupation by Syria. In the process, the Cedar Revolution nurtured a sense of possibility and community that inspired peace-and-democracy activists around the world.

Arrayed against the Cedar revolutionaries, however, was the majority of Lebanon's Shi'i population, long marginalized despite being Lebanon's most populous group. Along with a sizable segment of the Maronites and the Palestinian refugee population, they were either scared of a Sunni and Druze power grab, or they supported Syria's presence in Lebanon because of its support for Hezbollah's resistance against the eighteen-year-long Israeli occupation.

This split made it extremely difficult for the activists behind the Cedar Revolution to create an environment that would support national reconciliation, democracy, and an end to corruption and foreign interference. And when, despite these obstacles, the movement seemed to be poised to challenge the various entrenched interests behind the status quo, the Israel-Hezbollah war of the summer of 2006 ensured that arms and money, rather than a common, post-conflict vision of Lebanon's future, would continue to rule the country's politics.

While the Cedar Revolution ultimately fizzled, for the first time a peaceful grassroots democratic movement in the MENA managed to upset an existing system and throw the power elite on its heels, forcing it to adapt and compromise to stay in power. The memory of that accomplishment continues to inspire Lebanese, and activists around the Arab world, today.

A Long History of War and Music

Despite political stagnation, intermittent violence, and occasional war, Beirut remains one of the world's cutting-edge locations for dance music, hip-hop, and alternative rock. Before the 2006 conflict, well over 5,000 partyers would hit the clubs on a good night. The number is not that much lower today.

An evening for young Beirutis might begin with dinner or drinks at one of the innumerable trendy bars in the bohemian quarters of al-Hamreh, Gemayzeh, or Achrefiya (my favorite, purely for the irony, is the Che Bar, whose prices would make Che Guevara turn over in his grave), followed by a visit to one of the city's famed dance clubs. These include Acid, where for twenty dollars you can indulge in an open bar until dawn and dance the night away with Christian and Shi'i lesbians and/or Sunni and Druze gay men. Or you can go to what for me is one of the most interesting nightclubs in the world, the legendary BO-18, whose retractable roof, sleek and modern styling, and coffins for tables—it was built next to the site of a wartime massacre—allow you to dance under the moon and stars.

Add to these the underground parties that occur on a regular basis, and it's not surprising that only months before the 2006 Israeli invasion, at least one travel writer predicted that Beirut would soon be "the new Ibiza"—once the hottest party scene in Europe, if not the world. This would have been a good development not just for clubgoers, but for the country at large, since the emergence of freewheeling Ibiza coincided with the demise of Franco's decades-long dictatorial rule in Spain. Today Beirut still has an Ibizan air, but the political atmosphere remains as polluted as it's been at any time since the end of the civil war a generation ago.

༻✿༺

It didn't have to be this way. About six months after the assassination of former prime minister Hariri, I was standing on the stage of Club Nova, located in the upper-middle-class neighborhood of Sin el Fil. Some of the hottest clubs in the Eastern Mediterranean are located nearby, and the mix of modern architecture sprinkled with much older buildings gives the quarter, and Beirut, its unique feel.

Surrounding me on the stage were the members of The Kordz, one of the biggest rock bands in Lebanon and the Middle East, and to my mind, one of the best hard-rock bands anywhere. Also present were Reda Zine and Amine Hamma, who'd come with me from Paris for a conference I'd organized with Layla al-Zubaidi and the Danish organization Free Muse on the censorship of music in the MENA.

Earlier that evening the four of us had started work on the

song "Marhaba," and we were itching to translate the energy of our studio collaboration onto the stage. As big a thrill was that joining us was Salman Ahmed, founder and lead guitarist of Junoon. Labeled by fans and music critics around the world as "the U2 of Asia"—Bono is in fact a fan of the band—Junoon is unquestionably the biggest rock band in history east of Berlin (millions of albums sold, but, sadly for band members, most of them pirated). Organizing an impromptu all-star jam session is always a risky proposition. Luckily, our potentially discordant group of musicians—Lebanese, Moroccan, Pakistani, and American; Muslim, Christian, and Jewish—clicked from the moment we took out our instruments and began to play. "Isn't that what music is supposed to be about?" Salman asked rhetorically after the show, as audience members lingered around to meet the band.

Salman's happiness at playing a good set was overshadowed by the news that several members of his family were missing and presumed dead in a massive earthquake that had struck Pakistan earlier that day. Instead of flying home to New York with me as planned, Salman was now arranging to go to Pakistan to help dig through the rubble to search for his family members, who lived about 100 kilometers north of the capital of Islamabad. "My uncle is digging right now for them, but it's probably too late," Salman explained, with a calmness that caught me by surprise. "What am I supposed to do? I'm a Sufi, so I have to believe that whatever happens does so for a reason, and all we can do is remember our loved ones and honor them by bringing joy to others. Let's play some music."

We hit the stage for the next set, and Ahmed ripped through a few guitar solos before taking over the microphone to sing with Kordz lead singer Moe Hamzeh. After an impromptu version of one of Junoon's biggest hits, "Sayonee," he explained to the crowd what had happened to his family earlier in the day. With that, he called out U2's "With or Without You" and started strumming the chords. I'm not sure any of the rest of us had performed this song live before, but by the second verse it had taken on a life of its own.

By the time the second chorus was over, much of the audience, and the musicians as well, were in tears. It remains one of the most intense and meaningful performances I've ever been part of. Yet it was only a prelude to what was for me the most important moment of the night, The Kordz's Arabmetal version of Pink Floyd's "Another Brick in the Wall."

As I tried to play an Arabic-sounding yet funky rhythm under guitarist Nadim Sioufi's Arabesque version of David Gilmour's famous solo, it suddenly hit me: one of the most hopeful visions of the future of the Middle East I would ever come across was standing—well, headbanging, really—before my eyes. As I watched the reaction of an audience full of Lebanese, and foreigners of various persuasions to the song, the idea of rock 'n' roll helping to move a country away from violence and authoritarianism and toward greater tolerance, peace, and democracy seemed not just plausible but natural.

It also became clear that the anger exploding from the lyrics to "Another Brick in the Wall" was never intended to indict merely the stifling conformity of post–World War II Britain. It was equally relevant to the post-civil-war Lebanese political system. In post–Cedar Revolution Beirut—a city that Pink Floyd founder Roger Waters holds close to his heart, and has named a song after ("Leaving Beirut")—the wall evoked by the song is the one that has long closed various Lebanese communities off from each other, denied Lebanon an independent future, and sealed the Arab/Muslim world off from the rest of the world. As Moe pointed out a few hours later as we stood outside an all-night hummus-and-chicken shack ordering food, when the crowd pumped their fists in unison with "All in all, you're just another brick in the wall," they were declaring their refusal to continue being cogs in the machine of the occupations, violence, corruption, and repression that for so long have defined Lebanon.

Building a Temple of Rock

Moe Hamzeh has always loved two things, rock music and rocks. Before he became a professional musician, he received his BA and then his master's degree in hydrogeology. As he jokes, "Geology is rocks, I do rock 'n' roll. So it was a natural move. In fact, Beirut for me was the original 'school of rock.' I studied rocks in the morning and played rock 'n' roll at night."

Listening to classic heavy metal—Zeppelin, Hendrix, Deep Purple, Black Sabbath, and Iron Maiden—was his way of dealing with the strains of the country's long civil war. "I was always into rock, because it was my only way to forget where I was, with bombs going off all the time. The music was my only companion. I'd put on the headphones and listen to one of the great albums and try to sleep at night while the bombs exploded near my parents' house," he continued. "And when I'd wake up the next morning I'd put on Bob Marley in order to give me hope as I started a new day."

But what about Oum Kalthoum, I wondered, or even the timeless diva Fairuz, acclaimed as the "soul of Lebanon" because of her popularity among Lebanese regardless of creed or communal affiliation? "Honestly," Moe responded, "far more than Arab music, rock spoke to me because of how it reflected the reality of war. And when *The Wall* came out 1979, it became a symbol of tearing down the walls that kept us apart, and forced us to live with the worst kind of 'thought control.' "

Aside from music, what rescued Moe was attending the American University of Beirut (AUB), where he could enroll thanks to a scholarship from Rafiq Hariri, one of thousands the billionaire turned prime minister provided for young Lebanese to attend college. "It might seem ironic, since it was established by American missionaries to reflect Western superiority, but AUB opened me to different perspectives, a crucial experience because we were so closed off from other people outside our immediate community during and right after the war. It also gave me the ability to pursue a dream, music, that my parents thought was irrational. If I had gone to another university, where there wasn't the sort of interaction with other groups from Lebanese society, not to mention Americans and other foreigners, I would have become a much more narrow-minded person.

"I remember at AUB I had friends from Hezbollah—they would laugh at me as a rocker, but I wasn't a threat to them, nor they to me. We respected each other, studied, debated, hung out, and challenged each other, even during the war. Our discussions helped us all to learn to say to each other, 'Respect my space and I'll respect yours.' And it is precisely this that is no longer happening in the larger society today, outside of the music scene."

Indeed, today the trend in education has moved toward sectarian universities that cater primarily to one group or subculture within Lebanon's communal tapestry. For Moe, this development is a bad omen for the country's future. The chances of a twenty-year-old rock singer and his Hezbollah counterpart meeting and learning to understand and even respect each other are drastically reduced today, and are growing more narrow still. But as most every artist, activist, and scholar I know agrees, if these two poles of youth culture can't find some common ground, pulling everyone between them just a little bit closer in the process, Lebanon is doomed. And so is the Middle East.

The TRUTH of Music—and War

Moe may not have the air of authority of the talking heads who regularly appear on LBC (the main Lebanese television network) or al-Jazeera to comment on "the situation" in Lebanon, but his experience has taught him how complicated globalization has become in a small, multiethnic, and multireligious country like Lebanon that, paradoxically, has long been a primary center of cultural production for the larger Arab world. On the one hand, the "civilized chaos" that defines the urban fabric of Beirut meshes with the periodic violence wrought by forces inside and outside the country to produce a spirited, edgily innovative music scene. On the other hand, the country's diva-driven pop scene has been more or less taken over by the Saudi-owned media conglomerate Rotana, whose roster of cookie-cutter singers fits right in with the homogenization and vacuity of Lebanon's famous fashion- and style-obsessed culture.

And yet, at the same time, the forces that have produced this culture create a hit television show like *Superstar* (an Arab take on *American Idol*). As author Allegra Stratton wrote in her fascinating portrayal of millennial Arab hipsters, *Muhajababes,* such programs are among the most honest expressions of contemporary Arab pop musical tastes, since winners are chosen by the votes of 15 million viewers across the Arab world—more people, the program's producers never tire of pointing out, than have ever voted in a free election in the Arab world.

These contradictions fueled the uplifting yet ambivalent dynamics of the Cedar Spring. A photograph of the back of Moe's head, with the word TRUTH shaved into his hair as he stands on a balcony overlooking a million protesters, is one of the iconic images of the protests. A decade of full exposure to the globalized economy had forced Moe and his musical comrades to adapt to producing their art in the cracks of Lebanon's liberalized and corporatized cultural economy. But with Hariri's assassination, the cracks became chasms. The TRUTH shaved into Moe's hair was the truth staring up at Lebanese from the chasms dividing the country.

As Moe was surveying the huge crowd from the balcony on that beautiful spring day, three things became clear: first, that he and other young Lebanese had a positive obligation to rebel against the system—"our parents' system," as many Lebanese have described it to me—that produced Lebanon's intractable problems; second, that any such challenge had to be spiritually grounded rather than focusing merely on personal or cultural freedoms ("Both rebellion and spirituality are very important for me, and I think for the future of our people," he explained after one of our gigs together); and, third, that the violence, anger, and false hopes that have defined life for so many of his generation mean that nothing less than the most distorted guitars, the hardest beats, and the most fiery voices will convey what Moe and so many other Lebanese of his generation have felt in growing up as the children of Lebanon's long and brutal civil war.

"From a very early age we were taught to take sides, to differentiate between ourselves and the other sects and ethnicities," Moe reflects sadly. "But at the same time that I started to love rock 'n' roll, I started to ask questions, such as 'Why are we fighting?' 'Why would I hate a Christian?' 'What's the difference between us?' And this made me doubt everything and question everything, challenging everybody." As he gazed upon the sea of people below him, Moe felt that "there was really a chance for a sincere change, the kind Bob Marley sang about in 'Redemption Song,' which gave me so much hope during the war."

Artists like the Kordz and their fans were instrumental to the success of the Cedar Spring precisely because the older generation had become so disempowered and depoliticized by decades of Syrian dominance that it no longer believed it could have a critical impact. One well-known professor of history put it this way to me about a year before Hariri's assassination: "You know, in Lebanon we can say or write almost anything we want to, but that's because nothing we say or do matters." For members of the rock scene, this was certainly not believed to be the case.

But the Cedar Revolution never had the chance to transform Lebanese society at large. In good measure this was because the political elite managed to structure the national elections that the marchers demanded so that they were in fact less competitive than those held under Syrian control. The coup de grâce, however, was the Israel-Hezbollah war of 2006, which destroyed whatever momentum was left to the reform movement. In its wake, Hezbollah became the main power in Lebanon.

Even before the 2006 war, the potentially bright future for Lebanon heralded by the Cedar Spring—free elections, more-equitable economic development, the end of Syrian influence, and a more balanced political system—was by no means assured. As Moe explained when I was in Beirut shortly before the Israeli invasion, "The young kids are being brainwashed by their communal leaders and not being exposed to other people or points of view the way we were only a few years ago. They didn't have the war to force them to question things, so they just follow their leaders blindly because they haven't been forced to understand the consequences of such an attitude. And this, frighteningly, is giving me flashbacks of what led to the war."

It was also clear that many of the young and often secular activists (regardless of their religious background) participating in the sit-ins of the Cedar Revolution were there as much out of a desire for personal freedoms as they were to learn about how to transform the political system. There's nothing wrong with mixing personal and political liberation, or protest and pleasure, as long as the aims of each don't conflict with the other. But in this case, perhaps, the personal and the hedonistic shared a bit too much space with the political and the revolutionary. The U.S. media dubbed the protests the Cedar Revolution in celebration of its supposedly national character.

But according to one Lebanese colleague, an equally if not more apt characterization would have been "the Gucci Revolution," because, it seemed, so many of the protesters were as interested in high-end fashion as in refashioning a more equitable national arrangement among the country's various communities and social classes.

❦

Gucci or Cedar, for many of the young people at the heart of the protests of the spring of 2005, they took on the character of a giant dance party. Since the 2006 war, the dance scene is still going strong, but it's the city's small experimental music scene that has become most culturally, and politically, significant. Like Palestine's Ramallah Underground, some of Beirut's most innovative artists are more interested in creating soundscapes inspired by everything from John Cage to the latest fighting than they are in forging songs out of traditional melodies and harmonies. These soundcatchers and splicers overlap with Lebanon's hip-hop scene, and particularly Lebanese hip-hop pioneer Rayess Bek. Like other urban locales around the world stricken by poverty and violence, Beirut produces an abundance of artists who are adept at mining their harsh realities for aesthetic gold.

One particularly well-known group is the duo Soap Kills, which made a name for itself in Paris as well as Beirut when singer Jasmin Hamdan and guitarist Seid discovered that they could combine European electronica with Arab melodies, lyrics, and accents to great effect. They then changed styles from rock to the relatively slow-tempo combination of acid house and hip-hop known as trip-hop, and since then have been spreading their music via the Internet, which allows

"Searching for the Truth," Moe Hamzeh of the Kordz, looks onto a million-strong crowd at one of the Cedar Spring rallies in Beirut. March 2006.

Rock 'n' Roll is the soundtrack of the future. Poster from the 2006 Boulevard of Young Musicians Festival, with its blend of ultramodern and traditional imagery, reflecting the music of Morocco today.

Tens of thousands of fans rock out during the annual "metal night" of the Boulevard of Young Musicians Festival in Casablanca.

The first culture jam?
Muslim and Christian (or
perhaps Jewish) musicians
jamming on the Baldosas, a
precursor of the guitar,
in the golden age of
al-Andalus. Detail from
the thirteenth-century
manuscript known as
Cantigas de Santa Maria.

Poster for benefit concert in
support of jailed Moroccan
metalheads. Casablanca, 2003.

COURTESY OF REDA ZINE

Publicity
photo for the
Palestinian-
Israeli hip-hop
group Dam,
the most
famous rap
group in the
Arab world.

PHOTO BY
STEVE SABELLA

For Shady Nour, son of jailed presidential candidate Ayman Nour, playing metal in his bedroom helps ease the pain of his father's indefinite incarceration. Cairo, 2007. PHOTO BY MICHAEL SCHMELLING

Members of Hate Suffocation rehearsing in Cairo. May 2007.

PHOTO BY MICHAEL SCHMELLING

Reda Zine performing with the Kordz. Club Nova,
Beirut, Lebanon, 2005. COURTESY OF THE AUTHOR

The three members of Palestinian Rapperz standing in front of
Israel's eight-meter-high "Separation Fence" for a publicity
photo.

COURTESY OF MOHAMMED AL-FARRA

Arash Jafari, Mark LeVine, and Farzad Golpayegani,
performing at Barişa Rock for Peace Festival.

COURTESY OF ARASH JAFARI

Lebanese industrial death metal band Oath to Vanquish, publicity photo, 2006.

Drummer
Eddie Wastnidge
and bass player
Ali Sanaei of Farzad
Golpayegani's band
backstage at the
Barişa Rock for
Peace Festival.
August 2007.

Sherine Amr and
Sara El Kasraivy of
Massive Scar Era
performing at the
Sawi Culture
Wheel in Cairo.
August 2007.

Junoon cofounder,
Salman Ahmad.

Mark LeVine
and Moe
Hamzeh,
performing at
Club Nova.
Beirut, 2006.

Sheikh Anwar al-Ethari, the "Elastic Sheikh," from Sadr City, with Italian aid worker Simona Torretta, who was kidnapped in Baghdad for three weeks in 2004. COURTESY OF SHEIKH ANWAR AL-ETHARI

Egyptian metal guitar virtuoso Sherif Marzeban with legendary Swedish metal frontman for In Flames, Anders Friden, backstage at Dubai Desert Rock, 2007. COURTESY OF THE AUTHOR

them to be free of the corporate control that would constrain their creativity for commercial considerations.

Soap Kills seems to have imagined itself as an anti-Rotana. Picking up on the diagnosis of Morocco's ills by Hoba Hoba Spirit, Jasmin argues that it's "schizophrenic" that an adherent of Saudi Arabia's ultraconservative Islam (and a senior Royal, no less) would create a record label and multiplatform media company that promotes sexual fantasies via scantily clad singers in order to sell insipid, soul-deadening music. As important, this schizophrenia is inseparable from authoritarianism, which in turn is responsible for more personal problems. "Censorship is the reason for sexual frustration," Jasmin remarked, "and the female Arab pop singers serve as sex fantasies." That's why she and Seid decided they were going to use music to "break down the bonds of patriarchy and class bias that have made it so hard for alternative music to break through to the mainstream in the Arab world."

꧁꧂

While not quite so avant-garde, both rock and heavy metal have long been extremely popular in Lebanon. The genres were ubiquitous on the country's most popular radio programs because they appealed to young people during the civil war. Once the violence ended, an actual scene developed. But as in Egypt, the Lebanese metal scene suffered a serious blow in 1997, when a depressed teenage metal fan, Michel Jammal, whose father was a ranking army officer, killed himself. This was followed by a severe crackdown by the government on the music.

Yet the crackdown also carried the seeds of metal's renewal in Lebanon. Elias Abboud, a Christian from the north of Lebanon, was a classmate of Jammal's, and five years later he founded one of the most distinctive Death Metal/Grind bands in the MENA, Oath to Vanquish, with his brother Carlos. With his shaved head and goatee, Elias looks like a harder version of Moe; and indeed, Oath to Vanquish's music is a harder and more industrial version of The Kordz's classic rock metal sound.

"A friend slipped me a tape and that was it," he explained as we chatted in Moe's living room in the upper-middle-class neighborhood of Khoreitem. "You're exposed to so many kinds of music here that everything becomes a part of it. By the early nineties the scene was actually quite big, but there was also constant harassment that culminated in the 1997 scare. After my classmate's suicide we were brought into the principal's office and shown TV programs to teach us how bad metal is. They even showed a video of someone playing 'Stairway to Heaven' backwards in order to scare us."

The government also banned the sale of CDs by bands such as Metallica and Nirvana, although they remained easily obtainable in record stores and, increasingly, on the Internet. And the scene continued to grow, albeit slowly. By 2002, after returning from the UK, where both brothers obtained degrees in mechanical engineering, Elias and Carlos divided their time between running a profitable plastics manufacturing business and performing as Oath to Vanquish every few months at some of the biggest clubs in Beirut and at other venues across Lebanon. Their songs took on many social and political issues facing the country. "But not directly," both point out. Instead, playing off the same psychosocial distress that motivated Soap Kills, they developed what they call an "applied schizophrenic science," exploring and developing political commentary "through the veil of allegory and unsettling imagery."

The formula seems to have paid off. Oath to Vanquish is one of a handful of Arab metal bands signed to a foreign label, the UK-based Grindethic Records. But the farther you are from the mainstream in Lebanon, the greater the risk of persecution. "The police have continued to harass and even arrest rock musicians. So have the intelligence services, especially during the Syrian era, because metalheads were activists." Even today, Carlos added, undercover cops would come to shows and plant drugs on people, then raid the club a bit later and close it down.

Moe has also had his run-ins with the police in the last few years. "They asked me questions like, 'Do you think your fans worship Satan?' What they were really asking was whether our fans follow the official political line and obey authority." At one point the Ministry of Culture sent two men to film one of The Kordz's weekly shows. "We knew in advance, and made sure our crowd did as well. But after a half hour of a subdued set, I couldn't take it anymore and just said, 'Fuck it,' and played the rest of our set at full energy. Anyway, the owner made sure to get the guys drunk enough so that they couldn't remember anything. After the show, one of them actually stumbled over, slapped me on my shoulder, and slurred, 'Great job! Don't stop singing.' "

Perhaps the best evidence of the resilience of Lebanese rock are bands like Blend, Nadine Khoury, and the post-punk group the New Government. Founded only a year after the 1997 satanic scare, Blend was the first Arab rock band ever signed to an international label, EMI. Their biggest song was the 2003 hit "Belong," which deals with the post-civil-war generation's search for identity in the midst of the continued conflict and growing sectarian and class divisions.

On the other end of the sonic spectrum, Nadine Khoury's folk-inspired rock offers trenchant analysis of the violence, rampant inequality, and the easy escapism into drugs and alcohol to which many of her peers have fallen prey. But the most overtly political lyrics in Lebanese rock today belong to the group the New Government, whose debut album featured the lyrics "I killed the prime minister / I killed the famous journalist" as a way of critiquing the mafia-like tactics that continued to govern the country's politics after the Cedar Revolution.

Despite being well outside the Rotana mold, all these bands have used the Internet, festivals, and other networks for cultural transmission not controlled by the mainstream media to reach a growing audience. They have taken to heart the words of the Nigerian Afrobeat pioneer Fela Kuti, who declared not long before his death that "music is the weapon of the future." Beirut-based rock journalist and radio DJ Ramsay Short, who often began his popular show with one of Kuti's hits, feels that Kuti's point couldn't be more relevant to Lebanon: "Music is the one medium of expression with the power to cross all borders, speak the truth, be political, and affect change in societies across the globe."

Similar to the man from Morocco's Makhzen in Reda Allali's story, however, Short is only half right. Music is clearly a powerful motivator and organizing tool for change. But much like Morocco's Justice and Spirituality Association, in Lebanon Hezbollah sees itself as possessing the very same qualities Short and Kuti ascribe to popular music. And it has real weapons, not just good songs. The problem is that the majority of what could be termed Lebanon's musical jihadis are the well-educated, cosmopolitan, and politically progressive Lebanese young people of central and northern Beirut and other big cities. If they can't connect to the mass of working-class, often less educated young Lebanese, whether in the Shi'i neighborhoods of southern Beirut or the Sunni, Druze, and Maronite villages of the country's interior, it's hard to imagine how the outstretched arm with a Fender guitar can compete with the outstretched arm with a Kalashnikov—Hezbollah's brilliant yet disheartening riff on the cover of Bob Marley's *Uprising* album, which not so long ago helped a generation of Lebanese make it through another war-torn day.

The Sheikh Who Said Yes

Not far from Moe Hamzeh lives Sheikh Ibrahim al-Mardini, who has his own way of preaching peace and tolerance against the power of war. He lives with his wife and two small children in a tiny two-room apartment on the roof of his family's building in the working-class neighborhood of Verdun. Despite possessing a keen mind and an advanced theology degree, his unorthodox ideas—particularly that secular music, including rock and heavy metal, is not prohibited by Islamic law—have meant that he has to work in a pharmacy to support his family. "The Dar al-Ifta' [the official body responsible for issuing fatwas and approving Sunni imams] told me it would be better if I stayed away from mosques and madrasas," he said with a wan smile when explaining why he doesn't have a mosque at which to preach the *qutba,* or Friday-afternoon sermon, as do most religious scholars with his training.

Al-Mardini, whose smile and lotus-crossed legs radiate equanimity and wisdom even in the face of adversity, has refused to give up his interest in music despite the financial and professional costs. Though he doesn't have specific musical training himself, his writings on music and its permissibility in Islam have been circulated across the Muslim world. For him, support or opposition to music represents the fault line between an Islam that is open to the world and tolerant, and one that is not. As he explained to me, "There is nothing in the Qur'an that says music should be prohibited. In fact, it can play a positive role in society as long as it's not insulting or offers views against Islam."

Al-Mardini's writings on the subject are more explicit. He bluntly reminds readers that "there is no Qur'anic text banning music," and explains that seventy of the eighty sayings of the Prophet Muhammad traditionally used to prove music unlawful are considered legally "weak or very weak" (and so not binding for Muslims). For him, when the Prophet Muhammad said to one of his Companions, "You came with a very good ear," he meant an ear both for music and for wise political judgment. And if this is how the Prophet felt about music, its prohibition must "exist mostly to preserve regimes, not Muslim societies of some sort of Islamic personality."

Once again, we see a religious scholar offering a critique of his country's political establishment that echoes those offered by musicians. But Sheikh al-Mardini didn't take up the cause of promoting the Islamic legitimacy of popular music because he's a fan of heavy metal or hip-hop. His musical tastes are more traditional. What he does believe is that the opposition to music by conservatives indicates an even more serious threat to the public sphere in Lebanon. In a political environment riven with factionalism and hostility toward anyone who wants to change the status quo, music is one of the few channels for positively critiquing, and even transcending, the present situation.

As we concluded our first meeting, al-Mardini explained, "A musical culture is necessary for people to develop themselves; any limitations on the arts will encourage the opposite of what a healthy religious system should call for, because culture is something owned by everyone, and not something that a few persons should decide upon." Ultimately, al-Mardini wants Muslims to go back to the original sources and learn what they have to say about music and even more crucial issues.

Moreover, just as the opening of the Muslim public sphere allows seemingly marginal religious thinkers to reshape the contours of Islam, it allows musicians to claim a space in which a different vision of Lebanon can be articulated. As the Kordz urge listeners in their song "Deeper In," "Your mind is in despair and lost in a dream / Bring it out again from somewhere deeper in."

Rotana's "Dominate or Die" Versus Metal's DIY

It is no secret that religious forces can be regressive when it comes to artistic and musical freedom. Today, however, conservative religious groups like Egypt's Muslim Brotherhood, Morocco's Justice and Spirituality Association, and even Hezbollah, are adopting something approaching a live-and-let-live policy toward most artists. Direct government censorship, whether motivated by political or religious considerations, has also silenced musicians. But these days, being censored by the government in the MENA tends to increase sales in much the same way that "explicit lyrics" stickers do for artists in the United States.

In today's globalized media environment, many leading Arab artists have come to feel that today the growing power of the major Arab media companies poses a greater threat to their artistic freedom than do either government censorship or religiously grounded attacks. The epitome of this trend is Rotana. Founded in 1987, and with a market capitalization valued at over $1 billion, the Saudi-owned media conglomerate is the biggest Arab media company by far. Under its umbrella are television stations in Saudi Arabia, Lebanon, and Dubai; recording studios; record labels; at least six music video and cinema channels; production companies; management and publishing divisions; and even cafés where you can purchase the company's products and get them signed by one of the company's stars if they happen to be doing an in-store promotion.

As the company's publicity boasts, Rotana's "portfolio of more than 100 stars from the entire MENA region . . . certifies an 85-percent market share for Rotana in the Arabic music industry and four of the top ten channels viewed in the Arab world." Its roster includes perhaps the most popular male singers in Arab music today, such as the Iraqi Kazem Al Saher; Egypt's Amr Diab; Lebanese singers Najwa Karam, Julia Botros, Elissa, Georges Wassouf, and Wael Kafoury; and leading Kuwaiti singer Abdullah Rweished, who had a fatwa of death handed down against him by a Saudi cleric on an unsubstantiated charge of singing the opening verse of the Qur'an.

Along with its main Lebanese competitor, Future TV (founded by Hariri in 1993), Rotana's economic and cultural position in Lebanon epitomizes how deeply rooted globalization has become in the last two decades, thanks in good measure to the late prime minister's liberalization and privatization programs, which reshaped the country's economy toward the financial, service, and tourism sectors. But the price, as elsewhere in the MENA, has been increased inequality and poverty, skyrocketing foreign debt, and a retrenchment of sectarian and specifically Islamist politics, as personified by Hezbollah, in the poorer Shi'i communities that have experienced few benefits from the reforms. Not surprisingly, Hezbollah has developed its own increasingly globalized media structure centered around its al-Manar television network.

What makes Rotana different from its Western counterparts is that no Western entertainment company monopolizes every facet of the entertainment industry the way Rotana does, from managing an artist, owning her publishing rights, and distributing her album, video, and maybe even movie, playing them on its video music channels, and organizing her tours, the way Rotana does.

Rotana is both an international conglomerate and a "family business," one that remains tightly under the control of one person, Saudi Prince Walid bin Talal. In fact, Rotana is a new exemplar of the type of "family capitalism" that is not just typical of the wealthy Gulf petro-monarchies and sheikhdoms, but has long been the basis of Lebanon's grossly unequal distribution of wealth. While the company doesn't control every major artist in the Arab world, most of the ones not in its stable are established enough to demand similar budgets for recording, video production, and marketing their music from the few remaining labels that are willing to compete with it.

But with all but the biggest artists in the Arab world, Rotana doesn't have to negotiate or compromise. Operating under the same "dominate or die" philosophy that the *New York Times* once described as the modus operandi of contemporary corporate globalization, Rotana can make it very difficult for an artist to achieve mainstream success if he or she refuses to play by its rules, or decides to move beyond criticizing Israel and the United States to taking on the authoritarian political and social systems of the MENA, and especially the Persian Gulf.

In fact, what Moe Hamzeh describes as the "Rotana effect" has effectively put out of business both well-known local record companies such as Voie de l'Orient (the label of the seminal Lebanese singer Fairuz), the Saudi label Stallion, and the Egyptian label 'Alam al-fan. Even EMI closed up most of its local business in the Arab world because it couldn't compete with Rotana. And now other companies, especially mobile communications giants, are moving into the music production and distribution field, making it even harder for small producers to compete.

Thankfully, the categories of music that Rotana hasn't taken over yet have been Lebanon's alternative music scenes: rock, metal, and hip-hop. From Moe's perspective, Rotana's putting so many Arab labels out of business has actually created room for alternative groups to pursue a DIY strategy, not just in producing and distributing music, but also in producing their own videos, creating their own record labels, and even producing large-scale festivals. The only problem is that once these activities achieve critical mass, they wind up on corporate radar and become vulnerable to corporate co-optation, as happened with the Boulevard festival in Casablanca.

Two Months That Changed Everything

Around the time that Rafik Hariri was assassinated, a young Lebanese video producer had just returned from living in the United States for many years and took a job at Hezbollah's al-Manar television network. His particular talent was producing bloody music videos, in which the scenes of violence were timed to the beat of the music. His goal, according to one interview, was to remind people of the "power of blood"; more specifically, he wanted to encourage young Palestinians to become suicide bombers, which he could hope to do because al-Manar is the second-most-watched station in the West Bank.

The producer, who didn't reveal his true identity, is Moe Hamzeh's doppelgänger—his shadowy, somewhat nefarious twin. The two represent the poles of contemporary Lebanese popular culture; one is at the forefront of a politics of hope, the other of a culture of death. As Moe is the first to admit, it was the al-Manar producer who had the better time during the summer of 2006, when Hezbollah, almost simultaneously with Hamas, launched operations that kidnapped several Israeli soldiers for use as bargaining chips for their own prisoners, prompting a massive Israeli response that quickly escalated into full-scale war across much of Lebanon.

How did the hopeful promise of the Cedar Spring end up in a blood-soaked war between Israel and Hezbollah, a little over a year later? Conspiracy theories abound on all sides. But for me perhaps the most important, yet infrequently mentioned, reason for Hezbollah's unprovoked attack on Israeli territory was the fear by the movement's leaders that it was losing its once-vaunted social and political power. Almost a generation had passed since the civil war, and six years since Israel withdrew from southern Lebanon. Hezbollah's main patron, Syria, had been expelled by what started out as a ragtag movement of various Lebanese grassroots groups using nonviolent cultural events (e.g., rallies and marches). The push toward a new political order would surely leave the movement, whose claim to fame was violent resistance (even though it owes its enduring power to its extensive health, educational, and other social networks), far less powerful than it had been. Rather than engage in the hard work of competing on equal footing in a new and more robust public and political sphere, the Hezbollah leadership realized that war would both raise its profile around the region and weaken its domestic opposition, which is exactly what happened.

During the war, Moe sent me the following e-mail from Beirut: "Personally, I am not that well, physically, and psychologically. I am going into very depressive time, watching how this war affected our future . . . I am not performing anymore . . . my band members left the country during the war and the main people are not coming back, I am also not able to secure any more money to record the album, etc. etc. . . . So it is a very delicate phase I am going through." Not everyone was that paralyzed, however. Layla and most of her activist friends were deeply involved in housing refugees, sometimes in their own apartments in the relatively safe areas of downtown and central Beirut.

Among musicians, the band Scrambled Eggs, one of the most distinctive bands in the Lebanon scene (its unique sound is forged out of the raw materials of progressive rock, no-wave, ambient, noise, and straight-ahead American rock 'n' roll), stayed in Beirut, even organizing a show to help build solidarity and raise awareness in the foreign press about what it felt were the underreported realities of the war. The concert was titled "Musicians AGAINST Monsters" and was held at Club Social in the trendy, century-old neighborhood of Gemayzeh, located next to the downtown/Solidaire region. Although only blocks from the fighting, it was attended by a large share of the foreign journalists in Beirut, and became one of the few hopeful stories of the summer.

❧❦❧

Six months after the war ended, I was back in Beirut, lucky enough to see Blend and sit in with The Kordz on successive nights at Club Nova. Before Blend's show, Moe and his wife, Manal (pregnant with twins), and I met some friends at a restaurant in Gemayze. The last time I had been there, before the war, it was cordoned off by the army to provide security for a "National Unity" conference that was supposed to—but didn't—end the stalemate caused by the Cedar Revolution.

This time, months after the war, downtown was again cordoned off, but not for meetings between the competing members of the country's elite. Instead, the area had been turned into a refugee camp and protest site by Shi'is who had fled the Israeli destruction of their neighborhoods and towns. They knew, from press reports, of the tacit agreement between Hezbollah and Israel in which Hezbollah wouldn't fire rockets at Tel Aviv or Haifa if Israel didn't attack Solidaire and other upscale neighborhoods. A quarter that had been emptied of the poor and working class to make way for steel-and-glass high-rises, haute couture boutiques, and other attractions for the elite had been reoccupied by the same class that was expelled over a decade before.

"It's the revenge of the dispossessed," one dinner companion explained, who then pointed out that this tent city had lasted far longer than the one erected by the organizers of the Cedar Revolution. Hezbollah chief Hassan Nasrallah told his people that "your resistance and steadfastness dealt a severe blow to the New Middle East plan, which Condoleezza Rice said would be born in the July War. But it was stillborn because it was an illegitimate child."

It was clear from speaking with contacts in Hezbollah that the protesters were in no mood to relinquish their hold on Beirut's downtown until they received a bigger piece of Lebanon's already heavily sliced pie. In the meantime, each night the residents of the tent city shone a huge spotlight on the Parliament building at one end of the central plaza and blasted al-Manar programs through the loudspeakers. They re-created what the seminal postwar German philosopher Jürgen Habermas once dismissed as a "plebian public sphere," a public sphere for the working-class masses right in the heart of Lebanon's global city. In doing so, they were trying to ensure that Hezbollah would wind up with more power than before the war, despite the fact that Lebanon remains more divided than ever.

When I arrived at Nova for Blend's show, and then the next night at The Kordz's concert, it was clear that things had also changed in Beirut's music scene. On the one hand, the shows were attended by fewer people than attended the bands' shows before the war. But on the positive side, the smaller crowd exuded an intense level of camaraderie that was unusual even for the normally gregarious Lebanese. People were hugging and kissing hello with far more intensity, perhaps the result of the shared weeks of hell everyone had gone through.

There was another difference in the feel of the concerts, a kind of desperation in the bands that reflected the increasing lack of hope for most people who weren't Hezbollah supporters in any kind of positive outcome for Lebanon. This sentiment was on display when Blend played a walloping Oriental metal version of the classic Rogers and Hammerstein song "My Favorite Things" near the end of their show. When the band's new lead singer screamed lyrics such as "When the dog bites and the bee stings and I'm feeling sad, / I simply remember my favorite things and then I don't feel so bad," the absurdity of war couldn't have been more obvious.

The music was certainly symbolic, but it couldn't compare with the feeling of actually walking through the rubble of southern Beirut, which looked like a nightmare that even Gazans or Baghdadis haven't yet woken up to. Almost a year after the war, much of Haret al-Hreik, Hezbollah's home base, remained utterly in ruins. The streets were filled with pancaked buildings. Sheets and clothing still billowed in the wind out of the now-sandwiched floors. Yet, amid the rubble, Hezbollah was directing a frantic rebuilding effort, and gelaterias, cafés, and small boutiques were filled with customers, in what passed for a normal day in southern Beirut.

Alaa Abdel Fatah and his wife, Manal, who'd joined me in Beirut for a conference on youth and the public sphere that

Layla al-Zubaidi had organized, toured the neighborhood with me. Never having experienced war's devastation before, they were blown away. "It's so very intense," Alaa explained. "Lebanon was our—the Arabs' and Muslims'—hope. Everyone was very excited when they saw Hezbollah winning. But now, as I walk through here and see the result, it's so depressing. We always thought that if we brought hundreds of thousands of people into the streets, we could bring down the government, but this taught us otherwise."

As he processed his feelings during our tour of the rubble, two girls walked by wearing army fatigues, tight black T-shirts, and full headscarves. They were *muhajababes*, the object of media scrutiny ever since BBC producer Allegra Stratton published a book of that name, playing off the term *muhajaba* that was coined by young Arabs to describe their female peers who wore headscarves along with their tight jeans and T-shirts or designer clothes.

Having baited our eyes with their outfits, they glared at us as they walked by. As we passed, I noticed that each was wearing a yellow rubber wrist band, which looked a lot like the Lance Armstrong cancer bracelet worn by millions of Americans. But then my eye caught the Hezbollah logo on them, and I realized they were merely the newest item of Hezbollah chic, easily purchased, I soon discovered, in the local stationery store along with etched crystal paperweights bearing Nasrallah's likeness inside, and innumerable Hezbollah books and videos about the war with catchy titles such as *Nasr min Allah*, or *Victory from God* (the Arabic is a play on Hassan Nasrallah's last name; the text isn't nearly as interesting).

However distasteful Americans might consider their

accessories to be, the young women walking through the rubble in their funky outfits and Hezbollah charms are as much the future of Lebanon as are their funkily dressed sisters in Gemayze or Hamra, musicians and fans alike. Their perspective on the world is global, yet their allegiance is at least partly to Hezbollah, not merely (or even primarily) for religious reasons, but because the movement has managed to defy Israel and the United States, increase the power of their historically marginalized community, run a fairly corruption-free local government, and allow them the space to define their own cultural avant-garde, which is every bit as radical as the one that's been crafted a few kilometers to the north.

In fact, for all we knew the girls were on their way to class at AUB (they certainly looked like AUB students). Even if they were, however, it wouldn't change the basic equation that divides southern Beirut, and the Lebanon it represents, from the central and northern parts of the city, and the neoliberal vision of the future that, several years after Hariri's murder, still governs the worldview and policies of the country's pro-American elite.

Sheikh al-Mardini captured the despondency felt by most Lebanese I know over Lebanon's postwar paralysis when I went to check on him and his family on the last day of my trip. As we sat in his bedroom, he recounted how much more divided Lebanese society is after the war. There was a moment after Hariri's assassination, he explained as his children crawled over him, stealing the cookies his wife had laid out for us, when everyone could have worked together. But Hezbollah only wanted to lead, not participate as an equal, in any move toward the future. "Today, each side in Lebanon has its own culture, and religious and other ideas. At the moment of the Cedar Revolution we could have offered a model not just for the Arab world, but for the whole world. But Syria, Iran, Israel, and other powers all preferred that we be a failed experiment rather than succeed and challenge the existing system, which they all benefit from."

What troubled both the sheikh and Moe Hamzeh was how religion and culture were working against each other rather than for reform. As al-Mardini explained, "Religion and cultural reform don't just come with other reforms, they're crucial to them. That's why it's better for all of them [leaders of various factions] if everyone stays asleep, lazy and humiliated." Moe concurred, adding that "it's the role of culture to force those questions on their leaders, and it's the goal of leaders to stop those questions from being asked. And we're more important than ever because the gap between intellectuals and the rest of society is growing. Society is lazy, the system is lazy, but music can't be lazy."

One thing's for sure: both Hezbollah and Lebanon's hard rockers are expert at reminding people of the "power of blood." The difference is that Hezbollah and other political parties and militias use the symbolic power of blood to win support for shedding more of it when they deem necessary, while Lebanon's metalheads and their comrades across the musical spectrum use the symbolic power of blood for the opposite reason: to evoke the futility of violence.

It's hard to imagine who can initiate a dialogue on these issues, and in so doing give more space to the metaphorical, rather than actual, spilling of blood. Nevertheless, everyone agrees that such a dialogue is crucial to securing a peaceful future. (During one of the country's periodic political crises, in late 2007, a television ad was aired appealing for dialogue, "if not for us, then for our children. Talk to each other.") Putting The Kordz or Blend into heavy rotation on al-Manar might be a good place to start. But given Hezbollah's history of being ahead of the cultural-political curve, the movement might decide it's more efficient to train its own generation of Islamic rockers to take to the streets, airwaves, and satellite channels by storm.

The question is, will they, or their comrades in Hezbollah's political and military wings, be willing to share the stage with their peers? Or will an emboldened Hezbollah become more like Rotana and Wal-Mart, seeking merely to crush or buy out the opposition rather than engage it for the common good. Somewhere in the answer to this question lies the future of Lebanon, and of the Middle East as a whole.

IRAN

"Like a Flower Growing in the Middle of the Desert"

To travel from Beirut to Tehran is to move between two poles of the "Shi'ite Crescent" that couldn't be more different from each other. Beirut is a seaside city where even walking in the poor, Shi'i southern suburbs you can't escape the Mediterranean culture. Its legendary nightlife a few kilometers uptown doesn't stop even for suicide bombings and civil war. Tehran is roughly eight times the size of Beirut. With twelve million people, it is at least three times as large as all of Lebanon, yet the city seems devoid of character, and has no nightlife to speak of. At least aboveground.

My arrival at the recently opened Imam Khomeini Airport was quite a shock. The airport's hypermodern glass-and-steel design puts Milan's Malpensa or Paris's Charles de Gaulle airports to shame. It seemed a world apart from the stern-looking photos of Khomeini that stare down at you from various angles in the arrival terminal. I was nervous about getting into Iran—and even more so about getting out—given the tense state of relations between Iran and the United States and the United Kingdom. But the passport officer waved me through when he saw my American passport. No questioning, no heavy-handed security people following me. Just "Welcome to Iran," and off I went.

꽃

"Let's see . . . you've got the British hostages, the crackdown on insufficiently headscarved women, and the escalating nuclear showdown. There always seem to be at least three crises involving Iran these days, don't there?" Behnam Marandi asked as we walked down Jomuri-ye Eslami street in downtown Tehran, about a block and a half from the British Embassy. A computer programmer and Web designer by profession, Behnam is also one of the main forces behind *Tehran Avenue,* a semi-underground online magazine covering the arts, especially music in and around the city. Not only does Behnam know every important musician in Tehran, he knows what they have to do to survive in the era of President Mahmoud Ahmadinejad.

Behnam was actually off by at least one crisis. There was also an American "tourist"—who some people claimed was a CIA operative (it turned out that he was a former FBI agent)—who had disappeared on one of the small Iranian islands in the Persian Gulf. But where were all the protesters I had seen in front of the British Embassy while watching the BBC a few minutes earlier in my hotel room? This was only day five of the "British hostage crisis" that began when Iranian Revolutionary Guards detained a small British naval vessel patrolling the waters close to (Iran claimed inside) the country's territorial waters. Surely I should have heard them chanting their amusingly histrionic 1970s-era chants, this close to the embassy.

But, as with almost everything in Iran, reality rarely corresponds to the images of the country we see on television. Aside from the 150 or so protesters, many of them either "professionals" brought in for the cameras (and indeed, many milled around until given the cue to chant and march for the cameras) or die-hard regime supporters, Tehran's twelve million or so residents apparently had better things to do that afternoon. Even a block away from the protest site life went on as usual.

Officially, Iran is a country still obsessed with past humiliations. Newly printed posters of martyrs from the Iran-Iraq war, now a generation removed from public consciousness, cover buildings and utility poles. If you drive by Palestine Square, it's hard to miss the giant bronze sculpture of a map of Palestine, with life-size figures of women and children on one side, and fighters taking on the Zionist Goliath on the other. "But who thinks or cares about Palestinians?" a friend asked, with derision in her voice. As we walked by the former American Embassy, now home to a museum and offices of the dreaded Revolutionary Guards, we passed a huge, freshly painted mural on a building that read, ISRAEL SHOULD BE WIPED OUT, while the walls of the embassy featured numerous insults in Persian and English against the United States. No one pays much attention to them; and indeed the government allows Iranian Jews to visit the country's mortal enemy, Israel.

Most Iranians don't want revolution; they just want to manage their lives with as little interference as possible from the government. It's not easy to stay out of the government's way, however, when the Ahmadinejad regime constantly shifts the parameters of what's "Islamically acceptable" behavior, clothing, or music. Yet Iranians also seek to raise their standard of living by pressuring the government to maintain or increase public services and provide a better social infrastructure. It's the tension between these two desires that gives the ayatollahs and Ahmadinejad breathing room to enforce a social and political system that few Iranians care for.

Officially, I had been invited to Iran to give some academic lectures and meet with members of the religious establishment. But my real reason for coming to Iran was to meet with musicians. "The first thing you need to understand about music in Iran today," Behnam explained, "is that you can't show instruments on TV because that's considered against religion. You can have people playing them on TV, and you can hear instruments and the music, but you can't see the musicians playing the instruments, except for the daf [a type of drum] or flute—unless, of course, you've got an illegal satellite dish."

We were looking for a quick bite to eat, but that's not easy to find in downtown Tehran. In most cities of the Middle East, you can't walk a block without passing several restaurants or food stands. There are restaurants and fast-food-type storefronts in Tehran, to be sure, but compared with most of the region, there's never been much of a café and restaurant culture in Iran, so most meals are eaten at home.

Indeed, in a society where there's not much to do outside the home, dinner has become one of Iran's most important social lubricants. A member of Iran's top metal band, Ahoora, told me, "Our whole life is inside." Inside you don't need to wear your veil, you can blast your music, dance, watch pirated copies of the latest Hollywood—or Bollywood—movies, kiss your girlfriend, and otherwise feel free.

Of course, most Arab/Muslim countries try to control the use of public space by citizens—both where and how they can come together and what they can do and say when they do so. But in Iran the level of control is greater than in any other country aside from Saudi Arabia and parts of Afghanistan; it's surely the envy of the Egyptian or Pakistani Interior Ministries. As in the old Soviet Union, there simply is no public sphere in the traditional meaning of the term, as a space where citizens meet publicly and freely discuss issues of social or political concern.

There is one big difference between the Iranian regime and its predecessors behind the Iron Curtain: East Germany and the Soviet Union had elaborate internal intelligence networks that reached deep into the private lives of average citizens; in Iran, private space has become increasingly free of government interference in seemingly inverse proportion to crackdowns on the public sphere. Successive governments have come to understand that the majority of Iranians will not tolerate policing of their private lives anywhere near the extent that they'll accept control of their public identities and actions. And so, for the most part, the state leaves Iranians alone behind closed doors.

And even outside the home, Tehranians have long been adept at finding spaces to gather outside the official gaze—publicly, if not politically. They often take to the mountains north of the city in order, literally, to "get away from it all," particularly the control of the various arms of the state and its guardians of public morality, the *basij* (Persian for "mobilized"). This feared volunteer force is made up largely of young members of the Revolutionary Guards. For three decades now, when not engaged in war, the *basij* have roamed the country's main cities, harassing anyone who violates their interpretation of proper Islamic conduct or dress.

The *basij,* and the interests they serve, have made it nearly impossible to find a good place to play or hear heavy metal in Tehran. For the most part, nontraditional music, and rock in particular, is heard not just indoors, but quite literally underground, in basements, the storage rooms of apartment buildings, and parking garages. Performances are occasionally allowed, but only under tightly controlled conditions, and even then they can be canceled with little notice, sometimes in mid-performance. Few countries in the world have repressed non-official public culture, and particularly music, as thoroughly as has Iran.

 ❦

What most defines Iran for me is a particular musical interval, one traditionally unique to Persian and Indian music. Called the *koron* in Persian, and a "neutral third" by Western musicologists, the first time I heard the *koron* it literally stunned me, since it's almost completely unknown in Western classical or popular music. It is a microtone, an interval less than the semitone (for example, C to C#), which is the smallest interval traditionally used in Western music. The *koron* is formed by taking the major third of a key and lowering it by somewhere between a quarter-tone and a third-tone, which produces a very strange and unsettling yet somehow "neutral" sounding interval, so it's difficult for a westerner to tell whether the piece is being played in a major or minor key.

The *koron* is not used very often in Iranian metal because it's difficult for fretted instruments (and impossible for the piano) to play microtonal intervals. But it helps us understand the complexity of Iranian culture more broadly—that is, the ability to hold two seemingly contradictory positions and achieve a kind of reconciliation, or harmony.

The Roots of Iranian Rock

Rock 'n' roll has long been popular in Iran. It came of age in the mid-1970s during the reign of the secularizing Shah, who placed far fewer restrictions on foreign cultural practices and products than did his successors in the Islamic Republic (one metal musician explained that his mother "was a big fan of Pink Floyd, Hendrix, and the Stones"). Heavy metal joined the sonic environment around the end of Iran's brutal eight-year war with Iraq. Perhaps the first band to achieve something of a breakthrough in the metal scene was O-Hum (Illusions), founded in 1999. The band plays a well-orchestrated blend of Western hard rock and Persian traditional music and instrumentation, with many of the lyrics taken from the fourteenth-century poet Hafez. After its first album was rejected by the Ershad, or Culture Ministry, band members created their own website and offered free downloads of the album—one of the first Iranian examples of using the Internet to get around state restrictions on cultural production. By 2000, there were roughly fifty bands just in Tehran, but the scene had a hard time growing because it's so difficult to make it as a musician in Iran and the government routinely cracks down on alternative cultural expression.

O-Hum also began playing publicly—or rather, privately—at venues such as the Russian Orthodox church in

Tehran and at a few charity concerts. This was a period when the Khatemi government mainly policed public "Islamic" spaces. So churches, foreign embassies, and private homes became quasi-public spaces where musicians could perform for sometimes hundreds of people without fear of harassment or arrest. This would change in 2007, when the Ahmadinejad government began to invade private homes and arrest metal fans.

Paradoxically, during the last five years more underground bands have approached mainstream popularity, even when officially banned. For some this has been a sign of success: "Unlike in other countries, we're aggressive, we keep fighting to keep metal alive," one artist told me. Others would prefer never to see the light of day: "Maybe it's good that the best music is all underground. It keeps us on the edge. It keeps us fresh," another musician said with a sigh. But everyone believes that the music must go on. "The death of metal would be the death of Iran," explained a guitar player, "so we keep fighting to keep it alive."

Despite the crackdowns, as recently as 2007, 3,000 fans could be expected to show up for shows such as the one performed by the band SDS at the University of Tehran, even though it wasn't allowed to perform with vocals. "We were not allowed to headbang or even stand up," one fan present explained to me. "It was 'metal theater,' not a metal concert," continued Pooya, one of the founders of the scene who did the first, and to this day one of the only, public metal concerts with vocals. "Everyone had to sit politely. At one gig, at Elm-o-San'at (Science and Industry) University, we managed to play for forty minutes before the *basij* tried to force us to stop. They weren't supposed to enter the university. So they drove up to the front and started roaring their motorcycles, and the manager of the place begged us to stop. We were the last metal concert with vocals."

Even without vocals, explained another musician, when bands played classic death-metal anthems, like the songs from Slayer's classic 1986 album *Reign in Blood*, "the whole crowd would fucking explode with headbanging, nobody could control them. They'd go so wild, you know? Needless to say, the next gig was canceled, because the whole thing was about control, and we were out of their control. We were arrested and charged with satanism."

A professor who works closely with the Miras Maktoob Institute (Institute for the Written Heritage) explained the larger phenomenon reflected by Iranian metal this way: "On the one hand, in the current political situation you can't come to the surface here; the 'real underground' is in Iran these days, and one would imagine that because of this we are isolated from the rest of the world. Yet Iran has been at the crossroads of culture since Cyrus the Great. We've always been open, that's why the Iranian government has tried, and failed, to suppress our instinctual drive to reach out and absorb other cultures."

Censoring the Uncensorable, Foregrounding the Underground

The restrictions the regime has imposed on the performance of music are many. As Behnam explained, "The most important thing is that you can't see women singing on TV, and they aren't allowed to sing solo in public, so musicians have to do special arrangements of their music in order to have at least two women singing, or singing in the chorus of a performance featuring a male singer." Women are clearly the most heavily censored and filtered "item" on the Internet in Iran as well. Tens of millions of websites are blocked, as part of what one scholar terms the "gender apartheid of Iran," just because they contain the word "women" in them. The government automatically assumes that any website with women as a subject is "immoral."

Politicians, prophets, and even philosophers have been warning societies about the threat posed by music, and especially the female voice, to the social order since Homer introduced the Sirens to literature and Socrates urged the banning of eight types of music in the *Republic* on the belief that they encouraged drunkenness and idleness. Early Muslim leaders—although not the Qur'an—held similar views. After the Iranian Revolution, one newspaper explained, "We must eliminate music because it means betraying our country and our youth . . . Music is like a drug, whoever acquires the habit can no longer devote himself to important activities."

The mullahs weren't that far off the mark in comparing music-listening to drug use: more than one musician explained to me, in the words of one of the country's leading metal guitarists, that "buying music was like buying drugs" when metal first arrived in Iran in the late 1980s. Even getting a black-market cassette was comparable to scoring; you had to take two taxis and meet at a neutral location and make the hand-off as quickly as possible before hiding the tape in your pants for the ride home.

On the other hand, the late Ayatollah Khomeini wavered on his opinion of music. He argued that "music dulls the mind because it involves pleasure and ecstasy, similar to drugs," but he became more lenient after hearing a musician playing something he thought sounded beautiful outside the window of his home one day. Ultimately, the near-total ban on rock music during the Revolution's first fifteen years was loosened a bit under the presidency of Mohammad Khatemi, who was more responsive to the demands of the younger generation than had been his predecessors Khamenei and Rafsanjani. Metal bands even managed to get permission to hold a few concerts during this period, but President Ahmadinejad's election in 2005 led to the banning of all Western music from state-run TV and radio stations, making it harder—but not impossible—for fans to hear live metal in Iran.

To make a government-approved CD, without which you aren't allowed to perform legally, you have to take your music to the Ershad, or Culture Ministry, where several committees determine whether the music, lyrics, and presentation are technically professional and Islamically acceptable. The absurdity of the categories that must be approved in order to receive permission to release an album reflects the larger absurdities of Iran's political and social orders today. Bad grammar, shaved heads, an "improper sense of style," and even "too many riffs on electrical guitar and excessive stage movements" can all get your music banned. "It's like this," Behnam said. "When you submit a request, they have a department to check the music, especially vocal content. The Ershad will often order a singer or band to change the lyrics, melody, or rhythm in a song. Lyrics are especially important for them. They need to check whether it's against the system, which is forbidden."

By "system," Behnam meant the entire ideological, political, and economic apparatus of the Iranian state. So if a censor listening to a song decides that the guitar distortion is too intense, and therefore threatens state security by exciting emotions that the state can't control or that could be turned against it, the band will have to lighten up on the guitar. Or perhaps the melody is too Western, or just not Iranian enough, or the lyrics are a bit too risqué. You can imagine how death-metal bands might fare against an Iranian censor, which is why most don't bother trying to obtain government approval. But this tactic can be dangerous during periodic crackdowns by the government, which can use the "illegal" circulation of an artist's or band's music as a convenient excuse to arrest or otherwise harass them.

Schools have been on the frontline in the struggle for the soul of young Iranians since the Revolution. High schools were both where most metalheads were introduced to the music and where the government tried to clamp down on it from the start. Guitarist Ali Azhari, one of the most important artists in the Iranian scene, recalled with a smile, "The principal of my school had a shelf in his office filled just with my T-shirts and bracelets. He was trying to demetalize me," Ali said, coining a new word to explain exactly what was being done to him. "But it didn't work." Later on, when metalheads started to become a more public, if strange-looking, presence on the streets, the government began to accuse—and soon after, indict—them for being satanists, spreading Western culture, and simply for being in a metal band (which didn't seem to be part of the criminal code when I checked). Convictions of musicians were almost always overturned, but the government's point was made.

❦

Almost every Arab/Muslim country has some sort of official censor of music, but Iran's has proved more proactive and aggressive than others'. Iran's mullahs have legitimate reasons to fear metal: it reflects the mood of a young generation (65 percent of the country's population) roiled by drug use, prostitution, increasing AIDS, and, most important, a nearly complete rejection of the values of the Revolution.

Perhaps the best indication of how strongly the country's metal community—and, by extension, a large share of the rest of Iran's younger generation—oppose the ethos of the Revolution comes from the popularity of the pioneering British metal band Iron Maiden. "For sure, Iron Maiden would have to be the most important band for us," explained Armin Ghaouf, a twenty-eight-year-old mechanical engineer and guitar player who's been on the metal scene since its inception. Tall, with shoulder-length hair (it was much longer until the police cut it after arresting him) and a pleasant face, Armin plays a role similar to Slacker's in Egypt: he knows everyone and everything about the scene and connects all its dots, even though he doesn't play much these days. Sitting next to him, Ali Azhari agreed: "Maiden gives me a vision at a time when the chief symbol of Iranian culture is that of the martyr. Maiden is so visual—just think of the album covers with their tanks and other images of war and death—it's like a dream combined with music. The band allows you to imagine being somewhere else you can't physically be."

Just a few weeks earlier, Ali, Armin, and I had stood about twenty feet from the stage watching Maiden's first-ever performance in the Arab world, at the Dubai Desert Rock Festival. The images of war's violence and futility—particularly as embodied by the band's mascot, the skeleton-monster war robot Freddy, blundering across the stage pretending to shoot the crowd—served as the perfect rebuttal to Khomeini's valorization of war and martyrdom as the holiest acts within Islam. As Ali pointed out afterward, "There are so many images of war and guns on the streets and buildings of Tehran, it's the same symbolism really." Except that the Revolution's martyrs died "in the path of God," while Iron Maiden's die for nothing.

The mullahs celebrate violence; the metalheads critique it. Being a metal fan offers—however paradoxical it might seem—a "community of life" (as one musician described it to me) against the community of death and martyrdom propagated by the Iranian government. But the risks are both real and substantial. As Pooya explained, "Even my family thought I was dangerous." Pooya was arrested so many times he stopped counting. "I just wanted to dress like a metalhead, and I was arrested and beaten, first in the cars of the *basij,* then in jail." It wasn't just long hair that could get one in trouble. Ramin Sadighi, the founder of the innovative and respected Iranian world-music label Hermes Records, said that during the long period when Western instruments were effectively banned in Iran, he had to rent delivery vans and travel well before and after rehearsal times to get his upright bass to rehearsal and performances. "We sacrificed so much," he informed me, "more than the current generation of musicians can understand."

Other musicians were accused of being Jewish or of looking like "savages" because of their long hair and metal attire.

In response, one metalhead offered the most pejorative insult in the Iranian repertory: "The government is Arab! It's like we're occupied. That's why the music is so strong." (Many Iranians are intensely nationalist, and harbor a millennium-old grudge against Arabs for supposedly overshadowing them in the larger Muslim world.) Armin recounted one such incident: "I was walking down the street and a passing police patrol car stopped and the cops asked, 'Where are you going with long hair?!' I said, 'What's the matter? None of your business,' and they took me in and said, 'We'll call your father, we'll take his documents, and if you let us cut your hair he'll get them back.' What could I do? After that I started to put my hair in a ponytail, tuck it in my collar, and tie it up, and walking around on the street it didn't look like I had long hair. When we were playing or jamming, I took it out, that was it."

Of course, musicians aren't the only group targeted by the Ershad. Mojtaba Mirtahmasb, a well-known documentary filmmaker in Tehran, has also had his run-ins with the government, for two documentaries (*Back Vocal* and *Off Beat*) he made about the difficulties faced by Iranian musicians today. We watched the films in his apartment, since naturally they are banned from public view. Mojtaba explained that one Iranian jazz band had two concerts approved by the government, only to have the second show canceled hours before it was to start.

The government can prevent public performances, but in other ways music censorship is increasingly irrelevant in Iran. After three decades of a revolutionary regime, Iranian artists have gotten very good at making the best of a bad performance environment. Among the most interesting examples comes from Farzad Golpayegani, one of the top two or three metal guitarists in Iran, and one of the country's most talented graphic artists as well. Although he loves to play outside Iran, "where at least kids can headbang," Farzad remains committed to building the rock scene in his country, and has become expert at putting on shows that defy the restrictions placed on him, often at the last minute, by authorities. "The last concert was half unplugged because we were not allowed to bring drums, so I tuned my acoustic guitar like a setar," he laughed. (The setar is a three-stringed country cousin of the sitar.) "Another time I played with percussionists and a video of my paintings projected on a screen behind me; we had about 500 people for that show."

It's also relatively easy to buy foreign music in stores, while the Internet and music downloading have made it impossible to control the spread of "illegal" music. Yet if the central government has reached a seeming truce with young Iranians concerning what goes on between their headphones, local governments are closing music schools and jailing and even lashing people caught listening to "thumping tunes in their cars."

Is This Music or Magic?
How Metal Invaded Iran

The practice of tightly policing music goes back to the start of the Revolution, but it is one of the ironies of Iranian political culture that the very technology and clandestine means of communication that made the Iranian Revolution possible (in particular, the circulation of contraband cassette tapes of the Ayatollah Khomeini's speeches) were also used by the early metalheads to spread the word about, and the music of, heavy metal. Khomeini realized the possibility for cassettes to be used against him in the same way he used them against the Shah, so he banned them after taking power. Nevertheless, by the time Khomeini died, cassette tapes of the world's best metal were circulating to a small but fanatical community of metalheads in Tehran and other major cities like Isfahan, Shiraz, and Mashad.

Indeed, metal "fever" had spread among young Iranians at the very moment that the fever of the Revolution began to dim. As Pooya put it during yet another four-course meal at the home of a musician, "Out of the death of Khomeini the flowers of metal grew." Another musician picked up on the paradoxical image of metal as beauteous and life-affirming, explaining that when it first hit Iran, metal was "like a flower growing in the middle of the desert" of Iranian politics and culture.

⚜

I never thought it was possible to find a musician as devoted to death metal as Marz until I met Ali Azhari. "I remember when I was thirteen years old," Ali said during our first meeting in his apartment, "I was looking for serious music, not just party music or music to get drunk to. I was into reading books and wanted to be, I dunno, an important guy. And I remember I listened to—can you believe it—Def Leppard, and I said, 'Whoa! What is this? Is this music or is this magic? Is it a kind of spell?'"

I got lost trying to find Ali's house in northern Tehran, the upscale part of the city whose numerous high-rise condo developments, many of them with apartments costing well over $1 million, begin to look the same after a while (in one neighborhood the high-rises are all painted white, blending into the snow-covered mountains above them). Ali's apartment is in a nondescript building in a neighborhood where dozens of satellite dishes are illegally set up away from the street. "It doesn't matter, though," he explained. "They [meaning the *basij*] know it's here. They'll come by and rip them out eventually, and then everyone will wait a while and put them back in."

Ali is one of the best guitarists in Iran. He plays incredibly fast and cleanly, and he has a taste for the theatrical that gives his music an added sense of importance. His round face yet sharp features, long jet-black hair, and black metal T-shirt give him the look of a young Iranian Alice Cooper, although his videos might make even Alice Cooper a bit queasy.

The first thing you notice about Ali's apartment (after realizing that he seems to be one of the few metalheads in the Middle East who doesn't live with his parents) is that it's quite dark, even in the middle of the day. The second thing you notice is how neat it is. This is not the abode of the typical metaler; there are no beer cans or crumpled fast-food wrappers or potato chip crumbs lying around. Ali is much too artistic and professional for that.

As I inhaled the scent of Persian incense burned to keep out the malevolent spirits of the Revolution, my ears were assaulted by an extreme metal video by the group Hate Eternal, blasting from his television. Slowly the apartment came into focus. It was laden with 1970s goth-futuristic furniture and stuffed animals—real ones, including a fox with a squirrel in its mouth and a couple of birds of prey as well.

At the other end of the apartment is Ali's control room, a two-by-three-meter padded room with just enough space for his computer, a mixing board, and a window to connect to the even tinier "live" room. The walls are covered with posters and stickers of metal and rock bands, including Hendrix and Bob Marley. Ali's Marshall TLS 100 amp and a couple of microphones took up the entire room. "I used to have the dual-lead Marshall," he explained, but even though he had almost no chance of ever playing in a space big enough to use it, "I moved up to the triple," an even more powerful amplifier.

On Ali's computer desktop is a huge photo of Twisted Sister frontman Dee Snyder. "Metal owes him because he stood alone against the PMRC [Parents Music Resource Center], and others trying to demetalize the world," Ali said proudly. "When you're a kid in the middle of a war, it stays in your mind for a long, long time. Heavy metal was considered totally Western and unacceptable, but we heard it and said, 'We like it and we're gonna get it.' We started trading tapes and starting bands with old instruments not destroyed during the Revolution, and when people would travel we'd ask them to buy tapes."

Armin, a long-time friend of Ali, remembered, "Everyone was greedy and hungry to get albums, and they would be copied literally a million times, which meant you wanted to make sure to get one of the first copies, because cassettes lost quality with each copy. And we were also tricky. We'd always keep a song for ourselves, and people would have to beg to get it. Of course with the Web, you can't play those games anymore," he said with a laugh.

Ali laughed too, at the thought of all the changes that have occurred in the last decade. "I remember a female friend asking, like this sixty-year-old guy, 'Would you please bring me this CD?' and it was, like, a Cannibal Corpse CD. Naturally the guy hears the name and says, 'Lady, this kind of music is not for you!' And she lies and says, 'Oh no! I don't want it for myself, it's not for me, it's for someone else.' "

The clandestine "microshows" that characterized the early Iranian metal scene (and are still one of the few ways to hear metal performed live today) were ad hoc and improvised. To many of the attendees, the shows could be truly disorienting, almost like religious experiences—the perfect antidote to the hyper-ritualized, formulaic, and in-your-face Islam propagated by the Islamic state. For Armin, "The first show I played at left me so dizzy. It was in someone's home because there were no discos to play in, and there were maybe thirty kids. The host asked my band to play 'Altars of the Abyss' by Morbid Angel, and everyone just freaked out, they couldn't bear the level of extremity, they couldn't take it after five minutes. You know, the timing was perfect, because metal hit Iran at the same time DM [death metal] became big. It was the perfect time because it was just after the war ended and death was everywhere, and then, boom, it [metal] exploded."

Strolling Down Tehran Avenue

As the sun set, I headed with Behnam to the apartment of Sohrab Mahdavi, on a pretty, tree-lined street in the well-heeled Fereshteh neighborhood in the hills of northern Tehran. Sohrab is one of the gentlest and purest souls I ever met. He and his wife, Mahsa Shekarloo, a UNICEF official in Tehran working on women's issues, are keen observers of Iranian culture and politics.

Sohrab and Mahsa's apartment is a bit sparse, but tastefully decorated, with a nice sound system. As soon as we arrived, Sohrab laid out a delicious meal of *kuku,* an omelet with minced vegetable, rice, and yogurt, and some fresh *sabzi,* a plate of local herbs that normally includes mint, basil, dill, parsley, coriander, cilantro, tarragon, and watercress.

After dinner, we had tea and snacked on salted marijuana seeds. Not surprisingly, these are popular with college students because they help them to stay awake during long nights of studying for exams (before going to bed, students will chew poppy seed to come down). As we drank and ate, we listened to some traditional setar music.

Like the sitar, the setar has movable frets that make it possible to play various modes of Persian music and the combination of semitones, quarter-tones, and *koron*s that characterize it. I was aware of how versatile the instrument was, but I'd never listened to the kind of traditional Persian music Sohrab was playing for me, particularly the songs based on the *segah* mode, which combines a *koron* with a semi-flat *re,* or second, for a truly haunting sound.

Sohrab is the founder of *Tehran Avenue,* where Behnam works. The online zine was created in 2001 to explore cultural life in Tehran. "Basically, *Tehran Avenue* is a bunch of people trying to find out what's going on in their society," said Behnam. While it was started with only a small group of writers, in the last six years it has grown into a sizable community to "push the limits of understanding" of Iranian culture. Sohrab and his team see the site as a means of bringing the vibrant underground scene of Tehran aboveground. Aided by the "back alleys of the website," they employ both English and Farsi to bring expatriate and local Iranians into one community.

The activity that put *Tehran Avenue* on the global cultural map was Sohrab's idea to hold a virtual battle of the bands in

2004. Called Tehran Avenue Music Open, the competition prompted interest from hundreds of bands—itself an indication of how big the underground music scene is just in Tehran—with dozens sending in their music to be judged. A couple of years earlier, *Tehran Avenue* ran an "Underground Music Competition," the existence of which was spread entirely by word of mouth and, in a non-publicized manner, via the Internet. But sympathetic officials from the cultural establishment let them know that calling the competition "underground" could actually put the bands who participated in harm's way, so they decided to make it an open, albeit virtual, forum. Both competitions helped to solidify the identities of the country's emerging rock and metal bands.

The submissions showed how many great young musicians were coming of age in Tehran, and also pointed to the desperate need for an accessible space for them to get together and share their music. As of 2007, there were three Web-based competitions. Sadly, it's not yet possible to arrange live competitions to determine the winners, but the competitions have helped Iranian rock artists learn more about their own scene, and have opened their music to the world at large.

Like Walking Without Legs

Very soon after the Revolution, Tehran was transformed into what the anthropologist Roxanne Varzi aptly describes as an "Islamic revolutionary space." Old monuments were replaced by new ones celebrating the Revolution, billboards featured photos of clerics and Islamic symbols instead of ads for the latest Western goods, and women could no longer walk the city's wide boulevards in anything but the full-length outer

garment known as a chador. "An all-encompassing Islamic reality" was created, according to Varzi, and it didn't include
rock 'n' roll.

The Islamic public sphere became even more narrowly
focused once Saddam Hussein attacked Iran in late December 1980. The war intensified the already powerful cult of
martyrdom in post-Revolution Iran. The massive casualties
produced by the war, and particularly by the Iranian tactic of
using human waves to counter Iraq's superior firepower, required that Iranians—not just the young men fighting, but
the families sacrificing them—have a thirst for martyrdom.

After Khomeini's death in 1989, Iranian society gradu-
ally opened up during the Rafsanjani and particularly the
Khatemi governments of the next decade and a half. Increasing numbers of young people became disaffected with the
cult of martyrdom and complete self-sacrifice. Instead of the
religious idea of *bi-khodi,* or self-annihilation, being the dominant mode of religious expression, the more liberal idea
of *khod-sazi,* or individualistic self-help, began to take hold
among young Iranians disillusioned by the waste of war.
Some of them were led to metal as an alternative value system
rather than just as a form of musical escapism. As Armin
Ghaouf explains, "What makes heavy metal so important are
the eight years of brutal war—twice the length of America's
involvement in World War II. I remember the missiles coming to Tehran, so wearing a metal or Maiden T-shirt with a
tank on it is very relevant to me. We didn't know if we'd live
through the war. And even today, at twelve years old we are
still forced to learn how to use AK-47s and to defend against
chemical weapons."

With such experiences, it's no wonder that death metal

became popular among young people. But how do they make it part of their everyday lives on the streets of Tehran? They do it by blasting music in their cars until the *basij* pulls them over, or by wearing skimpy headscarves until the *basij* force them to pull them completely over their scalps; and by wearing their iPods or Walkmans, which, especially for women with their mandatory headscarves, has become a favorite way to tune out the existing regime and into one's own world while walking down the street. Some even tag the logos of their favorite metal bands on walls across Tehran—whether in their bedrooms or on the street—claiming their bit of territory from a society in which they feel they have little stake.

Finally, Iranians connect with their music through the Internet, not just in English but in Farsi as well (while only one in sixty people in the world speak Persian, the language ranks fourth in frequency of use in Internet blogs). As Behnam explained about *Tehran Avenue*'s focus on creating a Web-based community of artists and fans: "Increasingly we've chosen to go through the cyberworld because of the ban on live shows." But, I wondered, how do you do music without live shows? Behnam thought for a second and agreed, "Yes, it's like walking without legs. Music is supposed to bring people together and create communities—real, not virtual. If you can't do that, then something is missing."

But even without the chance to perform in truly public settings (and therefore in front of large crowds), metal musicians argue that playing metal gives them confidence for life, and a safe place to work out feelings of aggression and hopelessness that otherwise would lead to more-unhealthy activities (from violence to drug use), which are commonplace in Iran today despite the regime's self-image as a paragon of

Islamic virtue. As Armin puts it, "Metal is like an asylum. A mental asylum that rejuvenates you and gives you hope."

New Gods and Old Martyrs

"When you breathe in our country, it's political," admitted Ali Azhari. "But even so, we're not doing stuff to harm the system, we're just trying to survive." Ali was trying to convince me of his innocent intentions. But it was hard to take his protestations of innocence very seriously when he was wearing a T-shirt that read, YOUR GOD IS DEAD. Ali's T-shirt, but not his argument, made more sense when he introduced his new project, Arthimoth. "Arthimoth is a newborn god I created myself, a combination of an ancient Persian name with the Greek goddess Artemis [the goddess of the wilderness and fertility]. I thought that this is the time to re-create ancient gods as a legacy of our fathers. Musically, we try to remix very old, traditional Iranian village music with contemporary music and especially extreme metal. In other words, we root the metal in our culture."

Creating other gods, however metaphorically, is certainly a good way to get into trouble in Iran—even more so when it's obvious. As Ali and Armin admitted, "We chose this metal in order to communicate. We write on behalf of the kids." Yet if you watch Ali in the recording studio, Baphomet shirt drenched with sweat as he records a brutal vocal that sounds—and looks, if the grimace on his face is any indication—like it's coming from his bowels, it's hard not to take his theology seriously. Certainly the government does—to a certain degree.

As we were talking, Ali loaded the video for "Baptize"

onto his computer. Ali is rightfully proud of the video because it demonstrates his skills as a metal songwriter, guitarist, and filmmaker. It's among the most disturbingly powerful music videos I've ever seen, riffing on the futility of violence first brought to metal cinema with Metallica's groundbreaking video "One" (which depicts a horrifically wounded soldier—without arms or legs, blind, deaf, and mute—using morse code to tap out a message to his doctors to kill him). But "Baptize" takes the message of "One" to a far higher degree of intensity than Metallica's innovative video—both musically, as the chromatic minor riffs of the song have enough of a hint of the unsettledness produced by the *koron* to keep the listener constantly off balance, while the drums never settle down into a beat you can groove to, and visually (something I wouldn't have imagined possible before seeing his video).

Ali uses the word "baptize" to indicate how Iranians are forcibly submerged, body and soul, in a system in which there is no room for independent thought. The video's lead actor is a man, mostly naked, who is led, seemingly willingly, to a chair. Immediately upon sitting down, he has the top of his head sawed off; his brain is shocked with electrodes and then nibbled on by a rat while another man screams into his ear from an occult-looking book (Ali actually used a Hebrew book because using the Qur'an would have really gotten him into trouble). The images move back and forth between shots of the band headbanging in unison and Ali singing as the rat eats the man's brain. Finally, as the song ends, the "doctor" sews the man's scalp back on and he stumbles away, like a zombie, into the world.

Ali's studio was raided while he was completing production for the video. The original masters of the video were confiscated, and he was questioned by the secret police. But he managed to hide another master copy and upload the video onto YouTube, where he's received comments from both Israel and Lebanon with the same message: "Don't let religion ruin your art; 'keep it brutal.' " It's a sentiment that's shared by many Iranian metalheads. A member of Iran's hottest young metal band, Tarantist, put it this way: "Metal is in our blood. It's not entertainment, it's our pain, and also an antidote to the hypocrisy of religion that is injected into all of us from the moment we're born."

From Boom Boxes to Mobile Phones: Tehran's Streetcorner Public Sphere

Bahman, rhythm guitarist for Tarantist, explained that in Iran the idea of a unique Iranian identity is so strong that "anything that looks like a foreign culture is frowned upon. Especially if it comes from the U.S." Yet hip-hop, which even more than heavy metal is identifiable as a product of the "Great Satan," has had an easier time of it in Iran than its hard-rock counterpart (the baggy clothing preferred by rappers does have the advantage of being more Islamically acceptable than the tight leather pants, T-shirts, and menacing-looking jewelry that define metal style). Indeed, rap has played a central role in creating a broad sense of community against the grain of the regime's wished-for Shi'i utopia, very often without arousing the suspicion that it's doing just that.

The Iranian rap scene is still small compared to the much better established hard-rock scene, but its rapid growth is described by many metalheads with envy. That doesn't mean that rappers are off the government's radar screen; several were arrested around the time I was in Iran, including one of the country's leading rappers, Hich-Kas, for being too overtly political. But in general, hip-hop in Iran is more tolerated than heavy metal, as long as it doesn't deal directly with sexual issues or take on the government.

While it has strong working-class and lower-class roots, many rappers and fans are from the wealthier segments of society. No matter their origin, most Iranian rappers have chosen the genre both because of its connection to worldwide musical trends and because of rap's history of political and social criticism. One of Iran's rising female rappers, Salome, explained: "The true meaning of hip-hop culture [is] a lot deeper than it looks on the surface. It's become much more eclectic than it was previously, and much more out in the open. As important, it's become Persianized instead of just copying the West. For example, I only use natural instruments, without samples [the digitally recorded bits of instruments or other songs that have long been the foundation of hip-hop production] in my songs."

Salome is half Iranian and half Turkish, and makes her living as a designer since doing so as a rapper is out of the question. (That she can make a living as a fashion designer in the Islamic Republic says something about the complex politics of cultural production in Iran today.) When we met in the office of *Tehran Avenue,* she was dressed, fashionably, in black, including her headscarf, which she kept adjusting as we spoke. A connoisseur of alternative hip-hop in the States, Salome is a fan of Dead Prez, Immortal Technique, and Paris. She raps in Persian and Turkish on top of beats influenced by these artists, yet unlike her heroes, she goes out of her way to define herself as apolitical: "I'm not political, just social, so I'll do songs about our rage at all the Iranian rappers who say meaningless stuff imitating commercial American rap, stuff that has no connection to our culture."

When rappers in the Arab/Muslim world say they're "social, not political," it means they're not critical of their own government; foreign governments are another matter entirely. After the United States invaded Iraq, Salome wrote a rapid-fire, nationalistic America-basher called "Petrolika." But while she doesn't mind performing abroad (as she did at the Intergalactic Music festival in Amsterdam in 2006), in Iran "I want to stay underground. I don't want to do interviews, to make that sacrifice, particularly being a woman." Rapping is not high on the Ahmadinejad list of approved feminine vocations.

Iran's male rappers are equally aware of what lines they can publicly cross without getting arrested or otherwise harassed. This was clear from a visit to one of Tehran's best— but still underground—hip-hop recording studios. The studio, which has no official name, is located in a wealthy neighborhood, but—as usual—it's in the basement so that neighbors, at least those outside the building, won't know it's there (although the steady coming and going of young men in hip-hop clothing, or with instruments slung over their shoulders, must surely indicate that something un-Islamic— from the regime's point of view—is going on there). As soon as I entered, I had a case of déjà vu; its smell and look reminded me of almost every other studio I've been in. Cigarette smoke filled the air, mixed with the odor of fried fast food, while chips and empty soda cans were scattered on tables and the floor.

It was here that I met two of the leading rappers on the

Iranian scene, Reveal and Hich-Kas. Reveal grew up largely in the UK and is currently completing a degree in Persian language at the School of Oriental and African Studies in London. Hich-Kas, whose name means "nobody" in Persian, is a home-grown rapper who chose his name specifically as a play on rappers who try to blow themselves up with pompous-sounding names. "I just wanted to show that somebody that calls himself 'nobody' can say big things." Both rappers are critical of the current situation in Iran and the problems their fans face, but neither was very comfortable talking explicitly about politics.

Reveal is one of the most educated rappers I've ever met, but for sheer grandeur of vision the prize has to go to the eighteen-year-old Tehran rapper Peyman-Chet. "The 'chet' means 'stoned,'" Peyman explained to me as we sat in a tiny rehearsal/recording studio on the third floor of a working-class neighborhood of central Tehran. This was not the Tehran I had grown used to. The streets were narrower, the buildings older. Peyman chose his stage name not because he likes drugs, but rather as a play on the way rap and drug culture are mixed in the States—"It's quite the opposite in Iran, where it's more techno and rock and dance music that attract the drugs. I chose the dope imagery to focus on addicted people." Drugs are in fact a huge problem among Iran's youth. According to a 2005 UN report, the country has the highest addiction rate in the world, especially for heroin and related drugs. "Natural and synthetic heroin, even synthetic crack; we got it all in Iran," a member of the metal band Ahoora admitted. "Yeah, we have an abundance of everything here—drugs, oil, money—everything except freedom," another band member chimed in.

Ahoora and Peyman are seemingly from opposite sides of the tracks. Peyman practices in a dingy studio with old equipment, Ahoora has a state-of-the-art Pro Tools recording system in the villa of the guitar player's father, a wealthy pistachio merchant whose faux-1920s Hollywood-style home boasts an intricately carved wood-paneled barroom that must have seen its share of fabulous parties in the Shah's day. Peyman has a new Yankees cap, Ahoora's lead guitarist has five electric guitars (two Jacksons, one Ibanez, one BC Rich, and one I'd never seen before), three Marshall amps (a JCM 2000, a Valvestate 2000, and a G30R), sixteen effects pedals, and an eighteen-button effects board hooked up to a rack-mounted digital effects system.

Of course, being a rapper, Peyman doesn't need any of that stuff. All he needs is a pen, a notebook, and a few hundred dollars to record a song that will be downloaded by thousands, if not tens of thousands, of people all over the world soon after he uploads it to his site. And while his name parodies hip-hop's fascination with dope, his clothing is as authentic as it can get when you're living 8,000 miles east of New York: baggy pants, sports jersey, baseball cap, and a big gold chain. "I wear baggy clothes because when people see me it makes them think. It shows that I want change," he explained.

The small studio, which was normally used by rock bands, was filled with posters of Pantera, Megadeth, and Cowboys from Hell, a cheap drum set, and a small amp, on which rested, of all things, a menorah with *Shalom* written in Hebrew and English in the middle of it. "What's that doing there?" I asked incredulously. "I think it's cool. It's beautiful, and it pisses off the state," said the owner of the studio, who prefers that I do not use his name because, while Iran's

25,000-strong Jewish community faces little persecution in the Islamic Republic, thinking menorahs are cool is not something you want to advertise publicly.

Although he's very young, Peyman enjoys a certain notoriety as a result of his music's distribution over the Internet and a video of his being broadcast on Dubai or European channels. He doesn't just see himself as a rapper. "I became interested in Persian poetry and Irfan—mysticism—and try to mix all of that into my raps and send it to the streets with a bit of Tupac thrown in. We're like modern Firdusui or Rumi [the two most famous Persian poets]," he argued. He played me the rhythm of a new song he's working on while he rhymed in a strange mixture of classical and postmodern Persian. "Eminem inspired by Rumi," he said.

As I chatted with Peyman, I understood why rap was spreading so quickly and deeply in Iran: rappers have succeeded in reclaiming public space for themselves in a way that metalheads can only dream of. "There's around 1,000 rappers just in Tehran," Peyman explained, "and we constantly meet and have battles in the parks. One of the most important is [the appropriately named] 'Joint Park,' or 'Cigari Park' in Persian. Basically, when we want to meet and have a battle, the word goes out through SMS messages or announcements on Persian-language rap sites. At least two times a month we have these gatherings, and up to 200 rappers and fans show up. Once we have a critical mass of people"—and he took out his mobile phone to play me a video of one of these battles while he was talking—"someone takes out a mobile phone and plays a beat that's stored on it, and we start rhyming. But it's not just the park, we get together and rap on streets, sidewalks, corners, even though it's illegal. Usually the *basij* check us out and leave us alone, and so do the cops, but we can disperse and regroup very quickly if the cops hassle us."

Peyman is very focused on "doing something that will be loved on the streets." But in Iran, street cred doesn't come from the gangsta or thug life. Instead, it comes from writing a song that is an innovative combination of Persian and Western music and raps, and deals with real social issues without focusing the regime's attention on you. "The problem is, nothing is underground in Iran. You can do a political song in a third-class studio in Tehran and you'll be caught in a week. They have spies everywhere. My friend did a song called 'Objection' against everything that's going on, and he was caught and put in jail for a week. He had to sign something saying he'd never do a political song again. I just drop some of Tupac's more political lyrics into my songs. Those who know, get it."

Despite the government's overwhelming power, Peyman feels that "the only way to push the government is to grow the movement beyond the point it can easily be destroyed. That's why I focus not on gangsta rap but on our problems here. Yet those rappers who rap about drugs and sex, or are hard-core nationalist, get more famous than those who rap about social problems. Kids today are much more interested in drugs and sex than in fighting to change society," he said with disgust. "But if someone could give them the energy and inspiration to do something, things would change."

Needing Each Other, or Needing to Defeat the Other?

I thought about how the Iranian government must view the growing popularity of rappers like Peyman-Chet and their

metal counterparts as I sat in the Tehran office of Massoud
Abid, a professor of philosophy and human rights at Mufid
University in Qom (the center of Shi'i scholarship in Iran). Although he is a Hojatul Islam, the rank just below ayatollah, if
anyone from the establishment would be sympathetic to—or
at least tolerant of—the dreams of young music fans, it would
be Abid, who is well known to Iranian scholars and activists
as one of the more progressive religious scholars and officials
in Iran.

Neither my spoken Persian nor his English was fluent
enough to carry on a complicated conversation solely in either
language, so we spoke in Arabic mixed with the other two.
The trilingual texture of the conversation symbolized one of
Abid's key points, which is that Iran is becoming ever more
globalized today, even as the United States seeks to isolate it
politically and economically. And along with being globalized,
Iranian young people are becoming more politicized, he felt,
contrary to what Peyman-Chet had said. "Viewed from the
outside, it might seem that young people are increasingly depoliticized and alienated from the state today," Abid argued.
Yet, from his position on the inside, things looked very different. The public sphere was neither absent nor deep underground: "It's just developing in less noticeable ways, outside
of mainstream popular culture. Just look at the large increase
in the number of NGOs in Iran in the last last four to five
years."

But at an even more basic level, the universities are where
much of the most interesting developments are taking place,
according to Abid. He sees this especially in how students in
seminaries and "secular" universities are combining religious
and nonreligious courses of study. "Seminary students are

taking courses in human rights or sociological theory, more women than ever are enrolled in universities; you can see the change in the personality of students, as the focus on politics of the post-Revolution generation has also given way to more of a focus on personal issues," he explained.

Abid believes that most Iranians want better relations with the West. "We have to do two things: first, get rid of this conflict between Islam and the West; and, second, learn how to understand the West for both good and bad. The changing position of the religious establishment toward music is a good indication of the possibilities for such a rapprochement. Today most senior ulema [Muslim legal scholars] are opposed to rock not because of religious reasons as much as because it's not part of Iran's cultural heritage."

The hope is that as Iran's overwhelmingly young population expands the horizons of what is a legitimate part of Iranian culture, that too will change. Indeed, Abid expressed confidence that a rapprochement with the United States, and with the West more broadly, would ultimately occur. In the end, he told me as I got up to leave, "the two sides need each other a lot more than they need to defeat the other."

Abid's philosophy is certainly far from the politically dominant conservative philosophy of Khamenei and Ahmadinejad. But there is a well-developed strand of relatively progressive theology and social and political thought in Iranian Shi'ism today, especially around the issue of women. As Ziba Mir Hosseini describes it in her book *Islam and Gender,* "If clerics want to stay in power they cannot ignore popular demands for freedom, tolerance, and social justice." Whether it's women working through sympathetic ayatollahs to reinterpret Islamic law in less oppressive ways, or metalheads using online zines to pry open their society's public sphere, most Iranians refuse to yield to the repressive dreams of their leaders. This has produced a cultural tug-of-war that will continue for the foreseeable future, and metal and hip-hop will be an important part of its soundtrack.

Iran's Unplugged Heavy Metal Heroes

During my last few days in Iran, I was lucky to meet up with two of the bravest and heaviest musicians in the country. The first was Mahsa Vahdat, one of the best young singers of traditional Persian music in Iran, who gained international notice with her beautiful duet with British singer Sarah Jane Morris on the celebrated 2004 album *Lullabies from the Axis of Evil*. Mahsa's soft face, long dark hair, and captivating eyes draw people toward her the moment they see her, and her almost-whisper when she speaks brings you even closer. But when she starts to sing, her rich, sad, trembling voice is commanding.

"It's not easy to perform in Iran today," Mahsa explained, given the restrictions on women singing solo, and on live performances by women more broadly. "We are forced to perform outside the country if we want to perform our material as it's supposed to be played." But Mahsa has been lucky; at least she can write new music and record it in Tehran despite the cultural clampdown by the Ahmadinejad government. "The problem isn't religion. Everything in Iran is in the end about politics; religion is just the excuse."

It's also about power—wielded by men over women—which frustrates her more than most any other dynamic. "On the face of it, it's hilarious, their policy of restricting people and telling them that you can only sing for women. But it's also humiliating." Ironically, the very thing that limits her opportunities to perform in Iran—being a woman with an exceptional voice—makes it easy for her to get invited to international festivals and collaborations with artists from Europe and the United States. It's far harder for most rock bands, the success of Tarantist and Hypernova notwithstanding.

One artist who should be getting lots of offers in and outside Iran is Mohsen Namjoo, one of the country's most respected younger musicians. Mohsen plays the light and airy setar, though he looks like a weathered rock star of at least forty-five—a kind of Iranian Keith Richards with better teeth and skin. In fact, Mohsen is in his early thirties, but he's been through enough pain, drugs, and suffering in the last few years to last a lifetime.

When we finally managed to arrange a joint performance, at the apartment of one of Tehran's leading gallery owners, I understood just how heavy Persian rock could be, even unplugged. Most of the artists I've met in Iran believe, as one metal musician put it, that "you can't make a career out of music in Iran unless you are willing to compromise." Mohsen clearly hasn't heard about that philosophy. He lives purely and only to play music, and couldn't care less about the latest trends in pop music or the most recent three political crises. His years studying in some of Iran's most prestigious conservatories have produced an improbably wild yet somehow controlled style of setar playing, with a voice that can change from growled whispers to howls to tearful falsettos in the space of a measure.

With his talent has come quite a bit of ego (as more than one musician who's worked with him warned me); the best strategy I could think of halfway through our first song together was to play a simple rhythm on the guitar, or setar when we switched instruments for a couple of songs, and let him do his thing. This was certainly what everyone at this party had come to hear (several brought camcorders or mp3 players to record the "show," which quickly made its way onto YouTube). As I quickly learned, Mohsen's thing includes blues progressions seemingly shorn from Robert Johnson and heavy-metal riffs drawn directly from Deep Purple and Black Sabbath, interlaced with the intricate melodies of the *segah* mode, which he has transformed into an Iranian all-around blues-rock mode that left me, and most of the small audience, trying to figure out whether he was playing an Iranicized version of Western rock or blues, or a Westernized version of traditional Iranian music.

Mohsen might be an ex-junkie whose prodigious talent is matched only by his outsized ego. But he seems to have figured out the best strategy to defeat the mullahs and the repressive Iranian state that keep going after other musicians: ignore them. Rather than take them on with political lyrics, just get everyone high on your infectious music. Tear at the legitimacy of the regime with each *koron* and each three-stringed power chord strummed—when necessary, with a paper clip bent over a broken nail—with violent intensity on your setar. Get the metalheads and the traditional artists to give you props and support you, move from party to party and, when possible, from concert to concert, with a ferociously joyful music that links together almost every style heard in Iran, from the Zoroastrian era to the arrival of hip-hop.

As Mohsen explained in his very broken English, he just "lets the music do the talking, and the music will set you free." It's a sentiment that more and more members of Iran's metal, rock, and hip-hop scenes are taking to heart. It's not an easy task—at almost the same moment I was flying out of Tehran, an Iranian American colleague of mine at UC Irvine, Ali Shakeri, was arrested at the airport, and languished for months in jail or under house arrest with several other Iranian Americans on charges of being CIA agents and "velvet revolutionaries." Yet only a few months later I was able to meet up with Farzad Golpayegani and his band in Istanbul, where we—three Iranians, a Brit, and an American—performed before 30,000 fans at the biggest (and perhaps the only) peace festival in the Muslim world. That's the way life goes in Iran today, and however disheartening it can be, no one I know would risk the status quo for the risky and dangerous business of another revolution ("Look what happened last time we had one!" was the universal response I received every time I broached the subject).

Everyone agrees that the struggle for Iran's soul will be long and hard, but if the activists, intellectuals, and artists I've met, religious and secular alike, can muster enough patience and strategic foresight, there's a good chance that they'll succeed in cracking open the public sphere a bit more each year. And soon enough, it will grow so wide that no one—be it Ahmadinejad, the *basij,* or the ayatollahs—can force it closed again.

PAKISTAN

Shotguns and Munaqqababes
Along the Arabian Sea

Maybe it was the thirteen-hour time difference. Maybe it was arriving at 6:00 a.m., after two nearly sleepless nights in coach, at an airport that had recently been attacked by terrorists, where—at least in the arrival lounge—it seemed that hardly anyone was speaking a language I could understand. Or the fact that from all the news reports, conversations with friends, and even the tension on the plane, it was clear that Pakistan was entering another one of those violent periods that have defined its short history.

Landing in Islamabad, I was literally on the opposite side of the Earth, as my five-year-old son, Alessandro, pointed out to me a few days before I left, when he traced the longitudinal line from California over the North Pole and down (roughly) to Pakistan. Even Iraq, a far more violent and depressing place today than Pakistan—as of early 2008—somehow felt more familiar to me. At least I could speak Arabic. Pakistan was definitely not in my cultural and historical comfort zone. Yet the Himalayas were only a couple of hours away; for all I knew, the Buddha had walked not too far from where I was standing. And, quite probably, so had Osama bin Laden.

I had come to Pakistan on the trail of a friend and kindred spirit, Salman Ahmed of the Pakistani supergroup Junoon. Salman was home in upstate New York, preparing for a stint as artist-in-residence at Queens College. My journey was to find out how and why Salman, and Junoon bandmates Ali Azmat (vocals) and American Brian O'Connell (bass), managed to do what few artists I've met in the Muslim world—or anywhere else for that matter—have done in quite a long time: create a powerful, truly groundbreaking new form of rock 'n' roll, and use their fame to offer a direct challenge to a corrupt and despotic political and economic system.

It depresses Salman deeply that Pakistan today is in even worse shape than when Junoon first made its musical stand against the system in the mid-1990s. Indeed, the country seems to be more frayed than at any time since the eastern half of the country split off to form Bangladesh, almost two generations ago. A generation before, in 1947, the establishment of Pakistan had been accompanied by great bloodshed between Indian Muslims and Hindus and one of the greatest population transfers in world history. It also saw the creation of a country out of four regions—Punjab, Sindh, Baluchistan, and the North-West Frontier Province (part of Kashmir is also under Pakistani control)—that had very little in common culturally and linguistically.

At the root of the push to create a separate Muslim state for the Muslims of India was the belief by the community's leaders that Muslims would never be more than second-class citizens in a Hindu-dominated state. Creating a "spiritually pure" (*pak*) Muslim country (*stan*) that could link together the various ethnic groups of northwestern and eastern India was considered the best answer to this problem by the majority of India's Muslim elite. Offering a cultural alternative to the materialism of the Western culture bequeathed to India was also an important consideration for Pakistan's founders.

The drive to create a unique culture also provided a political and spiritual foundation for contemporary Pakistani music. In fact, the ideology behind "Pakistan" was far more successful as a catalyst for developing Pakistani music than it was in uniting the country's disparate peoples into a coherent nation. A semifeudal economic system, ethnic discrimination, and rampant corruption led the Bengali province of East Pakistan to split off from the more powerful western half of the country and establish Bangladesh in 1971. Similar problems have continued to plague the country since then, whether under the dictatorships of Zia ul-Haq or Pervez Musharraf, or the more "democratic" regimes of Ali Bhutto, his daughter Benazir, and her rival Nawaz Sharif.

The Passion of Pakistani Rock

Pakistan's corrupt and violent rulers did produce one good thing, albeit inadvertently: Pakistani rock. Rock 'n' roll in its various forms has flourished in Pakistan despite official prohibitions against the music (whether through censoring albums or prohibiting concerts) from the 1970s through the early 1990s. Even today musicians, especially bands that play the harder styles of rock and metal, find it difficult to find forums in which to play. Hotels, university halls, a few public theaters, and army bases (which are supposed to be free of the conservative religious sentiment that is opposed to rock music) remain the only venues where most metal bands can perform.

Yet out of this difficult soil a large and vibrant music scene has grown. In a reversal of the standard practice in the United States or Europe, in Pakistan bands tend to record their own music in home studios, then follow up by recording inexpensive but, thanks to digital technology, professional-quality videos. These are sent to MTV Pakistan, The Musik, or upward of a dozen other music video channels. Based on viewer response, the video might make it into heavy rotation, at which point a record company will pay a flat fee for the rights to sell a band's album. This leads to more-frequent and bigger concerts and, if everything works out just right, tours across Pakistan, India, the Persian Gulf, and the UK. (It's worth noting that Western rockers have recently picked up on this idea. As Sheryl Crow explains, "It's an interesting time because you used to make a video for a million dollars with a great director. Now you spend $10,000, if that, with no hair and makeup, and do it completely guerrilla style.)"

⧫

Rock 'n' roll would never have taken root, at least in its present form, without Junoon. The band is everywhere, despite being more or less split up as of this writing. Junoon remains the god of Pakistani pop music. The band's name is spoken of by other rock musicians in Pakistan with the kind of reverence—and occasionally jealousy—that was once inspired by the Beatles and Rolling Stones.

Junoon created a style of music, known as "Sufi rock," which mixes hard-driving guitar riffs with traditional melodies. In Arabic, Persian, and Urdu, *junoon* means "passion" or "obsession." The name was chosen to reflect the band members' objective of using music to confront the repressive political, social, and economic realities of the Zia and Bhutto governments. "The band was a specific counter to the legacy of the dictatorship," Ali Azmat explained to me. "The first political statement that I made was to get a rock band together. I wanted to sing about the social disparity and violence in society and articulate those issues through music." In short, the members of Junoon saw themselves as "musical guerrillas," and in response the government did its best to stop the band, banning it for a time, following members, and tapping their phones.

Salman, the band's cofounder, was born in Pakistan, but he lived in upstate New York from the ages of eleven to eighteen, during which time he was lucky enough to see Led Zeppelin perform during its last U.S. tour, in 1977. When Jimmy Page came onstage through a haze of smoke, wearing a white satin dragon suit and playing a double-necked guitar, Salman knew his future: to take the power and dynamism of Zeppelin's music and blend it with the beauty and spiritual heights of the Qawwali and Sufi music of his homeland to produce a style of music that the world had never heard before.

Salman's teenage years were spent literally bleeding into his guitar (that's what happens when you practice up to a

dozen hours a day for months on end). And so it wasn't surprising that when his parents persuaded him to return to Pakistan to study medicine, he spent as much time jamming
and playing in talent shows as he did studying anatomy. "My
guitar became my stethoscope and music became my medicine," he says. It wasn't easy to heal the nation, however, given
the ban against rock albums and concerts. Making matters
worse, militants regularly destroyed the band's equipment at
gigs, and even threatened to shoot its members.

Despite the numerous obstacles, by the mid-1990s Junoon
was attracting 20,000 or more screaming fans to their shows,
the majority of them women. In the process, the band became
the first Pakistani group to win the MTV India awards for best
rock band, beating out Sting and Def Leppard. But Junoon
was always more than just a musical group. With fame came
a more urgent sense of mission, which saw them step—literally, in front of a throng of Pakistani and Indian media—over
the border between Pakistan and India to promote peace between the two countries. They also took on the nuclear arms
race, arguing that Pakistan should be pursuing "cultural fusion, not nuclear fusion."

Needless to say, a public challenge to Pakistan's nuclear
program was bound to cause problems at home. But whatever
backlash they endured was mild compared with the reaction
of the government to the band's 1997 hit "Ehtesab," which
chronicled the corruption of the democratically elected Bhutto
government (which had replaced the military regime of Zia
al-Huq after the latter's death in 1988). One of Bhutto's aides
called and asked Salman if he was looking to commit suicide
by doing such a song. His reply, as he recounted in a VH-1

documentary about the band, was the perfect synthesis of heavy metal and rebellious activism: "Fuck you, mother-fucker"—with two middle fingers added for emphasis. The risks Junoon was taking with its music and politics were clear.

❦

If there could be no Pakistani rock without Junoon, there would be no Junoon without Led Zeppelin and Salman Ahmed's hero, Jimmy Page. The influence is obvious when you listen to riffs on Junoon songs such as "Ghoom," "Meri Awaaz Suno," and "Saeein." All are innovative blends of hard-driving riffs, "secret" Jimmy Page tunings (although I'm not sure how he learned them, since Page hadn't revealed them when Salman recorded the songs), and Qawwali melodies Salman had learned as a student of the great Sufi singer Nus-rat Fateh Ali Khan.

The band's powerful, no-frills performances also resem-bled the classic Zeppelin shows of the early 1970s. Yet listen-ing to Junoon, what stands out, paradoxically, are not the hard-rock riffs. Instead there is a softness to Pakistani metal, and rock more broadly, that is quite unique. Not soft in the sense of lacking power, but soft in the sense in which a ta'i chi master speaks of softness as the key to deploying far more power than is possible when the body is rigid.

Most metal bands I've discussed in this book, even the Gnawa-inflected scales of "Marockan roll," stick close to the traditional foundations of metal in their focus on the down-beat (even at ridiculously high speeds) and riffs whose melodies stay within the melodic parameters of traditional European minor scales. Junoon and other Pakistani bands such as Karavan, Mizraab, and Aaroh are too deeply grounded in the more fluid and tonally flexible music of the subcontinent to be limited by these structures. They don't have the Iranian *koron* as a tonal or political inspiration, but they do have the complex scales of classical Indian music, which offer twenty-two intervals to choose from in constructing the *that* or *raga*—scale—of a particular song.

You can hear the deep subcontinental roots of the band in songs like one of Junoon's biggest hits, "Sayonee," which features a catchy acoustic guitar rhythm driven by a tabla groove and a funky bass line, over which Ali Azmat and Salman Ahmed alternate haunting Urdu vocals and a fiery rock guitar solo. Perhaps most famous is the song "Ghoom," in which Salman plays a Jimmy Page–style red Gibson double-necked guitar in an homage to Led Zeppelin's "The Rain Song," with the addition of a hard-edged riff at the bridge. Such eclecticism might make Junoon's metal credentials suspect to hardcore metalheads, but it's what gives Pakistan one of the most interesting music scenes in the world.

Metal Rules in the Abode of Islam

Until a month or so before I arrived, Pakistan's capital, Islamabad ("Abode of Peace") was considered a refuge for the country's westernized elite to work and play. Then terrorists struck one of the city's most luxurious hotels, followed a few months later by a siege of the famed Red Mosque, which left scores of militantly religious students and police dead.

Islamabad's wide and relatively clean boulevards and gridlike pattern, common to the newly established capitals of developing countries in the postwar era, were intended to symbolize the efficiency of modern Pakistan, as was the division of the city into different sectors and zones (commercial, educational, residential, industrial, and diplomatic). Poor people get around on small, beat-up motorcycles. Women have to ride sidesaddle behind their husbands; it isn't uncommon for them to fall off as the bikes make their way through the country's potholed streets, especially if the women are old or carrying young children. Most of the wealthier inhabitants of the residential, diplomatic, and "defense" zones—the gated communities in most of Pakistan's major cities—have drivers to ensure that their wives and children can move around Islamabad, or Pakistan's other major cities, in the relative safety of their SUVs (the drivers often double as shotgun-toting home guards at night).

A few of the more flamboyant residents apparently also travel around in dune buggies. At least that was what was parked next to the half-dozen soldiers guarding a party being thrown by the son of one of the country's wealthiest families. I had come to the party on the invitation of Arieb Azhar, the leader of an emerging generation of Sufi-rock singers who are grounded in Sufism as a spiritual practice and not merely as a source of lyrical and vocal inspiration. Arieb started out as a rock singer when the scene in Pakistan was in its infancy. The difficulty in getting gigs and making a career in the country prompted him to leave for Croatia, where he spent thirteen years, including the civil war and its aftermath, studying and working. "When I arrived I was a Marxist, and I sang revolutionary songs with a very harsh voice. Then I moved on to singing Irish and country music because that was what was popular at the time. Now I'm trying to lose all the harshness, trying to become more of a human being as a singer. That's where the Sufism comes in, because being a Sufi forces you to focus on your own humanity and that of everyone around you as the core of being a spiritual person."

The party took place in the backyard of the family's home, which was the largest on a pleasant, tree-lined block of elaborate villas in Islamabad's swank "F-8 Sector." The entire yard was tented, with hand-woven oriental carpets on the grass, and was ringed by spotless white couches and tables. There was a delicious, fully catered buffet and barbecue. For entertainment there was a stage with a professional lighting and sound system, upon which half a dozen young rock and metal bands performed their best Guns N' Roses impersonations along with Pakistani hits. A professional cameraman and photographer recorded the evening, which as far as we could tell was in celebration of little more than the wealth and fabulousness of the young host and his guests.

The partygoers were slightly younger versions of the glamorous Pakistanis who inhabit the country's film, television, and music video industries. Tall, thin, with fine features and skin tones light enough to make their subcontinental exoticism seem almost safely European, the guests ranged in age from seventeen to about twenty-four years old. All were dressed in the peculiarly Pakistani fashion style that combines Armani A/X chic and the neotraditional fashions of rock star turned preacher and fashion designer, Junaid Jamshed. The young men looked like their lives were comfortably and enviably laid out before them, with no bumps on the horizon. The women perfectly fit their image on TV: modern, secular, yet ultimately there to be the objects, and servants, of men's desires.

Alcohol was being consumed in quantity, although not openly. So were any number of illegal drugs. Most disturbingly for the half-dozen or so guards—their discomfort was clear—the young men and women were behaving toward each other in ways that, to say the least, were not traditionally acceptable. You could feel the sex in the air. But however un-Islamic the gathering, for the parents of these kids such parties are a convenient, "modern" way to ensure that their children wind up marrying socially and economically acceptable partners.

The guests either didn't notice or didn't care, but it was pretty clear to me that the heavily armed guards (AK-47s and shotguns) were not too happy with the behavior of their charges. The scowls on their faces made it perfectly clear what they thought of the kids they were protecting. I couldn't blame them, honestly, since the guests were treating them with a kind of condescension and even contempt that was frightening considering the firepower at the guards' disposal. Within the space of three minutes, Arieb and I each turned to his friend Tamur, a veteran of the metal scene, and half-joked that one day a guard was going to snap and mow down the next generation of Pakistan's leaders (with Benazir Bhutto then still safely in exile, we had forgotten that there was still quite a bit of unfinished business with the current generation of leaders).

Yet it was hard not to be amused at the earnestness with which the bands were playing covers of nineties metal anthems and Pakistani rock hits—it seems that every rich teenage boy in Islamabad wants to be Slash. It stopped being funny, however, when it was our turn to perform. There was a definite buzz about our hitting the stage, since Arieb's video had been in fairly heavy rotation on MTV Pakistan and The Musik. But once Arieb started to sing a rocked-out adaptation of a Sufi melody, the rugs and couches emptied as everyone headed for the buffet. Clearly the kids weren't in the mood for anything that smacked of religion, even if it was clothed in metal. To Arieb's credit, however, he brought most of the crowd back by the second song.

As soon as we finished playing, the guests moved inside to begin the "rave" segment of the evening's festivities. One especially antsy guard, dressed in a uniform that was half Gurkha and half colonial-era hotel doorman, brusquely directed the partyers inside by pointing his shotgun at them. It was clearly time for us to leave, and we headed to a much quieter musical gathering, this time of devotees of Sufi inspirational music, a few blocks away. Arieb picked up a guitar and was joined by a friend on harmonium. They spent the rest of the night sitting on a small platform in a nice middle-class living room lit by aromatic candles, belting out songs of praise to the Prophet, while about a dozen middle-aged men and women drowned themselves in Rumi and Stoli.

❦

A few kilometers away, in Islamabad's downtown, 6,000 male and female students from the Jamia Hafsa religious seminary gathered to burn—literally—CDs, video recorders, and even televisions worth tens of thousands of dollars as part of a conference on "the enforcement of *sharia* and glory of jihad." They also issued warnings to the owners of music shops to shut down their "un-Islamic" businesses within one month or be attacked, a worrisome development for the country's capital, normally considered one of the most liberal cities in the country. These threats were not to be taken lightly. Extremists have killed government ministers with impunity. They also have burned down "Western" (in fact, Pakistani-owned and -operated) fast-food restaurants and banks, and threatened the president of one of the country's main universities. And, at the end of 2007, gunned down Benazir Bhutto while she campaigned for Prime Minister after returning to Pakistan under a deal with Musharraf brokered for the Americans and Brits.

As the university president explained to me at a closed forum we both attended that was sponsored by the Council of Islamic Ideology: "A commission I was on wrote a report about education reform, and when a conservative mullah read a copy, he called me a traitor. That may not mean much in your country, but here if someone like him calls me a traitor, someone will shoot me on the street. And if I call him a traitor in return because of his corruption and obscurantism . . ."

"Someone will shoot you on the street?"

"Exactly. So we shelved the report and the status quo continues. That's the way it works here, how religion and politics mix to maintain the current power structure in place." That is, the extremists feed off the widespread anger at the country's Westernized, secular elite, which in turn uses the threat of the extremists to maintain a quasi–police state that ensures their continued dominance of the country's politics and economy.

※

Extremists might target fast-food restaurants, but most Pakistanis still eat in them if they can afford to. I also sought out the local Pizza Hut after a few days of spicy Pakistani food when I met with the director of one of Pakistan's oldest private hospitals. He had graciously arranged for a car to take me to Peshawar and the North-West Frontier Province the next morning, and because he was from the region and had close ties to the tribal areas, I would have no trouble traveling around the otherwise less than hospitable, and potentially dangerous, region.

As we shared a remarkably spicy "plain" cheese pizza, my dinner companion (who asked that his name not be used) summed up the basic problem facing Pakistan. Quite simply, he explained, Pakistan does not exist. There is, of course, a state, such as it is, and a flag, and until its disastrous performance in the 2007 World Cup in Jamaica, one of the top five cricket teams on earth (no matter where you go in Pakistan, in the middle of rice paddies or garbage dumps, you'll find young boys and old men playing cricket). But there is no cohesive Pakistani identity. Poverty, inequality, and corruption are so rampant that few people have faith in the future. And the situation is only getting worse, as he sees firsthand as the administrator of a major hospital.

※※※

Some Pakistanis blame themselves for the range of problems affecting their country. Others, both religious conservatives and more-secular leftists, blame the United States and the West more broadly. And their attacks can be vehement, as I experienced while being interviewed by Talat Hussayn, the country's best-known news host, who challenged me, "Isn't it true that the U.S. has been continuously at war for over a century, that it's invaded dozens of countries?" Displaying the cover of my last book, *Why They Don't Hate Us,* on his monitor, he asked, "Why shouldn't people hate you? Why shouldn't Pakistanis be angry at America for what you've done? Surely you're being naïve."

More nuanced and encouraging are the views of the graduate students at the International Islamic University, who are pursuing an innovative curriculum that is combining 1,000 years of Islamic learning with the latest developments in American and European scholarship. The group with whom I spent the most time were all PhD students in comparative religion. I was quite nervous when I was introduced to them as someone who'd lived in Israel and speaks Hebrew—in fact, my stomach sank a bit—especially as their long beards and traditional dress reminded me a lot more of the Taliban than of the graduate students with whom I normally spend time.

But as is so often the case, appearances are deceiving. They explained that they were all learning Hebrew, as well as biblical criticism (Old and New Testament) and contemporary approaches to religious studies, as part of their course work. They had little time or desire to engage in spirited critiques of the United States or the West; they were much more interested in discussing how to better integrate "Western" and Islamic methodologies for studying history and religion, and, more troubling, how to criticize the government "without disappearing" into the dark hole of the Pakistani prison system.

Founding a Scene

Most of the students with whom I met were not Junoon fans (at least not openly), but it was clear that many appreciated the risks the band took to force a national discussion on some of the country's most distressing social and political problems. It wasn't Junoon that started the rock scene in Pakistan, however. The seminal band was Vital Signs, founded in 1987 by Junaid Jamshed, who was joined by Salman Ahmed on guitars for a few years before Salman left to form Junoon.

Until the creation of Vital Signs, and for years after, rock music traveled across Pakistan the old-fashioned way, through sharing old rock magazines and pirated tapes, and through borrowing music from anyone who already had it. What was missing until Vital Signs arrived was a certifiable hit song. That was provided by the band's patriotic smash hit "Dil Dil Pakistan," which in 2003 was voted the third most popular song of all time on BBC World.

What made Vital Signs and Junoon so important to Pakistani culture was the nerve they struck among young people. Vital Signs's videos depicted young men with relatively long hair having fun, driving around, smoking cigarettes, and hanging out with girls in a nonthreatening and not overly sexualized way. A few years later Junoon would offer an even more direct, positive, and uplifting alternative to the dour, oppressive, and violent ultraconservative, Saudi-sponsored vision of Islam.

From Junoon's Sufi perspective, religion must function as music does in linking people together rather than tearing them apart. Of course, such a view of religion is not going to be received well by an authoritarian system that for decades has used religion to divide and rule. And so Junoon was accused by officials of "belittling the concept of the ideology of Pakistan" and disagreeing with "national opinion" just for suggesting that their Pakistani and Indian fans were more alike than their national differences would suggest.

When Salman started receiving death threats for daring to play a supposedly secular style of music, he decided to tackle the issue head-on with a documentary film, *The Rock Star and the Mullahs,* that trailed him as he traveled through Pakistan speaking with religious leaders. "Unless you confront these critics directly, there's always going to be a sense that music is *haram* [forbidden]." With little regard for his personal safety, Salman actually brought a guitar into conservative madrasas and mosques and sang verses from the Qur'an.

What convinced Salman that his position on music was right was not the response the viewers see on camera, which depicted the Taliban telling him he'd burn in hell for putting the Qur'an to music, regardless of the purity of his intentions. Rather it was what happened once the cameras were off: teachers and students asked him for his autograph and admitted that they knew the words to all his songs. One mullah even started to sing beautifully. "He was clearly afraid of losing his gig! The mullahs are just hungry for an audience. They want people to listen to them, not to the musicians. But music can bridge the gap between religion and the people; that's why it's the soundtrack to peace."

The Final Frontier Is Inside Us

Driving into Pakistan's North-West Frontier Province (NWFP), there is a sign on the road that welcomes you to "the land of hospitality." This is not what I expected to find on my way to Peshawar, gateway to the region of the country controlled by the Taliban and al-Qa'eda, where Osama bin Laden is said to be hiding.

In the United States, and even in Pakistan, the NWFP is known almost exclusively as a haven for terrorists, ultra-traditionalists, and drug and arms smugglers. No doubt it has many of those, but it also has the ancient valley of Swat, known as the "Switzerland of Pakistan" (at least until the Taliban overran it in the fall of 2007) because of its famous ski resorts. The region is also home to some of the largest and most beautiful Buddhist statues in the world. And until Saudi-style extremism invaded the region—courtesy of the Pakistani intelligence agency, the ISI, which during the Afghan war turned the NWFP into the staging area for *mujahidin* activities in neighboring Afghanistan—the region was popular with adventurous Americans, from Texan gun enthusiasts, who flocked to the famed gunsmiths of Peshawar, to Robert De Niro, whose visit to the Khyber Pass is memorialized by photos of him eating in local restaurants.

When you arrive in Peshawar, road signs point to the "Imaginarium Institute for American Studies." Yet the U.S. Consulate's American Club changed its name for security reasons. The gates leading into the tribal areas warn, NO FOREIGNERS ALLOWED, yet Peshawar is awash in foreign money and people, its "smugglers' bazaar" awash equally in weapons, drugs, pornography, and cheap Chinese electronics. The U.S. Central Intelligence Agency, USAID, European NGOs, the Taliban—all have staked a claim to a city that has been at the crossroads of empire since Alexander the Great crossed the nearby Khyber Pass.

So has Sajid & Zeeshan, Pakistan's best rock duo, whose improbably beautiful album *One Light Year at Snail Speed*, filled with songs driven by acoustic guitars and keyboards, was recorded almost entirely in the home studio of the band's keyboard player, Zeeshan Parwez, using old synthesizers and guitars bought for a song at the smugglers' bazaar. The duo's music, which features lush vocals that flow over techno and house beats, acoustic guitars, and vintage synth sounds, symbolizes the contradictions of living on the frontier of Pakistani society and identity.

The day I arrived, an article about the band appeared on the front page of *Dawn,* the country's most important English-language newspaper: "Peshawar is not a place known for being very music-savvy, and the idea of a band coming from there was surprising for many music enthusiasts." In fact, as the duo explained to me, Peshawarians are called "walnuts" by other Pakistanis because they are supposedly "hardheaded or stupid. When we tour in other Pakistani cities, people actually ask us if we live in mud huts."

Such ignorance stems from the fact that so few Pakistanis from outside the region go to Peshawar these days, since the city and the surrounding tribal areas have become identified with the Taliban and reckless violence. Yet the rock scene there is almost two decades old. Sajid Ghafoor, the duo's singer and guitarist, was one of its founders, and from the start has been determined to show Pakistanis that Peshawar has a vibrant, creative cultural scene at the forefront of Pakistani society.

Sajid looks like someone straight out of the 1970s. His straight, longish dirty brown hair, pleasant face, and thin build remind me of Jackson Browne, a perception that was reinforced by his singing style, which is heavily influenced by 1970s California acoustic rock, Neil Young, and, more recently, Counting Crows. When he's not playing guitar, Sajid is an international and environmental law professor at Peshawar

University, with degrees from Hull University in the UK and the University of Oslo. Of the two professions, however, his haunting voice and catchy songs are what define him.

If Sajid writes most of the band's songs, Zeeshan, who's shorter, heavier, and a bit less stylish, is the duo's foundation. An MBA and a strong talent for computer technology allowed him to build a professional music and video production studio out of the musical detritus available at the smugglers' bazaar. When he's not recording albums, Zeeshan is shooting videos for many of Pakistan's biggest bands, and hosting the MTV Pakistan show *On the Fringe*.

Neither Sajid nor Zeeshan would leave Peshawar, which they regard as a refuge from the crass materialism and lack of social solidarity that pervade the country. As Sajid explained, "Peshawar might be light-years behind other cities, yet we don't deviate from our traditions and culture. People still look out for each other. Even if we party, we respect tradition."

Not that either of them have the chance to party that much. It's nearly impossible to perform in Peshawar since the last election put the ultraconservative Muttahida Majlis-e-Amal Party in power, and the government turned control of the NWFP over to local leaders in the vain hope that in return they'd curtail Taliban violence. "The only places one can play since then is at nearby army camps, or at the American Consulate's American Club," which in good colonial fashion doesn't allow Pakistanis inside unless they're working there. Alternatively, there are private parties, of a kind more discreet than the one I attended in Islamabad, in the burgeoning elite neighborhoods and suburbs of Peshawar. But it's hard to make a career of such infrequent gigs.

Sajid has deep roots in Peshawar (over lunch at Peshawar's best restaurant, Shiraz, Zeeshan bragged that his partner is a descendant of Genghis Khan, as Sajid smiled sheepishly), but his musical tastes range far more broadly than the traditional music of the NWFP. "One record shop here got the best music before shops in the big cities. And the coolest was metal. We grew up on metal. Megadeth, Metallica, Rush, Rage Against the Machine, and of course Floyd and Zeppelin; the sound just related to our feelings of aggression living in a dictatorship, and helped us get out the anger in a healthy way."

"There used to be so much culture here, especially music," Zeeshan lamented. "Junoon used to play here. We could play for crowds of thousands. But once Musharraf handed over control of the NWFP to the religious parties, that all changed." Zeeshan explained this as we headed toward the tribal areas. Neither of them was prepared to make a trip of it, and the armed guards standing next to the sign reading NO FOREIGN-ERS ALLOWED led me to agree, although I was well aware that if I entered under the "protection" of someone from the region, I would be all but untouchable by local custom.

But Sajid and Zeeshan also know that this tradition is under threat, and they are despondent about the growing extremism of Pakistani Islam and its intersection with government corruption—a combination that led the duo to record its first Pashto-language song, "Lambay," soon after my visit, for which we collaborated on a heavy-metal version of the song for the compilation album being released by EMI simultaneously with the publication of this book. Echoing the description by Moe Hamzeh of Lebanon's increasing religious-secular divide, Sajid said, "When I was in school I had religious friends. We respected them and they respected us. My brother is one of the most famous guitarists and producers in Pakistan, but prays five times a day. What you have to understand is that the Islamists who are against music are against it not because a fatwa has told them it's wrong, but because music opens minds and allows people to express themselves. They use Islam to stop others for political or economic reasons. But that's not Islam."

※※※

With a corrupt and authoritarian regime on one side, and the Taliban literally a few villages away, there's not that much space for Sajid and Zeeshan to stake out the kind of directly political positions that made Junoon famous a decade ago. Instead, they use their work to educate people and get them to question authority. Perhaps the most political song Sajid & Zeeshan has written is "Free Style Dive." Zeeshan's animated video of the song depicts a husband, whose wife has left him because he worked in a fast-food restaurant, fantasizing about robbing a bank. The clip shows him shooting several people before being arrested, at which point it becomes clear that he's imagining the scene, because it rewinds to his putting on his uniform and heading out to another dreary day. After clocking out at the end of his shift, the man spends the evening sitting on a bench at Khyber Park, staring despondently at the Pass. We drove by the park soon after I had watched the video. It has a spectacular view. But a bit outside the "frame" (of the scene in front of us, and of its video representation) are the luxury villas of the city's wealthy smugglers and the makeshift tents of Afghan refugees who've settled outside their gates. Between smugglers, refugees, Taliban, and corrupt government officials, the seeming futility of trying to transform Pakistan was hard to let go of.

Finding Pakistan's Most Globalized Music in Its Imperial Capital

Soon after I first met Zeeshan, he told me about an incredible guitarist he'd worked with in Lahore, Mekaal Hassan, who played heavy metal and progressive jazz with equal fire and precision. Before I could even say that I'd like to meet him, Zeeshan dialed his number on his mobile and handed me the phone. Luckily, Mekaal was in town for the next few days, so we agreed to get together once I arrived in Lahore. "Enjoy the drive," he exclaimed before hanging up. I wasn't sure whether that was meant truthfully or as a veiled warning, but Zeeshan explained that the first part of the drive passes through some of the most beautiful valleys in the country, which turned out to be true, especially the Kalar Kahar valley.

Lahore, however, is one of the more intense cities I've ever been to, a teeming city of nearly 10 million, and the cultural heart of Pakistan. The streets overflow with people, cars, and rickshaws and donkeys and the occasional truck that has been whittled away to little more than an engine, a frame, and four tires, yet still manages to navigate through the unmanageable traffic.

Peshawar and the surrounding tribal areas are often described as lawless and chaotic, but they are the epitome of order compared with the chaos and extremes of wealth and poverty that coexist in Lahore. The city feels like a crumbling former imperial capital, except that Lahore had already faded from glory before the British arrived almost two centuries ago.

Certainly the potent mix of poverty and spirituality shaped the music that came out of Lahore, including, most famously, Junoon. "My environment growing up in Lahore was a mix of poverty, violence, and religious extremism," Salman explained. "Because of this situation, the songs I wrote naturally yearned to express freedom, love, and hope." Not everyone responds to poverty and violence with love and hope, however, as the Taliban's growing power demonstrates. But it's undeniable that Junoon inspired many Pakistanis to look to the best of their culture and religion as the way to climb out of difficult circumstances.

I met one of the Junoon-inspired young Pakistanis the evening I arrived in Lahore. Ali Roooh is a young singer with a chic yet ruffian look, and a husky, versatile voice. Yet he's not a typical musician. Ali completed an MBA and worked as a customer-service specialist for multinationals like Shell and Citibank before quitting his job to focus on recording his first album and videos.

"We have no human development here. You can work for decades and not advance a centimeter in your life. And what happens when you can't get ahead no matter how hard you try? You give up and join al-Qa'eda." Ali, who comes from a respected religious family, shares Salman Ahmed's Sufi roots, and like him, he feels strongly that music is the best way to educate and motivate people to demand a better future. "But you have to find the right formula to reach people," Ali explained, as we listened to some of his new songs in the control room of Mekaal Hassan's Digital Fidelity Studios. Mekaal, who was producing Ali's new album, has worked with Junoon and almost every other major rock group in Pakistan. With a degree from the Berklee College of Music in Boston and years of recording and touring under his belt, Mekaal is recognized as one of the two or three best guitarists in Pakistan.

As we spoke, Mekaal put up a rough mix of Ali's newest song, "Mehfilay" (*mehfil* means any group of people gathered together for a single purpose, like playing music, having fun, or engaging in criminal activity). The song takes on the corruption of his society today in the same way Junoon's "Ehtesab" did a decade ago. Ali was taking a big risk, coming out with a song that strongly criticized the government. But growing up with a single mother who obtained three master's degrees and rose to the senior ranks of Pakistan's Atomic Energy Commission have made him quite determined to do his music his way, even after his mother disowned him for the unforgivable sin of quitting his high-paying job to pursue his musical dreams.

Mekaal has been far luckier getting support from his family for his music. He was a guitar prodigy, which is not surprising since his father, Masood, helped bring jazz to Pakistan in the 1950s after falling in love with it during a stint with the U.S. Army in Germany. As a child, Mekaal went to sleep listening to Miles Davis, Duke Ellington, Count Basie, Ella Fitzgerald, and Sarah Vaughn, among others.

Mekaal's jazz-infused upbringing gave him the perfect fulcrum on which to balance his other two loves, heavy metal and Qawwali music. The three have been blended in an inspiringly innovative way in his latest project, the Mekaal Hassan Band. While his guitar playing ensured the group an early taste of notoriety, what makes the band truly special is the unique combination of jazz, hard rock, and traditional Pakistani melodies, courtesy of the band's nay (flute) player, Mohd Ahsan Papu, who for years performed with Nusrat Fateh Ali Khan. Their vocalist, Javed Bashir, is considered by many to be one of the few singers who can lay claim to being Nusrat's heir.

As I stood in the studio listening to the band rehearse, the bond among the musicians was infectious. Mekaal's hyper-distorted sound was somehow balanced by Papu's flute, while Bashir's vocals soared up and down in the trademark Qawwali style made famous by Nusrat. Mekaal knows how good he and his band are, and he doesn't suffer fools kindly. His long curly hair and constant smile mask a shrewd businessman and musical entrepreneur. "I could have stayed in the U.S. and made a career there," he explained as his father nodded in agreement. "But I came back to use music to show that Pakistan isn't what we imagine it to be."

As I recounted my time in the NWFP, father and son smiled. "The thing is, things are a lot deeper here than they seem," Mekaal offered. "That's why I'm not as pessimistic as other people are about our future. The problem is that we're educating young people to see 50 Cent and think that he's the West. We've managed to get all the bad values of the West without any of the good ones, which makes it pretty hard to bring the two cultures into harmony."

"Mark, you've seen what Lahore is like," Ali said, picking up on the same theme. "Traditionally, Lahore was a city where everyone helped everyone else. But today everyone—including the Islamists, and don't let them tell you otherwise—wants to be Western, so they go after the money, even if it means ripping off people. I'm modern, but I'm not Western. I'm Eastern because I still believe in honesty and respect."

Consciously or not, Ali was channeling the utopian vision

of a fully modern yet fully Eastern man made famous by the great Indian Muslim poet Allama Iqbal almost a century ago. Iqbal is credited by most Pakistanis with being one of the fathers of the nation. Not surprisingly, his words were first set to hard rock by Junoon, a band that Ali worships with the kind of reverence one usually sees in the most devout Zeppelin or Dead heads. But Ali cherishes Iqbal even more, as became clear the next day when the two of us drove around Lahore searching for a good CD store (many shops were closed because of threats from firebrand preachers).

As we drove through the impossibly narrow alleys of Lahore's old bazaar, trying to find a store that would have a good collection of local CDs, I mentioned that I was anxious to see the famed Badshahi mosque, the largest mosque in the Mughal Empire. Ali smiled at my request; I realized why when we entered the mosque complex and came upon Iqbal's tomb, in front of which Ali stood and prayed silently for at least two minutes. When he was done paying his respects, Ali turned around and motioned to the dome of the massive Sikh temple standing right behind the minaret of the mosque. "Look at that. Sikhs and Muslims prayed right next to each other and it made total sense. We all worship the same God. You can't even imagine such a geography today."

Iqbal's poetry beautifully yet trenchantly explored the realities of life in early-twentieth-century British-ruled India. He spared neither Muslims nor the British for the difficulties his people faced. Junoon endeared itself to Pakistanis by adapting Iqbal's words (perhaps most famously his poem "Saqi-nama") to their music. For his part, Ali felt that the words to another poem by Iqbal, "Shikwa," which he planned to record, were even more appropriate today: "You reserve your favors for men of other shades, / While you hurl your bolts on the Muslim race. / The tragedy is while kafirs [infidels] are with houris [maidens] actually blest, / On vague hopes of houris in heaven the Muslim race is made to rest!"

It's not surprising that such sentiments would find a home in Pakistan's small but powerful extreme-metal scene. Ali Reza, guitarist of the group Black Warrant, explained it succinctly when Ali Roooh and I met him at a KFC not far from Mekaal's studio (it was guarded, like most "Western" restaurants, by a shotgun-wielding security man). For Ali, this kind of exasperation at the seeming inability of Pakistanis to grasp hold of the future fueled his music. In Black Warrant's most powerful song, "Corroded Peace," Ali gives voice to a Pakistan on the verge of imploding. "Bomb those who want freedom / Kill those who say 'no' / Love the silence and solace after everyone is dead." Such depressing lyrics are the standard fare of extreme metal, but when you sing them long enough without seeing any change in your society for the better, it's hard not to burn out, which is why Ali is leaving Pakistan for a freer future in Australia.

Pepsi, Munaqqababes, and Metalheads on the Arabian Sea

For most bands in Morocco or Egypt, getting a video on MTV is a dream; here it's a necessity. "I mean, all the guys have videos on TV," explained Layla al-Zubaidi, who'd met up with Mekaal, Ali, and me in Lahore, where she was organizing yet another conference, this one on women and NGO activism. "Imagine that in Lebanon or Morocco. You can really feel the Indian influence here with the videos and commercialism of the scene. And I'm not sure in the end if, as in Lebanon or America, the videos aren't going to take over the music, which will really be a shame."

The commercialism of the Pakistani music scene is in fact more evident in Karachi, the original capital of Pakistan, and its largest city (at more than 20 million people, it is officially the second largest city in the world). So are the extremes of wealth and poverty, secularism and conservatism that increasingly divide Pakistani society. As I moved through the first-class cabin to my coach seat on the flight from Lahore to Karachi, I walked past four women, all of them in complete purdah, covered from head to toe in black, including gloves. Even their eyes were covered with large, 1970s-era sunglasses. Each woman had a security tag hanging from her veil; they had been inspected and tagged like carry-on luggage.

An hour later I saw them outside the airport in Karachi, and the paradox of their position was clear. A swirling wind blew up their abayas, revealing their clothes underneath. All were wearing expensive designer pantsuits, which matched their expensive handbags and luggage. A brand-new Land Rover came to fetch them. The tone of their "Urdish" (Urdu mixed with English) conversations on their sleek cell phones confirmed their status as among Pakistan's young and rich elite—the religious counterparts of the partyers Arieb and I had performed for in Islamabad the week before. They were "munaqqababes" (a woman who wears the niqab is called a *munaqqaba*), equivalent to the young and fashionable muhajababes of Cairo or Beirut.

༄

"Don't take a cab in Karachi or you'll be Daniel Pearled," the bass player for the Karachi-based band Mizraab warned me.

Luckily I was the guest of Amin Hashwami, a scion of one of Pakistan's wealthiest families, who controls a number of industries: hotels, resorts, tourism, welfare, information technology, oil and gas, minerals, pharmaceuticals, real estate, and investments. He had sent a car.

Although he could spend his time either building his family's empire or living it up with his peers, Amin is more interested in running his new chain of coffee bars, called Coffee Café, where he sponsors jam sessions for Karachi's best young rock musicians. Amin is a good friend of Salman Ahmed. He regularly lectures in the United States and is a founder of an international group of young Arab, Muslim, and Israeli businesspeople who meet to discuss pragmatic ways of engaging in mutual recognition and conflict resolution, and he helped set up most of my interviews.

Karachi is home to three bands that together define the past, present, and future of metal in Pakistan: Karavan, Aaroh, and Mizraab. Karavan is the godfather of Pakistani metal. The band was established in 1997, but founder and lead guitarist Assad Ahmed has been on the scene since he played guitar with Vital Signs back in the late 1980s. Considered one of Pakistan's "supergroups" alongside Vital Signs and Junoon, Karavan is one of the few Pakistani bands to sell over a million records, based purely on legally purchased (rather than pirated) copies. At one point the band was pulling in so much money, Assad explained, that he thought little of spending $25,000 to charter a plane from London to New York for a weekend of partying with his girlfriend and fifteen of her closest friends. But these days the band members are more into saving for retirement than spending their hard-earned money on the usual rock-star frivolities (for their upcoming album, the band decided to use art students for the video, both to save on production costs and promote young talent).

Like most Pakistani rock and metal bands, Karavan's music is, even at its hardest, more grooving than headbanging. Assad's influences are more Ace Frehley, Jimmy Page, Ritchie Blackmore, and Jeff Beck than the great sitar or sarod masters of his country. Yet his sharp riffs sound far different over the band's languid, if clearly heavy-metal, grooves than they would over more-traditional metal tracks. "That's for sure," said Assad. "Just look at the success of our unplugged album, which has already been downloaded over 200,000 times even though it hasn't been officially released yet."

After spending a decade playing closer to the fluff end of Pakistani pop, Assad worked hard to give Karavan as much substance as possible, in both the band's lyrics and music. Some songs, like "Gardish" (one of their biggest hits from the album of the same name), mix hard-driving riffs with lyrics that tackle the lack of equilibrium in Pakistani society and the dangers facing a culture which seems to be in constant motion, but doesn't seem to be getting anywhere. On the other end of the spectrum is the balladlike, arpeggio-driven "Yeh zindagi hai," which describes the campus violence in Karachi during the late 1980s and early 1990s, when thousands of students were killed or disappeared during clashes between secular and religious groups. At a time when violence is again erupting across Pakistan, the song's admonition to Pakistanis to "break down the walls of hatred and come together as one" is especially relevant.

However important the message of "Yeh zindagi hai" and other consciousness-raising Pakistani rock songs, the reality is that at least half the target audience for the song—the militant students willing to use violence to enforce their view of Islam on their classmates—is unlikely ever to hear it. And unless, as Salman Ahmed has done, you're willing to take your guitar and start traveling to madrasas around Karachi and Lahore, it's hard to imagine how Karavan's brand of progressive metal and lyrics will get that audience to change their intolerant position toward the rest of Pakistani society. This doesn't diminish the power of the group's music, but it does highlight the fact that even the most powerful music has a hard time moving beyond the larger social networks and relations in which it is embedded.

๛

If Karavan is the gold standard of Pakistani hard rock, two younger Karachi-based bands are producing some of the most innovative and popular hard rock today: Aaroh and Mizraab. The name Aaroh refers to the ascending part of a scale in classical Indian/Pakistani classical music, and in fact lead singer Farooq Ahmed trained extensively in that style as a child. He used that knowledge for the vocal and melodic foundation of Aaroh.

Aaroh first hit the big time when it won the Pepsi-sponsored Battle of the Bands in 2002 (they came in first out of a field of 171 bands). The Pepsi Battle has in fact launched many of the top rock bands in Pakistan of the last decade, and its importance in the Pakistani music industry reflects the disproportionate importance of major corporations—both foreign and domestic—in Pakistani popular culture.

The battle for signing the best young bands has been likened to a "battle of the brands" between giants like Pepsi, who signed up Vital Signs soon after their hit "Dil Dil Pakistan," and Coke, which became Junoon's main corporate sponsor after the band hit it big in 1996. Both cola companies had the same goal of building brand awareness among their young customers through music, following the practice perfected in the United States over the last two generations of using the allure and mystique of music to sell otherwise uninteresting products.

Because Pakistani record companies don't as a rule nurture new music, such sponsorship deals help support artists on tour, pay for video production, and ensure that videos are played regularly on the major music channels (in fact, most good videos are sponsored by brands, not record labels). Even successful bands need good sponsors because CD piracy greatly limits their income from record sales. "The money from sponsorships is crucial to our survival," one musician told me. The problem, at least according to respected rock journalist Nadeem Paracha, is that the power of Pepsi and other Pakistani companies to shape popular music is starting to resemble Rotana's, with equally negative results. In the end, he argues, "There is hardly any difference, really, between a cynical corporate exec and a foaming fat mullah." Of course, corporate execs don't issue fatwas or declare jihad, but neither do the vast majority of religious figures. From Farooq's perspective, in Pakistan today both are part of the same system of corruption, intolerance, and oppression. Both stifle creativity, and both stop music from doing what it does best: challenge society's conservative mores and push it forward toward more openness and tolerance.

Aaroh learned about the power of relying on corporate sponsors the hard way. Band members claim that Pepsi never came through with the money the band was awarded for winning the Battle of the Bands. This left Aaroh in legal and musical limbo until its contract expired, during which time several members of the band left in search of better prospects. Luckily the band's two most important members, Farooq and bass player Khalid Khan, remained. Freed of the need to write specifically for Pepsi and its favored demographic, the reformed band began to produce its own music. Since that time, Aaroh has become one of the best songwriting hard-rock bands on the subcontinent, with powerful yet catchy riffs, funky drum and bass grooves, and vocally expansive melodies that give Aaroh a sound that few rock or metal bands can match, in or outside of Pakistan.

The members of Aaroh, like Karavan, enjoy being rock stars. You can see it in the way they walk around, and in the care they put into presenting themselves to the public, including the rock-star-style clothes they wear even when just going about town. But for sheer musicianship and drive, perhaps the most important guitarist in Karachi is Faraz Anwar, founder of the band Mizraab. "We don't live in the fancy part of town," Mizraab's bass player, Rahail Siddiqui, said mockingly, when we first met at Amin's Coffee Café. Faraz's house was a half hour away, near the airport, in a decidedly working-class part of town.

Now in his thirties, Faraz looks like a teenager who doesn't get out in the sun much. That's because he spends most of his time in his small studio working on new material (like Prince—and Mekaal Hassan—Faraz plays all the instruments on his record, and acts as his own engineer and producer). "I basically taught myself how to play guitar," he said. "Mostly through cassette tapes, and then videotapes of my favorite guitarists that I ordered out of guitar magazines."

Those tapes, plus an eight-to-sixteen-hours per day practice regimen, have served Faraz well. He is known in musicians' circles as one of the premier guitarists in the country. His first album, *An Abstract Point of View*, was released by Gnarly Geezer, the boutique record label of his hero, the British progressive jazz virtuoso Allan Holdsworth, who's known to go out of his way to find the best young talent to expose to his quirky but devoted following. Faraz has done more than any other artist to bring progressive jazz-rock to Pakistan, wrapping it in Pakistani melodies and sheathing it in heavy-metal riffs and drums. The eclectic style has yielded several hits, the most popular among them being the song "Ujalon Main," which features a catchy chorus and a jazz-rock solo that demonstrates his unique style, placing him in the virtuoso company of Mekaal Hassan and Assad Ahmed.

It's not just Faraz's fanatical technique and dedication that separate him from most other musicians in Pakistan's rock and metal scene. He's also deeply religious. "He prays five times a day," Rahail explained (even many religious Muslims don't pray the required five times per day). Faraz's lack of rock-'n'-roll narcissism, the absence of themes involving sex in his music (unlike Aaroh's videos, none of Mizraab's feature beautiful women in sultry poses), and his religious and working-class roots, all offer Mizraab the chance to reach out to precisely the section of the Pakistani population—young, working-class, and religious, but not under the spell of militant ideologies—who are crucial to uniting the economic, social, and political factions that have divided Pakistan.

❦

Junaid Jamshed, the founder of Vital Signs, is perhaps the biggest-selling artist in Pakistani history. But these days it's not music that keeps his spirits high. Instead, it's his faith. If Junoon was the Led Zeppelin of Pakistan, Junaid's good looks, charismatic personality, and powerful voice made Vital Signs the country's Beatles. But beneath the fabulous life of a mega-celebrity, something wasn't right. As he recounts it, "It was ten years ago, around 1997, and I was at the peak of my career, almost an icon in my country. I had everything at my feet, but I was unhappy and discontented. Then I met an old school friend, Jhani, who had returned to his faith. He was a very successful businessman, yet he led a peaceful and uncomplicated life, with time for friends, family, and charity.

"Jhani never spoke to me about Islam or any ideology; he didn't preach. But as I spent time with him I began to think that maybe this way of life could give me spiritual material for my albums—new directions—as far as music was concerned. Then I realized the music I had been doing up till then was often without substance. Everyone was doing it. People took from me, just as I had taken from Sting, Genesis, Deep Purple, or Madonna, grabbing elements from here and there, sugar-coating them, and putting the result in front of an audience as if it was Junaid. So I started sitting with him and going to the mosque. You know, all the things about gun-running and terrorism, that the West and even many in Pakistan relate to mosques and Islam, they had nothing to do with what I was seeing."

Junaid's discussion of his slow return to faith is quite interesting because it has opened him to other faiths in a way that most "born-again" Muslims—like their Christian or

Jewish counterparts—have not been. "That's true. For the first time I began to respect Hindus, Christians, Jews, and other religions because I realized that everyone is created by the Almighty. Everyone deserves respect because we're all part of a global family. That helped me musically too, because with a spiritual background I radiated different emotions toward people. My motivation was no longer Jack-and-Jill songs, but rather the predicament of the whole world. I also learned that if we all want to live happily, we need to give more and expect little in return. The Qur'an is all about this, and other prophets also had the same message."

Sadly for most Vital Signs fans, one of the things Junaid decided to stop giving was his music. In talking with many other of Pakistan's most well-known artists who have known Junaid since the old days, it seems that like Cat Stevens, he left the music business because the rock-'n'-roll life was taking a dangerous toll on him. If true, it can help explain why, when he openly embraced his religion, he decided that all music besides religiously inspired vocals and drum is *haram*. Such a view follows the logic behind the prohibition against alcohol in Islam: the potential for abuse outweighs whatever good it can do. (Junaid's renunciation is not unequivocal, however; he performed "Dil Dil Pakistan" to celebrate the twentieth anniversary of its release. "I felt strange, but the song is like my child, it's so beloved by people, so I had to do it.")

Naturally, Salman Ahmed, who is an old friend from their days together in Vital Signs, has had many arguments with Junaid about his belief in the prohibition of music. "I know what Salman says, but the fact is that the Prophet forbade us to use other instruments besides the voice to create music. You can debate it, but that's the way it is. And even with the music, all those great bands, the Doors, the Beatles, and the rest, all wanted to be against the establishment. But they didn't have anywhere to take people once they led them away—there was never really an 'other side' to break *into*, rather than just out of. As for me, I still sing, but now I record *naat*s [traditional Pakistani songs in praise of the Prophet, with just vocals accompanied by a traditional drum], which are much purer. The last album I did just won the award for the best-selling album in Pakistan last year, and I'm doing *naat*s in English now, which are selling all over the world."

At the same time, however, Junaid's spiritual awakening hasn't led him to turn away from or criticize his old friends in the rock and pop world. "Look, if I just tell society, 'Don't do this!' they will be flabbergasted. 'What the hell is this guy talking about?' 'Who is he, a musician, to tell me music is *haram*?' etcetera. You must give them a better alternative. If I don't have a better alternative, I shouldn't tell them to stop or leave something."

As we spoke, Junaid was getting ready to go out on one of his frequent *da'wa*, or conversation tours, around Pakistan, in which he travels around preaching his views of Islam to as many people as possible. These frequent trips have brought him close to the grassroots of Pakistani society. "Yes, there's a lot of pain, suffering, and poverty, but I'll tell you something, I'm optimistic. The other people you mention aren't optimistic because they don't have the answer. I do, and the answer is God. We just need to return to Him, and be willing to listen to others, and talk, and the rest will follow. And until then, Pakistan, the U.S., the whole world, will be disintegrating and disgruntled. It's that simple."

Junaid has managed to cross the cultural divide while

keeping his respect for the world he left behind. But the dialogue he advocates is increasingly difficult to have in Pakistan, just as it is in Lebanon and most of the other countries of the MENA. Pakistanis from the country's artistic, religious, and journalistic elites have all complained to me that the lack of communication, and the loss of young people to extremism that it encourages—extreme consumerism as much as extreme religion—"is killing the country."

I asked Junaid why, since he is so involved in the plight of his people, he hasn't become more explicitly political. Echoing the view of Orphaned Land that if you preach too hard, people will refuse to listen, he explained that "I'm an artist at the end of the day, and I have to think like one. If you want to tell people something this difficult you have to sugar-coat it."

Although he didn't participate in it, one example of sugar-coated politics is the 2006 song (and foundation of the same name) "Yeh Hum Naheen," which means "This Is Not Us." The official English title is "Say No to Terrorism." The song features about a dozen of the biggest pop artists in Pakistan, and sounds like an American-style acoustic guitar–driven pop song, except it's sung in Urdu, with a background track of Qawwali vocal improvisations.

"Yeh Hum Naheen" was written to persuade young Pakistanis that the violent and intolerant Islam they are being fed by so many religious quarters is both wrong and doesn't represent the true Islam of Pakistan. The lyrics include lines such as "These stamps of death on our forehead are the signs of others" and "The stories being spread in our name are lies." But while the song reached number one on MTV and The Musik, its Western sound and bevy of secular pop stars seems geared more to the young ravers in Islamabad than to their much poorer and more-militant peers in the madrasas. It's hard to imagine the song encouraging the much-needed dialogue about both terrorism and the forces that nourish it, even if Junaid Jamshed sang the chorus.

At heart, according to one senior government-appointed religious figure whom I know, the problem is that Pakistan is divided by vested interests that are beyond the reach of any conceivable medicine to heal, no matter how much sugar is added. At best, if enough money is thrown into the medicine chest, one could hope to produce a strange simulacrum of Islamic and Western society, such as have evolved in Dubai or Doha, where huge amounts of wealth and an invisible foreign underclass allow a few lucky Arabs to live the "liberal" Muslim dream next door to their expatriate Texan and British neighbors.

Indeed, if you walk through the airports in Lahore and Karachi, you'll find advertisements for Emaar Pakistan's latest luxury development, Crescent Bay, along Pakistan's Arabian Sea coast. It's a lovely-looking development, with happy-looking families living in homes that could easily be in Dubai, or Minnesota for that matter. But only a few Pakistanis will be lucky enough to live there—or even work there as the guards, cooks, gardeners, and drivers that make the lives of Pakistan's elite livable. As I walked past the munaqqababes with their tags on their veils, something Ali Roooh said to me as we drove through one of Lahore's poor and overcrowded markets rang inside my head: "Mark, Pakistan is doomed unless we can return to our traditions of taking care of each other."

❧❀❧

A few months later, as I sat at home watching on television the assassination attempt of Benazir Bhutto, followed by

Pervez Musharraf's declaration of a state of emergency, I contacted many of my friends in Islamabad, Peshawar, Lahore, and Karachi, and asked if they had any plans to join the pro-democracy protests. None had any plans to join, or even write a good song, as Junoon and other artists had done a decade ago. A few laughed at my naïveté; "Most of the musicians I know are busy with video shoots and recording," Ali explained, "or enjoying the show—which mice are going to get which scraps of cheese. Otherwise life goes on as normal, which means people are watching their dreams, and Pakistan, rot in front of them."

A few days after Bhutto's assassination, I called Salman Ahmed. He was emotionally torn, considering the news of her assassination reached him just as he was coming down off the high of performing with Alicia Keyes and Melissa Etheridge at the Nobel Peace Prize ceremony for Al Gore in Oslo. But while most of his fellow musicians in Pakistan sat shocked on the political sidelines, he was already thinking of ways to build a new social and political movement by creating a television show that would feature some of the country's brightest young activists, artists, and scholars discussing how to rebuild civil society from the ground up.

No one knows how bad the situation has to get before Pakistanis, including musicians, take to the streets in large enough numbers to force a change in the system. *Insha'Allah*, Ali, Mekaal, and most of my friends said that some sort of miracle will pull the country out of its current mess. But as of early 2008, it seems that Pakistan—or at least large swaths of it—has gone beyond the point where either music or religion can save it.

EPILOGUE

Which Way to the Future?

Five years ago, when I began this journey in a hotel bar in Fes, Morocco, I had only the faintest inkling of the incredible variety, richness, and sophistication of the music, musicians, and cultures I would soon encounter. Twenty trips and sixteen countries later, I have gained a strong appreciation for the role played by "Western" forms of music like heavy metal and hip-hop in helping young people across the MENA cope with the stress produced by lives spent, at least on the surface, on the margins of their societies.

Some are doctors, others law professors, MBAs, or just plain musicians. Whatever their original training or day job, almost everyone I've met has chosen to make rock, metal, or hip-hop their life's work in the belief that music can help them heal themselves, and their societies. As Junoon's Salman Ahmed (an MD) put it, "I could heal a lot more people using my guitar as a stethoscope than I could using a real one."

The question remains whether the MENA's metal and rap scenes can help stimulate wider cultural and political transformations in the societies of the region. The answer depends on whether the increasingly transnational communities of

fans and activists can outwit the policies of "repressive tolerance"—as the twentieth-century German philosopher Herbert Marcuse described it—pursued by governments and
corporations since World War II. This strategy involves public support by political and economic elites for greater tolerance and freedom of speech, but only after they've rigged the
game so that genuine alternatives to the status quo are either
co-opted and depoliticized, delegitimated and marginalized,
or harshly repressed.

Such strategies have often helped to stifle or defang
dissenting voices in so-called advanced democracies. As
Thomas Frank demonstrated in his *Conquest of Cool*, this
process enabled corporations to "conquer" the 1960s counterculture before hippies could transform their cultural revolution into large-scale political and economic change. More
recently, the Bush administration used repressive tolerance
during the lead-up to the invasion of Iraq to discredit its critics (indeed, Marcuse's analysis of repressive tolerance is focused on the United States and other democratic societies).
In the authoritarian systems of the MENA, this strategy allows a veneer of democracy—or merely promises of democratization—to mask continued marginalization and even
intensified oppression of anyone who threatens the power of
elites.

Metalheads, and musicians more broadly, have little
chance of overcoming the repressive tolerance that passes for
"liberalization" and "democratization" in the MENA on their
own. But their struggles and successes remind us of a past,
and offer a model for the future, in which artists—if inadvertently at first—helped topple a seemingly impregnable system of rule. The model, as the Iranian and other MENA

governments are well aware, is the Velvet Revolution that swept across Eastern Europe in the mid- to late 1980s. A generation later, the Iranian government jails activists for being "velvet revolutionaries" precisely because it realizes what a threat a culturally grounded rebellion against the political status quo can be.

The original Velvet Revolution in Czechoslovakia was a society-wide nonviolent revolt against a repressive Communist government spearheaded by students, playwrights, philosophers, novelists, filmmakers, and musicians. The "Prague Spring" of 1968 inspired a cultural scene in Czechoslovakia that bolstered the country's pro-democracy struggles during the Soviet occupation and the hard-line Communist governments of next two decades. The most famous group presence on the scene was the Plastic People of the Universe.

Named after a Frank Zappa song, the PPU started out playing covers of bands like the Fugs and, of course, Velvet Underground. Fairly quickly, however, the musical talent of the core members of the group helped the PPU become one of the most innovative bands in Czechoslovakia, one that occupies a unique place in the history of rock 'n' roll. The PPU combined Western and local styles of rock with an ability to reach both international and domestic audiences (after being "demoted to amateur status" in 1970 by the post-Soviet-invasion government, the band hired a Canadian singer to help them reach an English-language audience). Their wide appeal helped them to become a potent political symbol as a result of the state's crackdown on freedom of expression and dissent.

Indeed, the PPU was not political by intent, at least at first. But their defiance in the face of the professional and personal costs they suffered for their music inspired other bands and culture producers to join them in their refusal to bow down to the Czech government. Together they nurtured a truly "counter" cultural scene under the political radar that exploded out of the underground just as the era of contemporary globalization commenced in the late 1980s, sparking the wider political rebellion that forced the Communists from power.

There is no reason to assume that Muslim metalheads and rappers who are picking up where Ozzy Osbourne or Tupac Shakur left off can't play a role similar to that of the Plastic People of the Universe. But any Velvet Revolution that emerges in the MENA will have to look also at the Polish experience in toppling Communism, where religion, in the form of the Catholic Church, and labor activism, in the form of the Solidarity movement, played prominent roles in overthrowing the regime. If the musicians and more-secularly oriented intellectuals can join with the rising generation of progressive religious activists and the leadership of the still-suffering working classes, they stand a good chance of creating the kind of broad community that was behind the revolutions in Czechoslovakia, Poland, and the rest of the Eastern Bloc.

※☆※

"Finally, a real metal community!"

It was a hot March afternoon, and Marz had just spent several hours in the desert being interviewed for *Global Metal*, the sequel to the documentary *Metal: A Headbanger's Journey*, directed by Sam Dunn. We caught sight of each other as he entered the field of the Dubai Desert Rock Festival, increasingly known as the Mecca of the Middle Eastern Metal Scene.

As we kissed hello, Marz surveyed the crowd of 20,000 metal-heads, most of them Arab kids, quite a few of them the metal equivalent of muhajababes—jeans, Iron Maiden T-shirts, and headscarves. He had trouble taking it all in.

Though exhausted from the heat, Marz had the wide-eyed, wonder-struck grin of a boy who'd suddenly walked into the world's biggest candy store. "I never thought I'd see something like this in the Middle East," he confessed later as we walked around the giant stage, chatting with members of the Atlanta-based group Mastodon while we watched the Swedish death-metal band In Flames run through a powerhouse set.

Already in its third year, Desert Rock's headliners included Incubus, Prodigy, Robert Plant, and, in the biggest moment in Middle Eastern metal history, Iron Maiden (although it's not widely known, one of the band's original lead singers, Paul DiAnno, converted to Islam in the early 1990s). Few crowds have erupted with more energy than did the fans at Desert Rock when Maiden, with its full twenty-ton show, hit the stage. And I don't think I've witnessed a more poignant moment at a concert than when the crowd sang Maiden's anthem, "Fear of the Dark," in unison with lead singer Bruce Dickinson, lighters aloft in one hand, cell phones in the other to record it for You Tube posterity.

Audience members were literally in tears. One girl, in a muhajababe outfit, told me that she'd been waiting her whole life for this moment. "This is our first time playing in an Arab country," Dickinson told the audience, visibly taken aback by the crowd's reaction to the previous song. "I know Dubai is the melting pot. Everybody is here. We have people from Saudi Arabia, the United Arab Emirates, Scotland, Lebanon, Egypt, Sweden, Turkey, Australia, Wales, America, Canada, Kuwait. We have the whole world, just about, here tonight . . . And we'll be back." Robert Plant's set the next night was equally inspiring. And when he spoke briefly to the audience in Arabic and Urdu—the only artist to do so—the crowd roared in appreciation.

Desert Rock was never intended merely to be a great concert. But what made it so special was, as Marz exclaimed, the sense of community that permeated the air. However fleetingly, a pan-Islamic metal *ummah* had come into being; one that most metaliens, including Marz, see little chance of building in their home countries, even if, as in Egypt, the situation has improved recently. "The stage would literally have to be right here," Marz told me, referring to Dubai. "There's no way our kind of metal [death, doom, and other extreme forms] will ever be accepted in Egypt. Dubai is the future." Marz was more prescient than he could have imagined. The next year his band played Desert Rock as part of the Battle of the Bands right before the festival.

Finding a Way Toward the Future

The phrase "Dubai is the future" has been used by everyone from Halliburton executives to mega-real-estate developers to describe the unbridled possibilities for satisfying the greed of globalization's elite in the emirate. One official promotional video refers to it as the "mind-blowing fantasy land in the heart of the desert." Never mind that Dubai is located on the sea, or that the existence of this supposed utopia depends on the world's deadly addiction to petroleum, along with the uneasy presence of a super-exploited army of South Asian workers, who keep the city-state running for about five dollars per worker per day.

Giant malls with indoor ski slopes, man-made peninsu-
las shaped like palm trees and maps of the world, all dot
Dubai's postmodern landscape. But it's the skyscrapers along
Dubai's main strip, Sheikh Zeyd Road, that the emirate's leaders have determined should be the visual marker of its wealth,
modernity, and global reach. Their steel-and-glass superficial-
ity stands in marked contrast to the lush, soulful, yet violent
landscape of Pakistan, which I'd left only hours before.

Unlike much of the Arab world, Dubai's level of foreign
investment, and its economy more broadly, have grown
steadily, as have standards of living and other development in-
dicators. Moreover, in contrast to most of the MENA's authoritarian leaders or monarchs, the leaders of Dubai and the
other Gulf emirates have moved away from wasting much
of their oil-derived wealth on military spending and vanity
projects; instead they are investing in world-class architecture,
museums, publishing, education, and media "cities" that are
becoming regional hubs for global commerce and cultural
production.

Because of these positive developments, the United Arab
Emirates' relatively liberal economy and social mores are
touted as the "model for the future" of the Arab world, as the
New York Times columnist Thomas Friedman titled one of his
columns. While admitting that it's not yet a democracy, he argues that "Dubai is the model we should want the Arab world
to follow" because it offers a "decent, modernizing model" for
other countries of the region.

This is wishful thinking at best. Neither Dubai nor the
other emirates have moved close to having a functional
democracy. Moreover, Dubai's small population and large per

capita income, coupled with its large, low-wage foreign work-force, makes it an unlikely model for other countries in the MENA. Even the Emirates' relative cultural tolerance, a neces-sity given the overwhelming number of foreigners living there, will not easily be emulated by larger Arab/Muslim countries.

Dubai, however, has had little choice but to accept the powerful impact of globalization on its culture. As one senior Gulf minister explained in reference to the foreign influence on the Gulf sheikdoms: "The effects on our culture [are] un-avoidable. The world today is one big village. Cultures are melting and a mixed global heritage is being formed. Yes, we might lose some identity, but that is the price we must pay."

A more optimistic version of this view is shared by Jackie and Laura Wartanian, the founders of the Desert Rock Festi-val. Indeed, Desert Rock is perhaps as close to counterculture as you can get in Dubai, although it remains well within the limits of the accepted morality there today. "We wanted to cre-ate a special community," Jackie explained to me. "One that starts to know each other, and meet each other at Desert Rock every year. We call our fans 'disciples,' and while it's still in its early stages, every year we can see the disciple community grow."

She continued, "We wanted the Middle East to experi-ence the same atmosphere, energy, and passion of rock music that we've seen at major festivals around the world." While the festival is decidedly not political, by focusing on still-taboo subjects like AIDS awareness and condom usage, and offer-ing a space where young Arabs of both genders can meet and have fun, together with fans from around the world, the festi-val can serve as a model for the region. "If one person or two take this message from the Festival with them, they will tell their friends and then the friends will tell the other friend and so on."

Faraz Kahn, a Pakistani VJ who hosts *Rock On,* a weekly show from Dubai for the Musik, has a unique perspective on the larger significance of Desert Rock. As he explains, "While there are clubs that cater to hip-hop and trance, until Desert Rock there was nothing dedicated to rock 'n' roll here. And more than helping to grow the metal scene, the festival creates a unified space rather than the barriers normally constructed in the region. In doing so, it's become a gateway for kids to experience life in a slightly different way, where it doesn't matter if you're Muslim or Christian, Buddhist or Hindu, black, white, or brown . . . Everyone sings together, jumps together, and respects one another."

Rocking for Peace at the Crossroads of the World

Despite the many positive accomplishments of Dubai Desert Rock and its counterpart 3,769 miles to the west, Casablanca's Boulevard des jeunes musiciens, neither festival can push the boundaries far enough to challenge their countries' political systems. A more relevant political and musical model for the future of the Arab/Muslim world lies at the crossroads of East and West: Turkey.

It was in Istanbul that I joined Iranian guitar virtuoso Farzad Golpayegani, along with the Egyptian rock band Massar Egbari, at the fifth annual Barişa Rock for Peace Festival (in Turkish, *barişa*—pronounced "barisha" in English—means peace). The experience reminded me of how much further along Turkey is on the path of democratic development than other countries in the Arab world.

Despite three or four coups (depending on who's counting) during the last forty years, and the heavy hand of the military in Turkey's political and economic life, there's no denying that democracy is strongly rooted in Turkey today. This fact is what led the European Union to begin the long process that could ultimately lead to Turkey's accession to the EU. But this process has also generated intense debate in Europe over whether Turkey is "European enough" to justify its membership, with even the Pope opposing Turkey's joining what many European leaders would like to keep a "Christian club."

For their part, most Turks I've met don't want to be forced to choose between "East" or "West," between being European or being Muslim. Ethnic Kurds and Armenians retain a strong ethnic (and in some cases separatist) identity, but the majority of Turks consider themselves just plain Turkish. As anyone who's listened to Turkish pop, rock, or Arabesque music knows, "Turkishness" (*Türklüğü*) includes a range of identities that come together with varying degrees of compatibility and success. Indeed, Turkey's ravenously hybrid music scenes offer innumerable examples of how music moves across national, cultural, and civilizational borders, whether or not politicians and business leaders support such exchanges.

Gergo Barcza, founder and saxophonist of Besh o Drom, one of the hottest Gypsy-inspired bands in the world, explained it to me this way when I met him in Budapest about a month before the festival: "The point is that all these people, the Arabs and the Jews, Armenians and Turks, Bulgarians and Romanians, they all hate each other, but they all listen to the same fucking music. Stupid, no?" He laughed as he considered the absurdity of the dynamic he'd just described. "And in many ways it's the Turks today who have the most globalized music. It's taken over popular Romanian music, for example. No one wants to play what we would consider real Gypsy music today. Now they just play variations on Turkish pop. That's globalization, for better or worse, and it shows how music is deeper even than nationalism. The musicians might be Romanian, Serbian, or Macedonian, but musically their roots are clearly to the East."

By "East," Gergo meant Islam, and it's precisely Islam that has not only Europe up in arms, but millions of secular Turks as well, who fear the rise of a religiously centered culture that is represented by the ruling Justice and Development Party (AKP). The irony is that today it's Turkey's Islamists who support greater democracy and integration with Europe, while the country's once pro-Western military and secular elites are turning to Central Asia and farther east in search of allies who won't demand they relinquish as much political, economic, and cultural power as would be required to join the European club.

The complex nuances of Turkish politics today are well understood by the organizers of the Barişa Rock for Peace Festival. One of the festival's main organizers, Avi Haligua, picked up on a theme I've heard in countless meetings with musicians and Islamists alike during the last few years: "The problem with the AKP government is not Islam, which has nothing to do with anything since most everyone is Muslim and the country remains as socially open as before. The problem is with the government's neoliberal policies, and their impact on Turkish workers, the environment, and the cause of peace."

Such an analysis explains why the Barişa Rock for Peace Festival has next to nothing to say about the secular-religious debates that still roil Turkish society. Its organizers understand the core issues facing their society, and so the festival—which began in 2003 as an alternative to corporate-sponsored summer music festivals such as the "Rock 'n' Coke"—focuses on the environment, war and militarism, globalization, and various social issues (including, quite loudly, gay and lesbian rights). This combination of great music and progressive politics has helped the festival to grow from around 10,000 fans in its first year to more than 130,000 attendees in 2006. When I played with Farzad Golpayegani in 2007, the number of attendees approached 150,000.

There are many reasons why Barişa Rock has become something of a Turkish Woodstock. To begin with, the festival has been able to grow in size and stature while remaining grassroots because its organizers could build on Turkey's well-developed network of leftist, peace, environmental, and anti-corporate globalization movements. Together they have more organizational as well as financial resources than their counterparts in most other countries in the region, including the organizers of the Boulevard des jeunes musiciens or Dubai Desert Rock. As important are the social and sexual freedoms experienced by the tens of thousands of fans who camp out for three days in a space that is free of outside interference or prying eyes, with dozens of activist booths and stages for poetry, lectures, and theater, to enrich the experience.

Musically, Barişa resembles the Boulevard des jeunes musiciens at the other end of the Mediterranean in the trampling of musical boundaries that is featured in its line-ups each year, which include bands from Ireland to Iran. This is nothing new in Turkish music; as Cahit Berkay, guitarist and saz player for the "Rolling Stones of Turkey," Moğollar, explained it to me. "You think mixing Eastern instruments over rock grooves is new? We were doing that forty years ago. The key for us is that we never just copied the West. It was always us taking what we heard to a new level. That's why we still can play in front of 20,000 people after all this time."

Pulling this off is not as easy as Berkay makes it sound. "There's a delicate balance we have to keep," Avi Haligua said. The balance between politics and partying, metalheads and muhajababes, had to be just right: "Politics is the driving force. The environment, peace and justice, women's issues—all these messages have to get through to the crowd, otherwise what's the point? They might as well just go to Rock 'n' Coke. But we have to do it as much through the music, and especially through the sense of community and conversations we create each year and the long-term connections we help forge, as through the information we try to get into fans' hands and minds."

The Funky Iranian

For me, round one of the conversation Haligua has tried to create occurred on the festival's opening night, when I sat in with the group Massar Egbari, whose soulful combination of rock, Latin, and Egyptian melodies and instruments has quickly made it one of the premier bands in Egypt. "We're about having conversations that can challenge enforced identities and politics," guitarist Hani El Dakkak explained the morning after their show. "In a situation like ours, where mosque and state are far more powerful than here, you have to be positive, create conversations, not allow the political situation to stop you from reaching out and spreading the word that another future is possible." But the conversation has to extend beyond Egypt to really succeed. "Like when you came onstage, and without having met us, started trading solos with us. It has to be free, honest, and push the boundaries but with respect," Hani continued.

Farzad Golpayegani's British drummer, Eddie Wastnidge, agreed with Hani's assessment of the role of music in generating such conversations. "And performing such music in Istanbul—it's the ultimate fusion where East and West can meet, and have met for centuries." It wasn't surprising, then, that in the context of ever-worsening relations between Iran, the UK, and the United States, Eddie jumped at the idea of rejoining Farzad and an American guest guitarist at Barişa Rock. It was hard for any of us to pass up the chance to make such a public statement against the political and cultural status quo on all sides.

The most meaningful demonstration of just how powerful that communication could be occurred when percussionist Arash Jafari called out to the crowd, to great applause: "Muslims, Christians . . . Jews [he paused for a second before adding Jews]. Together, for peace, not war!" It was clear from the crowd's reaction how important it was for the fans to hear such a statement from a group of musicians whose countries were engaged in a war of words (over Iran's alleged nuclear weapons program) that threatened to move toward military confrontation as the festival was taking place.

The musical highlight of the evening occurred moments later, when we broke into a funk-blues jam we'd come up with earlier that day during our final rehearsal, and more than 25,000 fans began to jump up and down with the band in unison. The audience went so crazy that, for the only time during the festival ("Ever!" one of the organizers told me later), the stage manager had to grab a microphone in the middle of the song and scream at the crowd to move back or he'd stop the show.

Bass player Ali Sanaei had come up with the groove during a break in the run-through of our set. I was shocked to hear Ali play such a groove because I'd never before met a musician from the MENA who had an authentic feel for the soul and grooves of American blues or funk. (The same is true also for most heavy-metal musicians I've encountered; regardless of their country of origin, they rarely play blues or funk very well.) I pestered Ali about this fact, and finally he explained how he became the funkiest bass player in Iran, if not the entire world of heavy metal.

It turns out that under his extroverted, wild-man metal warrior exterior, Ali is completing a major in orchestral composition at one of Tehran's prestigious conservatories. "I started with some jazz and blues and a little bit of funk and built my musicianship on that. Then I found metal, which I started playing because you can find the bloody roots of metal in the blues. The more I listened, the more I realized that the pentatonic scale that defines blues and rock is very close to the folk scales of northeastern Iran, where I grew up. The music just sounded so familiar, it was easy to play it as if it was my own."

I smiled at Ali's sense of connection to the blues, since the blues owes its origins in good measure to the melodies and rhythms brought to America by Muslim African slaves, which were in turn influenced by centuries of contact with the Islamic Middle East. In a small but powerful way, a historical and musical circle was completed when Ali fell in love with the blues, cut through centuries of musical accretions that had separated America's roots music from its Islamic (among other) roots, and created a playing style that captured the essence of both.

"Music is so powerful because it can bring people close to each other," he continued, "even if one person is from Afghanistan and another from Mars. It flies above the borders and finds its audience no matter how hard governments try to restrict it. That's its magic. When I met all those people at Barişa, I found myself a tiny drop in the heart of an ocean."

Ali's metaphor called to mind Led Zeppelin's "The Ocean"—like most metalheads in the MENA, Ali is a big Zeppelin fan—whose title refers to the band's appreciation of the "ocean" of fans before whom they performed. The song's lyrics, "Play for me, play for free, play a whole lot more . . ." sum up the attitude of most metalheads I know, for whom "DIY" (do it yourself) has made a virtue out of necessity, and helped give the music cultural resonance far beyond its growing fan base. But the symbolism of the ocean also points us to something deeper than just the cultural power and aesthetic embeddedness of heavy metal: the religious sensibility of the heavy-metal experience, and that of other extreme forms of music, especially when performed live—whether in a basement in Tehran, in a dilapidated villa outside Cairo, or on the main stages in Casablanca, Istanbul, or Dubai.

Such twenty-first-century "happenings" hold the potential for transcending individual identities into communal solidarities, which, however tentative and insecure, are in marked contrast to the kind of violence-laden "self-annihilation" demanded of young people by the more extreme forms of Sunni and Shi'i Islam. In fact, seven hundred years before Led Zeppelin celebrated its communion with its ocean of fans, the twelfth-century Persian Sufi Farid ad-Din Attar and his more famous contemporary, Jalaluddin Rumi, wrote of the "ocean of the soul" that grounds human experience, and makes possible union with the rest of humanity and ultimately with God. As Rumi describes it: "Like the birds of the sea, men come from the ocean—the ocean of the soul . . . When the vessel [of the body] is broken . . . by the wave that comes from the soul . . . the vision comes back, and the union with Him."

৯চ৯

The heavy metal of the Muslim world is often quite angry; as Sheikh Anwar al-Ethari pointed out to me when I began this journey, that anger is what reminded him of the intense form of Shi'i practice of his native Iraq. But Ali's point, like that of so many metalheads I've met, is that heavy metal is about a lot more than just anger and violence. The ocean is not always angry; the music can be positive and life-affirming. It reflects the attempts by young Muslims, Christians, and Jews across the MENA to create a positive and open "project identity," as the sociologist Manuel Castells describes it, against the grain of the negative "resistance identities" that dominate the experience of Islam today for too many Muslims. And when that project identity takes on a political edge, as it has in Istanbul, and—at least for a moment—in Casablanca and Beirut, a new "Spring," and perhaps even a velvet revolution, becomes possible to imagine.

Corleone to Baghdad?

Ali was describing the ocean as we drove along the ring road passing through Istanbul's modern financial center, filled with modern skyscrapers and corporate offices, on our way back to the historic Ottoman heart of the city. As our driver careened through the traffic, I recalled Jimmy Page's interpretation of the famously obscure cover of *Led Zeppelin IV*: "I used to spend a lot of time going to junk shops looking for things that other people might have missed. [One time] Robert was . . . with me . . . and found the picture of the old man with the sticks and suggested that we work it into our cover somehow. So we decided to contrast the modern skyscraper on the back with the old man with the sticks—you see the destruction of the old, and the new coming forward. Our hearts were as much in tune with the old ways as with what was happening, though we weren't always in agreement with the new."

Page's attempts to achieve some kind of reconciliation between the old and the new while remaining more sympathetic to the past well summarizes the sentiment of most metalheads—in fact, most people—I've met in the MENA. It also sums up the reason for the popularity of the genre more broadly: the combination of anger and positivity that drive metal in the Muslim world is motivated by the larger struggles of the region's peoples to reconcile a powerful past with a troubled present and an uncertain future.

The greatest obstacle to converting the anger expressed by heavy music, or religion, into a positive cultural and even political force is the violence that suffuses most societies of the Muslim world—whether it's the "pinpoint violence" deployed by authoritarian governments to stifle dissent, or the wholesale violence of war, occupation, and terrorism. That's why the message of festivals like Barişa Rock for Peace and Dubai Desert Rocks is so important. As DDR's Jackie Wartanian describes it, "Fans come here from across the world and they form a community, and it reminds us that whatever governments might do, peace is possible."

But violence is also powerfully seductive to young people who have little hope for changing their societies through politics, never mind music. Lebanese-French rapper Clotaire K described it this way: "The level of violence and racism against France's blacks and Arabs is hard for an outsider to imagine. This is why some in today's generation are becoming more violent in response. Remember [during the protests of 2005 and 2006], millions of peaceful marchers achieved nothing politically, but a week of rioting got the country's, and the world's, attention."

The kind of limited violence described by Clotaire K has long been deployed by marginalized groups to force governments to listen to their complaints. The problem is that violence is by nature hard to limit or control; it often blows back on those who turn to it, regardless of the perceived justness of their cause. Nowhere is this more obvious than in Iraq, whose tiny metal scene was devastated by the post-occupation violence set off by groups who couldn't imagine coming together to resist the occupation through nonviolent means. In fact, when the lead singer of the country's only metal band, Acrassicauda, was interviewed for the documentary *Heavy Metal in Baghdad,* the first thing he did was hold up a copy of Iron Maiden's *Death on the Road,* and say, "This is what life looks like here," before explaining just how bad a life has become to make it resemble an Iron Maiden album cover. Sadly, the band members were living in exile in Syria when Iron Maiden made its triumphant debut in Dubai.

But it wasn't the violence of Baghdad that I was thinking about as I struggled to stay awake at Attatürk Airport a few hours after the close of the Barişa Rock for Peace festival so as not to miss my flight home. Rather it was one of the rare moments of tranquillity during my travels in Iraq: a warm early-spring afternoon spent drinking tea in the courtyard of the Hiwar (Conversation) Café and art gallery with acclaimed "guerrilla filmmaker" Oday Rasheed, director of the prize-winning 2005 *Underexposure,* the first movie filmed in Iraq after the fall of Saddam.

After experiencing a week of steadily increasing violence as the insurgency focused on central Baghdad, my conversation with Oday, who is also one of Iraq's best hard-rock and blues guitarists, was a much-needed respite from the encroaching insanity around us. But I had no answer for him when he chided me gently for the cultural myopia of most Americans. "I know all your artists and cultural figures—Jimi Hendrix, John Coltrane, F. Scott Fitzgerald. But I also know my culture—Oum Kalthoum, Farid al-Atrash, and Adonis. How many Americans even want to know my culture, let alone take the time to do so?"

I met up with Oday a year later when I invited him to

Messina, Sicily, where he joined Reda Zine, Sheikh Anwar al-Ethari, Layla al-Zubaidi, and the Italian scholar of Islam Armando Salvatore, for the workshop on heavy metal and Islam that gave birth to this book. It turned out that Oday and I were both big fans of *The Godfather;* and we pledged not to leave Sicily without making a pilgrimage to Corleone, on the opposite side of the island, after the conference. As we took turns driving along the rugged, switchback-filled landscape of the SS118 *superstrade* (in reality a two-lane road without a shoulder), we returned to our earlier conversation about the problems of cultural transmission between the Muslim world and the West. As we talked, thousands of years of history passed around us. Greeks, Romans, Vandals, Goths, Byzantines, Muslims, the Spanish, Bourbons: all had controlled Sicily at one time or another, and all had contributed to the richness and diversity that define the island's unique culture. The imagery, and the history behind it, helped put the disaster of Iraq, and the Middle East more broadly, in perspective.

"I fell in love with blues, rock, and metal because it was a way of being against Saddam without being obviously political," Oday admitted as we tried to find the little square through which the young Vito Andolini (and future Don Corleone) was smuggled inside a basket on a donkey. "You might get roughed up a bit because of your long hair or clothes, but you wouldn't get shot or your parents tortured for being a metalhead or rock 'n' roller." No more, he explained.

"I am an Arab, a Muslim, and I lived under Saddam," he told one interviewer when *Underexposure* came out. When the violence of the U.S. invasion and occupation was added into the mix, they become "reasons enough to put a wall around your thoughts, as in a prison." But Oday was lucky; filmmaking and guitar playing gave him the means to break out of the prison in which most of his fellow Iraqis remain trapped.

The problem is, for every Oday Rasheed risking his life to capture the chaos of life in post-invasion Iraq, or Clotaire K using hip-hop to force French society to recognize the rights of its Muslim immigrants and their children, there's a paranoid government willing to do what's necessary to silence them, a superpower bent on invading their country to liberate them, a Rotana or Coca-Cola out to defang them in order to secure greater profits, or a fanatical religious leader trying to convert or kill them to further his cause—sometimes all at the same time. The stakes in this contest couldn't be higher.

Luckily, the metalheads, hip-hoppers, rockers, and punks of the Middle East are no longer alone. They not only have each other; helped by the Internet and an increasing number of international festivals of various sizes, the world is starting to listen to their music and their stories. A real dialogue between cultures and countries is emerging, one that will not be cowed by authoritarian governments, silenced by war-crazed administrations, overshadowed by jihadi propagandists, or co-opted by multinational conglomerates. It is being conducted by young people around the world, on their terms, and if they're lucky, it will be free of the stereotypes, prejudices, and conflicting interests that have doomed their elders' conversations for generations.

As we ate dinner in a small restaurant on the road to Corleone, Oday, his partner Furat al-Jamil (a respected documentary filmmaker based in Germany), and I agreed that if Sicily could rise out of the ashes of centuries of occupation and from the powerful mafia culture it produced to become one of the most rapidly, yet sustainably, developing regions of Europe, then maybe there's hope for the Middle East, and even Iraq. It's a vision none of us wants to give up, even though every time I hear from Oday or Furat, it seems that another close friend or family member of theirs has been killed.

The fear, the violence, the hatred in the Middle East can seem deafening, but it's still not loud enough to silence the voices of resistance. A generation after Twisted Sister's 1984 smash hit, kids across the MENA are screaming, in English, Arabic, Urdu, Farsi, Hebrew, Turkish, and French—online, onstage, and, however tentatively, on the streets—"We're not gonna take it anymore." It's a message that used to resonate with Americans and Europeans. The sooner we rejoin the chorus, the sooner real peace, democracy, and reconciliation will be achieved—not just in the heartlands of the Muslim world, but in the heartlands of the West as well.

ACKNOWLEDGMENTS

Nearly every person mentioned or interviewed in this book provided important help in my attempts to understand the dynamics of the metal, hip-hop, and larger rock scenes in the Middle East and North Africa, and their relationship to popular cultures of the region more broadly. I extend to all of them my deepest thanks for their time, openness, and help. In addition, there were numerous people who were either not mentioned directly in the book, or who provided invaluable inspiration or organizational help during numerous trips to the region, including the following:

Sami Abu Shehada, Howie Alper, Pegah Arzi, Hicham Bahev, Noam Ben-Zeev, Ishay Berger, Bill "Freedom" Bremner, Emil and Dennis Culic, Chuck D, Davey D, Lara Deeb, the Dryer Brothers, Ted Dunbar, Sam Dunn, Jordan ElGrabli and the staff of the Levantine Center, Mona Eltahawy, John Epstein, Kevin Eubanks, Ezgi Evcil, Omar Fadel, the Farmer family, James Fittz, Thomas Frank, Michael Franti, Richard Gizbert, La Famiglia Guidotti, Hassan Hakmoun, Avi Haligua, Amine Hamma, Rema Hammami, Amin Hashwamy, Myke "Shyndigg" Henney, Dr. John, Akbar Irani and the staff of Miras Maktoob (Tehran), Junaid Jamshed, Ritchie Johnson,

Deborah Kapchan, Shawana Kemp, Naz Khan, Ben E. King, Liisa Ladouceur, the Lane family, the MacDonald/Hertel family, Abdessalam Maghraoui, Sohrab Mahdavi, Behnam Marandi, Russel Martone, ash-Sherif Marzeban, Mahmoud Omidsalar, Jonas Otterbeck, Anton Pukshansky, Ghidian Qaymari, Dr. Zahoor Qureshi, Todd Ray, Ole Rietov, Marie Korpus and the staff of Free Muse, Dan Rabinowitz, MC Rai, Haroon Rashid, Todd Ray, Yuval Ron, Violaine Roussel, the Rubel family, Sameh Sabry, Michael Santiago, Gershon Shafir, Anwerali Shahbuddin, Jonathan Shannon (the next drink in Fes is on me), Jerjees Sheja, Mahsa Shekarloo, Samora Smith, Paul and Yuki Soares, Sami Syed, Alyce Thomas, Jackie and Laura Wartanian, Charles Wheeler, Oren Yiftachel, Rebecca Young, Sameh Zakout, Maor Appelbaum, and David Ziegler.

❧❦❧

A very special thanks and extra love to the following people, without whom this book could not have been imagined or completed: Salman Ahmed, Sara Alexander (my teacher and soul sister), Moe Hamzeh, Jean Dupré, Armando Salvatore (*Visto che non ero pazzo!*), Reda Zine (Le Dude, A+), and, of course, Layla al-Zubaidi (four continents and counting).

❧❦❧

Special thanks to Adrian Cheesley and Mario Choueiri of EMI, for their support of the compilation album "Flowers in the Desert," featuring many of the artists discussed in this book.

❧❦❧

Barry Siegel, Benjamin Horbert, Ted Swedenberg, Dani McClellan, Samuli Schielke, and Amy Willentz all provided much-needed comments and/or editing suggestions on drafts of various chapters. Sandy Dijkstra, Elise Capron, and Taryn Fagerness of the Dijkstra Literary Agency provided invaluable advice and support in the conceptualization and completion of this book. Kate Kennedy of Three Rivers Press undertook a heroic effort to turn the completed draft into a coherent manuscript. John Glusman, my editor at Three Rivers Press, and Tom Peters, editor of Verso Books, exhibited great patience, foresight, and sculptors' hands in editing the final manuscript.

❧❧

Research for this book was made possible by grants and other assistance provided by the School of Humanities, Department of History and International Center for Writing and Translation, UC Irvine; the United States Institute of Peace; the Open Society Institute; the Fulbright Senior Researcher Grant program, Italy; l'Ecole des Hautes Etudes, Paris; the European University Institute, Florence; the Central European University, Budapest; the Mediterranean Studies Association; and the Higher Education Council, Pakistan.

BIBLIOGRAPHY

Most of the research for this book is the result of in-depth fieldwork and interviews with the individuals mentioned in the various chapters, along with many others who provided background or other information on the condition that their names or any other information that could be traced to them not be given. Unless otherwise indicated, all names are real. In addition to interviews, quotations or specific information were taken from the following sources, listed by country/chapter. A comprehensive list of metal bands in the MENA is available at www.metal-archives.com, searchable by country.

For a detailed bibliography and analysis of economic and cultural globalization in the MENA, and in particular countries, see my *Why They Don't Hate Us: Lifting the Veil on the Axis of Evil* (Oxford, England: Oneworld Publications, 2005).

INTRODUCTION

Bolman, Philip. *World Music: A Very Short Introduction*. Oxford, England: Oxford University Press, 2002.

Dale, Dick. "Dick Dale's History." Official website of Dick Dale, www.dickdale.com/history.html.

Elmandjra, Mahdi. *Humiliocratie à l'ère du méga-impérialisme*. Casablanca: Annajah Al Jadida, 2003.

Kahn-Harris, Keith. *Extreme Metal: Music and Culture on the Edge*. Oxford, England: Berg, 2007.

Population Reference Bureau. "Youth in the Middle East and North Africa: Demographic Opportunity or Challenge?" Washington, DC, April 2007. www.prb.org.

Walser, Robert. *Running with the Devil: Power, Gender and Madness in Heavy Metal Music*. Hanover, NH: Wesleyan University Press, 1993.

Whitaker, Brian. "Highway to Hell." *The Guardian*, June 2, 2003.

Weinstein, Deena. *Heavy Metal: The Music and its Culture*. New York: Da Capo, 2000.

Morocco

Basbous, Antoine. "La menace du wahhabisme au Maroc n'est plus un tabou." *El Watan*, September 29–30, 2002.

Center for Defense Information. "U.S. Arms Transfers to America's Newest 'Major Non-NATO Ally.' " May 3, 2004.

Dilami, Abdelmounaïm. "La monarchie en réponse à nadia yacine." *L'Economist*, June 12, 2005.

Hamma, Amine. "De l'Internationale-metal au conflit sociétale local: La scène de Casablanca." Interview with Gérôme Guibert. *Tribune* 5, no. 2 (2007).

Human Rights Watch. *Morocco's Truth Commission: Honoring Past Victims During an Uncertain Present* 17, no. 11 (2005).

Pfeiffer, Tom. "Despair and Desperation Thrive in Casablanca Slums." Reuters, April 13, 2006.

Samie, Amal. "Metal Intifada." *Maroc Hebdo*. Online archive, 2000.

Tozy, Mohamed. *Monarchie et Islam Politique au Maroc*. Presses de Sciences Po, 1999.

U.S. Department of State, Bureau of Economic and Business Affairs. *2001 Country Reports on Economic Policy and Trade Practices*. (Washington, DC: U.S. Government Printing Office, 2002).

———. *Country Report on Human Rights Practices, 2005*. (Washington, DC: U.S. Government Printing Office, 2006).

Yassine, Abdesselam. *Rasa'il al-ustadh al-murshid* (Letters of the Surpreme Guide). Accessible at www.yassine.net.

———. *Mihnat al-aql al-Muslim (The Muslim Mind on Trial)*. Rabat: 1994.

Yassine, Nadia. *Toutes voiles dehors (Full Sails Ahead)*. Paris: Le Fennec, 2003.

Websites:

boulevard.ma

H-Kayne.com

hobahobaspirit.com

lazywall.co.uk

maroc.attac.org

myspace.com/biggthadon

myspace.com/cafemiralegroupe

myspace.com/syncopeaband

nadiayassine.net

yassine.net

EGYPT

Amnesty International, U.S.A. Country review, Egypt. www.amnestyusa.org/By_Country/Egypt/page.do?id=1011147&n1=3&n2=30&n3=897

cbsnews.com. "Rockin' in the Islamic World." August 13, 2006.

Lynch, Marc. "Young Brothers in Cyberspace." *Middle East Report,* #245, Winter 2007.

Sinan, Omar. "In Egypt, Heavy Metal Is Making a Quiet Comeback." Associated Press, August 16, 2006.

Websites:

anaikhwan.blogspot.com

arabist.net/arabawy

egyptmetal.net

ihoudaiby.blogspot.com

ikhwanonline.com

ikhwanweb.net

manalaa.net

myspace.com/beyondeast

slacker.foolab.org/ (archive of Slacker's photos and reviews of all metal shows in Egypt)

ISRAEL/PALESTINE

Golan, Riviv, Lpanion; Hem mishtinim 'al.matzavot, yorekim 'al ha-tzionut . . . Interview with Useless ID in *Leilot,* weekly magazine of Yediot Aharonot, June 30, 2006

Sagi bin Nun. "Kiss the Fat Woman Good-bye." *Haaretz,* October 26, 2004.

Martinelli, Robert. Interview with Kobi Farhi. *Maelstrom,* December 11, 2002.

Newman, Jason. "Shalom/Salaam/Word Up." Undated article in *Urb Magazine,* accessible on urb.com at www.urb.com/online/features/141_israel_palestine.php.

Sagol 59, interviewed by riotsound.com (undated).

Shabi, Rachel. "Palestinian Political Rap Attracts Growing Crowds." *Middle East Times,* January 2, 2007.

"Street Language and Experience." Nox-mag.com, August 2006.

Tamari, Salim. *al Jabal didd al Bahar (The Mountain Against the Sea).* Beirut: Institute for Palestine Studies, 2005.

Ungerleider, Neal. "Levantine Hip-Hop 101: Who's Who in the Middle East Rap Game." *Slate,* August 18, 2006.

Yassin, Dir. Interview in *Profane Existence* magazine, 1999. www.angelfire.com/il/deiryassin/peinter.htm.

Websites:

dampalestine.com/
khalas.net
myspace.com/palrapperz
orphaned-land.com
ramallahunderground.com
sara.alexander.free.fr
slingshothiphop.com/

Lebanon

al-Manar, Dar. "Nasr min Allah." Media material on 2006 war. Beirut: Lebanese Committee for the Arts, 2007.

Aspden, Rachel. "Islam and the Porno Devils." *The Observer,* July 23, 2006.

Aubin, Benoit. "After Syria Leaves, War-weary and Fractious, Lebanon Dares to Dream of Unity." www.MacLeans.ca, April 21, 2005.

Butters, Andrew Lee. "Sex, Drugs and Rock 'n' Roll in a Failing State." *Time,* August 31, 2007.

Charara, Walid. "Transition sereine au Liban." *Le Monde Diplomatique,* May 1999.

Chassey, Clancey. "Hizbullah Is Lebanon's Bulwark Against Al-Qaeda." *Daily Star*, December 24, 2005.

Förch, Christina. "Arabic Rock Music of International Caliber." Qantara.de, 2004.

———. "Trip Hop from Beirut: Soap Kills, a Band that Sets Itself Apart from Commercial Arab Pop." Qantara.de, 2005.

Frank, Robert. "A Merger's Message: Dominate or Die." *New York Times*, January 11, 2000.

Kassir, Samir. "Désordre établi au Liban." *Le Monde Diplomatique*, February 1997.

Ibrahim al-Mardini, Sheikh. *At-tibyan fi ahkam il-musiqi wa-l-alhan*. Beirut: Dâr al nohmania, 2001.

Nasrallah, Hassan. *Risa'il qa'id al-muqawama*. DVD. Beirut: Dar al-Manar, 2006.

Ohrstrom, Lysandra. "Demand for Plastic Surgery Rises Despite Political Tensions, Economic Downturn." *Daily Star*, April 18, 2007.

Rosen, Nir. "Hizb Allah, Party of God." www.truthdig.com, October 3, 2006.

Shadid, Anthony, and Alia Ibrahim. "Lebanon Fails to Elect New President." *Washington Post*, November 24, 2007.

Stratton, Allegra. *Muhajababes*. London: Constable and Robinson, 2006.

Websites:

almanar.com.lb

boell-meo.org/ (Heinrich Böll foundation, Beirut office)

futuretvnetwork.com

freemuse.org

ghaliboun.net (Hezbollah official website)

moqawama.org/english/index.php (English site for Hezbollah)

oath-to-vanquish.com

rotana.net

soapkills.com

thekordz.com

Iran

Arash BT. "An interview with one of the organizers of 'Tehran Avenue Music Open.' " *Zir Zaman,* October 2003.

"Arthimoth: Death Metal Band from Iran." Danish TV documentary, on YouTube in three parts.

Basmenji, Kaveh. *Tehran Blues: Youth Culture in Iran.* London: Saqi Books, 2005.

Mir-Hosseini, Ziba. *Islam and Gender: The Religious Debate in Contemporary Iran.* Princeton: Princeton University Press, 1999.

Peterson, Scott. "You Say You Want a Revolution? Iran Bands Rock On." *Christian Science Monitor,* October 1, 2003.

Tala'i, Darius. *Radif Mirza Abdallah: Natnavisi Amuzishi va tahlili (The Traditional Persian Art of Music: The Radif of Mirza Abdallah).* Tehran: Nashreney Publishing, 2007.

Varzi, Roxanne. *Warring Souls: Youth, Media, and Martyrdom in Post-Revolution Iran.* Durham, NC: Duke University Press, 2006.

Websites:

ahoora-band.com

arthimoth.com

farzadonline.com

mahsavahdat.com

mohsennamju.com

myspace.com/hichkas21

peyman-chet.com/

revealed

Tarantists.com

tehranavenue.com

PAKISTAN

Crow, Sheryl. "Interview on Motherhood." huffingtonpost.com, November 22, 2007.

LeVine, Mark. "Heavy Metal Muslim." *OC Weekly,* February 9, 2006.

———— with Salman Ahmed. "Led Zeppelin: A Force for Peace." *Boston Globe,* December 8, 2007.

Paracha, Nadim. Review of album by Irtiqa. chowk.com, October 15, 2003.

Shaukat, Zeenia, and Fareeha Rafique. "Battle of the Brands." News International (Pakistan), July 2003.

Syed, Madeeha. "Instant Karma." *Dawn,* March 4, 2007.

Websites:

aaroh.net

akashtheband.com

haroon.com

iiu.edu.pk

junaidjamshed.net

junoon.com

karavanonline.com

Mizraab.net

sajidandzeeshan.com

CONCLUSION

Batarfi, Khaled. "Best Model for the Arab World?" Arabnews.com, April 18, 2007.

Castells, Manuel. *The Power of Identity*. New York: Blackwell, 1996.

Chatterjee, Pratap. "Ports of Profit: Dubai Does Brisk War Business." *CorpWatch*, February 24, 2006.

Batarfi, Khaled. "Dubai: Best Model for Arab World?" Arabview.com, undated.

Cameron Crowe. "The Durable Led Zeppelin: A Conversation with Jimmy Page and Robert Plant." *Rolling Stone*, March 13, 1975.

Economist. Ankara and Istanbul, Jun 7, 2007.

Frazer, Suzan. "Former Islamist Wins Presidency." Associated Press, August 28, 2007.

Khouri, Rami G. "New Possibilities Beckon the Arab World." *Agence Global*, June 9, 2007.

Frank, Thomas. *The Conquest of Cool: Business Culture, Counterculture, and the Rise of Hip Consumerism*. Chicago: University of Chicago Press, 1997.

Friedman, Thomas. "Dubai Is Model We Should Want Arab World to Follow." *Deseret News*, March 17, 2006.

Kettelhake, Silke. "Oday Rasheed's *Underexposure*: Blinking Incredulously at the Sun." Qantara.de, 2005.

Khan, Faraz. "Rock On." Interview with Mark LeVine, April 10, 2007 (available on YouTube.com in two parts).

Marcuse, Herbert. "Repressive Tolerance." Online text of 1965 original, www.marcuse.org/herbert/pubs/60spubs/65repressivetolerance.htm.

Pera, Marcello, and Joseph Ratzinger. *Senza Radici (Without Roots)*. Milan: Arnoldo Mondadori Editore, 2004.

Tuncer, Hatice. "Müzik Doğu'dan gelir." *Cumhuriyet*, August 26, 2007.

Welch, Chris. *Led Zeppelin: Dazed and Confused: The Stories Behind Every Song*. New York: Thunder's Mouth Press, 1998.

Websites:

barisarock.com

beshodrom.hu

desertrockfestival.com

edition.cnn.com/video/#/video/international/2007/10/09/
ime.amman.music.cnn (CNN report on my performance at
Barisa Rock for Peace Festival)

heavymetalinbaghdad.com

nervecell.net/

underexposure.com/

vbs.tv/player.php?bctid=452299431 (*Vice* magazine
documentary on heavy metal in Baghdad)

wastedland.net/

For additional interviews, songs, videos,
forums, tour dates, documentaries, and other
information related to the artists and
other people profiled in this book, please visit
www.HeavyMetalIslam.net.

INDEX